❧ Contents ❧

Illustrations

❦ 1 ❦

Memories

The passage of time brings about irreversible physical changes to the body. The arteries become hard, the heart loses its strength and rhythm, the skin loses its elasticity and muscle, bones become brittle, the body shrinks in size and physical activity diminishes. The brain, and with it the mind, also undergoes changes, and in some the ravages of dementia are added to the list of miseries that old age brings. In my own old age I have followed the general pattern of bodily change, but mercifully I have been spared the last named affliction. However, I sometimes find it difficult to recall my actions of only a few days ago, or where I have left certain objects, my keys, my reading glasses and so on, but in compensation I seem to have acquired the ability to recall vividly and in detail happenings that took place three quarters of a century and more ago. My own old age has brought with it also an inability to fall readily asleep, and as I lie awake in bed I have taken to probing deeper and deeper into my mind's river of memory and to dwell on happenings that took place a long time ago. There is a twilight zone between wakefulness and sleep where the mind takes wings and soars free. Long-forgotten and indistinct images appear, gradually take shape and become as real.

The memories of my early childhood until the age of five or thereabouts are vague and unclear. The first hazy recollection I can bring to mind is that of the figure of my father bending down over me as I lie in bed and presenting me with a toy wooden locomotive. As they came back to me I would sometimes discuss these old memories with my brother Ralph, who was six years older than I was. When I told him of my vague recollection of having been given a wooden train by our father, he recalled a Christmas in the early 1920s in our tenement flat in Surrey Street in the Gorbals, when father gave us both a present of little toy locomotives which he himself had fashioned out of bits of wood. Sadly I shall no longer be able to compare such memories with Ralph; he passed away last year after what could be described as a very good innings of ninety-two years. But no matter how long the path trodden may have been, the passing of a life is a sad occasion, and the death of my big brother, bringing with it the realisation of my own mortality, affected me more than I would ever have believed possible.

1

Surrey Street in the old Gorbals was the first home the Pieri family, my brother, father, mother and I, lived in when we first came to Glasgow. My father, Francesco, came to Scotland in 1919 from a little hamlet named Bacchionero, (Blackwoods) set high in the foothills of the Apuan Alps. It lies a few kilometres above the hilltop town of Barga in Tuscany, on the steep wooded slopes above that picturesque town. All that is left now of the hamlet are the ruins of a small stone chapel. In front of this there is a paved clearing, and on either side there are the ruins of a farmhouse and some small barns. The area is remote, deserted and difficult to access. There is no road, only a few overgrown paths no better than goat runs give access to the area, but the climb up from Barga, a lung and leg testing three hour trek, is well worth the effort, for the view from the clearing down into the valley beneath is spectacular. Since the end of the Second World War I have trudged up these paths many many times, although the walk seemed to become ever steeper for me as the years went by, finally rendering the journey impossible for me on foot. My last visit took place a few weeks ago, and that had to be done by means of a jeep, leaving me only a few hundred yards to negotiate unassisted. It was here that I was born eighty seven years ago, and it was here that as a boy of twelve in 1931 I spent what in retrospect was probably the happiest and most carefree year of my youth.

At the time of my birth at the beginning of the year 1919, the hills above and around Bacchionero were dotted with hundreds of tiny hamlets, whose inhabitants lived at a bare subsistence level, and whose way of life had not changed in a century. Most of the land above Barga was owned by an absentee landlord, Pietro Bertacchi, who let out little parcels of his huge estates to tenant crofters and their families. The bigger the family, the bigger was the croft offered, for everyone in the family, no matter how young, worked the land and thus the land could be made to produce more for the owner. These sharecroppers were known as *Mezzadri,* from the word *mezzo* (half). The rental paid to Bertacchi was not in cash, but consisted of one half of everything the land and the work of the sharecroppers yielded: grain, cured ham and meats from pigs, cheese from sheep and goats, milk products and, if the croft was big enough to sustain more than just a few sheep, some wool. At 900 to 1000 metres above sea level, vines could not be grown on these crofts, and a grape harvest, which could have given the families some extra income, was denied them. From time to time Bertacchi's agents would go round his estates with trains of mules (there were no roads, just trails which even a mule found difficulty negotiating) to collect his share of the produce, and whatever remained was for the crofter family to live on. They existed on what they produced, and barter was a common form of trading. One hamlet with a surplus of cheese would trade with another which had a surplus of grain, one with a surplus of wool would trade with another with a surplus of leather. A family with the skills to make wooden *zoccoli* (clogs) would trade with another which could make iron implements, and so on. Cash money was seldom used between these sharecropper families. To obtain cash would have meant selling some produce in Barga or in the Lucca valley beneath, and the lack of roads made the transportation of farm produce a daunting proposition.

One hamlet in the area which was the envy of all others was that of Bacchionero, the name given to about 450 acres of land in the centre of which stood a group of farm buildings set round a tiny square graced by a small church. Bacchionero was my birthplace and the birthplace of my mother Maria, and of her mother before her. Mass was said here every Sunday by a priest who came from the village of Renaio in the valley below riding on a mule, but who returned home after the service on foot, with the mule laden with offerings from his parishioners: eggs, cheeses, hams and, a great delicacy, chestnut flour.

The church was the proud possessor of an organ, housed on a tiny balcony facing the altar, and during the year I was to spend in Bacchionero as a boy of twelve, I was given the task of pumping the handle so that the attached bellows could feed air into the pipes of the organ. One day each week the church would be used as a school, run by the priest for those who wanted to learn how to read and write, and such was the hunger for literacy among these sharecroppers that the church was always packed with persons of all ages for the lessons, from the very young to the very old.

The relative affluence of the Carani family, about fifteen in all including my mother, generations of whom had worked the land for the Bertacchis over the years, was based on the fact that the few houses and the tiny church that made up Bacchionero had been built on good fertile land in the middle of a huge forest of chestnut trees which produced tons of chestnuts every year. The trees shed their load of chestnuts at the onset of autumn, and these had to be gathered immediately or else they would lie and rot on the ground or be carried off by the wildlife of the region. Every year at chestnut harvest time, scores of families congregated in Bacchionero, either from the Lucca valley beneath or from the other side of the Apuan Alps, journeys of many miles made on foot over rocky and dangerous paths. Men, women and young children, they all set themselves to gathering the precious chestnuts until mountains of them had accumulated in the area in front of the church.

The harvest could last for a week or more, with the peasants sleeping in barns or stables or wherever could afford shelter from the cold autumn nights. The chestnuts were taken to a neighbouring farmhouse known as Carletti, named after the family who had originally lived there, and now occupied by the Santi family, my mother's in-laws through her sister Rosa. Built on the steep side of a hill and with no livestock except a few pigs and chickens, Carletti produced nothing. It had a mill wheel driven by the power of a fast flowing stream over which the house had been built, and to this wheel all the corn and grain and chestnuts of the neighbouring crofts were brought to be ground into flour. The Santi family who lived there in the early part of the twentieth century and who operated the mill, received payment in the form of some sacks of flour in addition to cured meats and cheese or whatever else might be offered by those who had made use of the their water-driven grinding wheel.

The mill had been there for all of living memory. I used to wonder, and still do, as to how the huge millstone, weighing many hundredweights, could have been dragged up those steep hills from the valley below. In 1943, the Santi family became the proud possessor of the first electric lighting to be seen in those remote hills, generated by a dynamo stripped from a German jeep which had been ambushed and destroyed in the neighbouring hills by a group of partisans. The dynamo was fitted to the mill wheel drive and produced enough current to light a few low wattage bulbs.

As soon as their work was done and the last chestnut gathered, the chestnut pickers returned to their homes. Payment for their work consisted of as much flour as they could load on their backs. Father and mother and children, all heavily laden like beasts of burden with as many sacks of chestnut flour as each could carry, took to the rocky paths, some to descend into the valley below and some to climb back over the Apuan Alps into the valleys there, a backbreaking journey of two or three days.

One half of the remaining flour was collected by Bertacchi's agents and the Carani family of Bacchionero kept the rest, this to provide them with luxuries such as olives and wine, bartered for the chestnut flour by crofters from the Lucca valley below.

The chestnut trees provided another source of income for the Caranis. In the winter months old trees would be felled and the trunk and branches cut into logs and charred over open fires. The charred logs were then tied into bundles and sent to the valley below by means of a primitive one-way funicular cable, there to be sold as firewood.

This had been the way of life in the hills above Barga for centuries, and was the way of life of thousands of peasant families in the hills of Tuscany, a life of work and drudgery which kept body and soul together but offered no hope or opportunity for a better life in the future. These were the conditions that confronted my father when he returned to his family from the First World War. Strong and ambitious, he had no desire to follow the way of life of his ancestors, and so he turned to the escape route which had been taken by millions of Italians before him—emigration. Before the war he had spent some years in America, where my brother Ralph was born, but the introduction of a quota system by the government there, in an effort to limit the influx of immigrants from the Mediterranean countries, thus severely restricting the number of immigrants from Italy, had closed that door to him. It did not matter that my father had lived and worked in the USA for a number of years before the war or that my brother Ralph was born there. In a society where neither merit, need, nor right counted for anything, my father had neither the connections nor the money to bribe corrupt officials to be put at the top of an emigration list as thousands were doing, and so he would have to take his place in the queue, which meant a wait of many, many years. Now that I had arrived on the scene, he was faced with the bleak prospect of scratching a living in Bacchionero to feed not only himself, but a wife and two sons. With the door to America closed, he set about searching for another place where work was available and where effort would be rewarded.

My father turned to the one agency which could offer help—the Church. The local priest, who came to say Mass in the little chapel in Bacchionero every Sunday, was consulted. He was well-informed in the affairs of the outside world, and spoke of a city called Glasgow in the country of Scotland in the far north of Britain. A number of families from the district had found jobs there, a man from Barga named Primo Marchi had set up some fried fish shops in Glasgow and was looking for good and willing workers to man them. There were, as yet, no travel restrictions to that part of the world, so the decision was made, and with the promise of work and lodgings from this man Marchi, my father and mother packed what few possessions they had, wrapped us up well to face the reported rigours of the Scottish weather and set off on the four-day journey to Glasgow.

Primo Marchi provided the family with a two-room tenement flat in Surrey Street in the Gorbals district to live in and my father was put to work in one of Marchi's newly opened fish and chip shops, the Savoy, at the corner of Hope Street and Renfrew Street. I was to learn later that the only furnishings contained in the flat were a table and some chairs and two mattresses for us to sleep on. The beds came later, when father had put together a few shillings to buy them. The one good feature of the flat was that since it was on the ground floor with no neighbours, the outside toilet did not have to be shared with other families, as was the case in the upper floor flats, where one toilet had to serve for three dwellings.

In the Savoy he learned to prepare and to serve a dish completely unknown in his native Barga, fried fish and chips, and although the working day was of twelve hours, six days a week, it was not as heavy and as concentrated as some of the work he had known in America. By the standards of the day his weekly wage of £3 was adequate, and each week a few shillings would be set aside towards the day when he would be able to set up a little shop of his own, for that was the dream of every Italian immigrant: to have a business of your own, and to own a home of your own.

I don't remember much about our time spent in Surrey Street, for more than eighty years have now gone by since then. We lived there until 1925 or so, and the only distinct memory I have is that of a constant red glow in the sky, day and night, which as I was later to learn, came from the nearby iron works, Dixon's Blazes, where, in the interests of a cost-effective use of the coal which fuelled them, the blast furnaces were never extinguished. These furnaces were also the source of an all-pervading smell of sulphur and of a fine red dust, which on still days constantly covered everything in the neighbourhood. This brought about the birth of a much spoken phrase in the family which Ralph and I used throughout our entire lives to wish away some unpleasant event: 'if only the wind would blow!'

I also remember the rumble and clanking and puffing noises of trains as they passed over a railway bridge which almost touched the roof of the tenement and the soot which drifted down after they had passed. After a while, a practised ear could tell if the wagons were heavily or lightly laden. The wheels of an engine pulling heavily loaded wagons would tend to slip on the rails as the engine accelerated, giving rise to a blast of increased noise from slipping wheels and escaping steam. Driven by nostalgia, I motor through that district now from time to time. Surrey Street and Dixon's Blazes have long since been demolished, and in their place there is some derelict open ground, but the railway bridge over the road is still there and still in use.

Sometimes, whilst on such excursions through what remains of the areas I lived in all those years ago, the sight of an old street or building seems to re-awaken in me the recollection of vague smells and odours, for the Glasgow of those days was a city of stenches and odours which have now vanished from the environment, but which still linger in the memory. On the northern side of the river Clyde and acting as a counterpoint to Dixon's Blazes in the south, the huge Buchanan Street railway goods station was the source of a variety of ripe odours which could spread over the Cowcaddens and into the city centre itself. The station housed hundreds of carthorses in a vast stable, whose emanations served as a foundation for the smell of oily steam and smoke belched out by the hundreds of goods trains which puffed in and out of Buchanan Street every day. Mixed in with this sea of smells was the all pervading stink of a tannery in a neighbouring street, Dobbies Loan, which vied with the stench of an animal fat rendering factory in the same area. These emanations would mix in with the distinctive subway smell from the Cowcaddens and Buchanan Street undergrounds, all of which went to create a suitable mix for the slum smells rising from the ripe backyard middens and common stairhead lavatories of the surrounding tenements.

In later years our family was to make our own small contribution to these smells, in the form of the odours produced by the frying of fish and chips in the Savoy restaurant, which was to come into our possession in the early 1930s, and which was situated just a few hundred yards from the railway station. There were no filters or ducts to take away the heavy smell of cooking in animal fats in those days; this was allowed to float free into the surrounding atmosphere, where it blended in with the wide spectrum of smells already there. The scene was rendered more Dickensian in the winter, when soot from the coal fires which heated the city tenements would mix in with the fog and mist which often descended over Glasgow. A black and smelly and impenetrable darkness at noon would then prevail over the entire city.

After a few years working for Marchi, my father had acquired the reputation of being a dependable and trustworthy man, and was offered a fish and chip shop in Crown Street for a year's hire. The owner, a Mr Guidi, was an immigrant from our same Barga district who wanted to go back home for a spell and needed a reliable person to run his shop for the period of his absence.

There, at about the age of five, my clear memories begin. We now lived in much better accommodation in Crown Street in a tenement flat above the shop, far enough removed from the rumble and soot of the trains and the fine red dust of the smelting furnaces. It was a first floor flat, so we had to share the toilet on the landing with two other families, but I remember that mother told us that they were "*Gente Pulite*" (clean people), and enjoined us to leave the toilet in good order after using it. To this end she provided a neat pile of suitably cut newspaper to be drawn on when visiting this communal lavatory.

I started school at St Francis in Cumberland Street, and it was there I first realised that I was somehow different from the other boys. I was a "Tally", my parents spoke English with a broken accent, and when one of them came to pick me up at school they spoke to me and I answered them in a language my school colleagues did not understand, all of which made me feel vaguely and inexplicably uneasy and almost ashamed of being different from the rest.

A strangely dichotomous way of life had begun for myself and my brother. We were language-perfect in Glasgow English, so we merged well into our Scottish environment. But then after school hours our home environment was of a purely Italian nature, where only Italian was spoken, so my brother and I grew up to be completely bilingual. On thinking back over the fifty and more years that they were part of my life, I don't think I ever spoke a single word in English to either of my parents. My brother and I could slip easily and effortlessly from one language to the other and from one set of cultural values to the other, and we were at all times aware of the difference in origin and way of life between ourselves, our school companions and our Scottish neighbours.

To some extent this feeling of displacement, I suppose, could well have been created by ourselves. The vast cultural differences and the language barrier between Tuscan and Glaswegian made close contact with the locals impossible for our parents. For them socializing was limited to the occasional Sunday visit to one or other of the few Italian families in the neighbourhood, and my brother and

I were never actively encouraged to introduce outsiders into the family circle. By the same token, although I played quite happily with the other children in our street, I cannot remember ever having been invited into a local household as a boy.

I remember the Sundays in Crown Street quite clearly. On that day the shop did not open. Our mother dressed us up in our Sunday best, and proudly marched the family off to Mass. Sometimes on the Sundays when the Xaverian fathers organized special Masses for Italians, we were taken to the cathedral in Clyde Street to listen to the fire and brimstone sermons from the pulpit. I remember one priest vividly, Padre Calza, I think his name was. He had lost an arm during the First World War and used his remaining one to thrash the air and pound the pulpit as he warned us of the fate that awaited if we did not obey the ten commandments. He was a powerful orator with a deep and commanding voice, and on the Sundays when he said Mass and preached and quoted the Gospels from the pulpit, there was not a seat to be had in the packed Cathedral. His sermons were in Italian, and although many of the faithful present were locals with no knowledge of the language, the congregation sat as if hypnotized by his voice and flamboyant gestures. His powerful voice led the singing of the hymns, and I can clearly bring to mind the high-pitched keening voices of the Italian women present as they joined in.

Afterwards, our mother would have prepared a traditional Italian meal for the Sunday lunch. She was a marvelous cook and Ralph and I would fill ourselves with a pasta dish of some sort, served in a sauce that only a devoted Italian housewife can conjure up, with homemade ravioli always a great favourite. This would be followed by a variety of roasts, to be rounded off with some sort of traditional Italian dessert. At this meal Ralph and I would be allowed a glass of wine, poured with a flourish by my father from a straw-covered bottle, probably bought in Fazzi's delicatessen in Clyde Street. Ralph's glass was much larger than mine, as befitted his greater years. Our mother was an intensely religious woman, and after the Sunday meal the family was made to say the rosary together to give thanks for all the blessings God had bestowed on us. In retrospect I don't think that my father was all that religious; he led the answers to the prayers at quite a speed, as if he wanted to get it over with so as to enjoy the rest of the day.

In summer we took a penny ticket on the tram to Queen's Park at the top end of Victoria Road, followed by a walk in the park, perhaps stopping for a while to listen to the brass band which usually played in the semi-circular bandstand close by the entrance. We would then walk through the park alongside the boating pond to arrive at the Bluebird café at the Pollokshaws Road entrance for an ice-cream wafer, and then, pleasantly tired, a penny ticket on the tram towards home. I also remember Sundays in Crown Street because of the backyard singers who used to sing in the back court of our tenement in the hope of having a penny thrown to them from one of the windows above. These singers all had loud, high-pitched nasal voices and all sang the same plaintive songs. My mother never threw them money, but would always wrap up some food, 'a piece', and lower it down to them on a piece of string from our third storey kitchen window. This method of delivery was resorted to after some dropped 'pieces' had burst open on impact with the ground.

On Saturdays there was no school, and on those mornings I helped in the shop preparing the fish and chips for that day's business. I hated that job despite the sixpenny bit I was given as pocket money at the end of it, for I always finished with some fish bones sticking out of frozen fingers. I remember the Saturdays too for the pitch and toss sessions which took place in our backyard. Because of its situation on a corner site, ours was far bigger than the neighboring ones, so that was probably why it was chosen by the punters for that particular pastime. In a pitch and toss game a half crown or two shilling piece was thrown on the ground and coins were then tossed at them, the one landing nearest the target picking up all the money. The game was controlled by a 'belt man', so-called because of the leather metal-buckled belt he wielded as a weapon against rule-breakers and cheats. A blow delivered to the head by the heavy metal buckle was enough to lay a man senseless, and seldom did an afternoon go by without some transgressor being laid low by a blow from it. With an audience of children standing on the midden roofs the better to see the action, the pitch and toss sessions were rough and rowdy affairs which often ended in fights, and the police were always on hand to break the games up and arrest one or two of the troublemakers.

Fridays I remember only too well. Before going to bed on Fridays we had to submit to a wash-down in a hot tub of water, since there were no such luxuries as baths in the tenement flats of those days. After the body wash came the de-lousing procedure, where a week's accumulation of head lice acquired from your school companions was combed from your hair by the use of a fine comb. I can still remember the sharp crack as a scurrying louse was trapped and disposed of by mother's thumbnail. Finally your head was submitted to a wash in a basin of hot water laced with Lysol, a strong disinfectant, which, I am told, is in use to this very day. These were necessary procedures, but not to be enjoyed.

I remember too, the General Strike of 1926, which took place during our time in Crown Street. The entire workforce of the nation had gone on strike in support of the miners, who had been subjected to a wage cut by the government and had gone on strike in protest. Railwaymen, transport workers, dockers, printers, builders, iron and steel workers, engineers and shipyard workers, a total of four million men, all stopped work in protest at the government's action. I don't know how, but my father managed to get hold of a horse and cart, and on Sundays he searched the neighbouring countryside for supplies to keep the shop going. There was no coal to be had for firing the fish frying range, so I remember going with him and my brother Ralph to the coal bings in Kirkintilloch to gather as many pieces of coal as we could from the mounds of coal dross piled up near the pits, a labour which as I recall left us covered from head to toe by the fine coal dust.

On the road back to Crown Street we sometimes stopped at various farms to load up with potatoes. Some of these farms also kept us going with lard rendered down from slaughtered pigs, which would go to augment the scarce supply of cooking fats available. The pig lard very often got mixed in with the fine debris from the coal, and no matter how many times a fine wire mesh sieve was passed through the hot dripping, some of the fine coal dust could not be filtered out, resulting in coal dust speckled fish and chips. I don't remember how we managed to get fish; maybe we sold just pies and black puddings with the chips, as they were made locally and didn't need transportation. I don't suppose I'll ever know now that Ralph is no longer around to ask. During the General Strike, despite the use of precious coal to heat the water, the Friday hot tub was in use every night to rid us of the coal dust which adhered to everything we touched.

Crown Street was a main road leading directly into George Square, and during the strike crowds of demonstrating workers would often pass our shop on their way to protest meetings in front of the civic buildings in the square. There were frequent clashes with the police and at times even the Army was called out to maintain order. One day after one of these disturbances, a man was brought into the shop by some friends, blood streaming from a cut on his head, and mother washed the wound and tied a makeshift bandage round the man's head. His friends too were covered in bruises, and I remember how tired and gaunt they all looked, and how profuse they were in their thanks when mother made them some sandwiches and mugs of tea.

Having seen how much more money could be earned by working for yourself rather than for others, at the end of our lease in the Crown Street shop, father sought the hire of another shop, and found one in Butterbiggins Road near Queen's Park. With it came a change of home and our first taste of luxury, for we now actually had an indoor toilet which did not have to be shared with anyone, and for me there was a change of school to Holy Cross primary, in Dixon Avenue, I think it was. Compared to St Francis, Holy Cross was very posh, and I didn't get called 'a dirty wee Tally' there so often and didn't have so many fights in the playground. The headmistress there was a Miss Kampf. She was very nice and used to organize tram outings for the pupils on Sundays. Since this clashed with our family arrangements I remember her coming to our house to ask my parents if it was all right for me to go on these trips. As I recall, the trams went out as far as Milngavie, and she used to take us for long walks up to Mugdockbank and round the reservoirs.

I made my first communion at Holy Cross Church, and afterwards we would be taken by the school to confession there once a week. There was a priest, Father Graham, I think his name was, who put the fear of God in you every time you confessed to him. He used to thunder at you in the confessional in the same way that the Italian priest Padre Calza did from the pulpit. His condemnations could be heard quite clearly by the penitents waiting outside, and all the boys did their best to avoid going to him. I remember someone saying that he had been a Church of Scotland minister once and had converted to Catholicism, which made him much more severe than the usual priest.

I sat my qualifying exam there and did well enough to go on to a 1A class in St Mungo's in Duke Street by the side of the Molendinar burn. The school was directly opposite a woman's prison, and the boys used to vie with one another to run errands to the top of the school tower where our janitor, a Mr Grace, kept his cleaning supplies. From the top of the tower we could see down into the prison yard where the women took their exercise.

In Butterbiggins Road, for the first time, I began to form friendships with some of the neighbours. Next to the shop there lived the McMeighan family. Mr McMeighan was a cornet player in the Empire pit orchestra, and his son John, who was about eighteen or so, played the violin, and they would invite me in to listen to their gramophone. They had some marvellous records of Caruso and Tetrazzini and Lawrence Tibbet, and of a Spanish guitar player named Segovia; and at the more popular end of the musical spectrum they introduced me to the music of Louis Armstrong and Paul Whiteman, and to the singing of Rudy Vallee. They had recordings of an American negro singer, Paul Robeson, and when they played his records they used tell me of the bad treatment and oppression the negroes in America were subjected to. They had a daughter, Nan, who was a librarian, and she used to bring Ralph and me books to read about such matters, even though I was perhaps still too young to understand them fully. Their favourite recordings were those of Duke Ellington, and I would sit entranced as Mr McMeighan identified the various instruments in the orchestra as they weaved their tapestry of rhythmic jazz music. He could name each player in the orchestra, and I soon became familiar with the names of the Ellington musicians, Cootie Williams, Barney Bigard, Juan Tizol and so on. It was the first time I had ever been asked into a Scottish home, and the McMeighans opened up a whole new world of fascinating music to me.

I made another friendship at that time, one that was to last a lifetime. Francis Traynor was a quiet likeable boy a few years older than I was, who lived round the corner in Inglefield Street and who came in occasionally to buy some chips. My mother felt sorry for him and would see to it that he always got a few extra chips in his pennyworth, and took to asking him into the back shop to eat a hot pie or some such delicacy. Francy came from a very poor family, and undernourishment as a child had left him with badly curved shinbones, the result of rickets. This condition was prevalent in Glasgow in those days, at a time when many a family did not have enough to eat and children were starved of the minerals necessary for proper growth.

Francy was a very intelligent and likeable youth, and mother took to teaching him a few words of Italian. He was fascinated by the amount of food lying around in our back shop, and would often say that his ambition was to work in a restaurant, so that he would never be short of food again. True to his word, he became a chef and finished his working days as a cook in the kitchens of the Central Hotel in Glasgow. During the war he joined the merchant navy as a cook, and survived the sinking of eleven of his ships, which I am sure must be some sort of a record. He loved music, and we both spent many an enchanted hour listening to the McMeighans' gramophone. When I eventually married, twenty or so years later, Francy acted as my best man, but he himself remained a bachelor for the rest of his life. He was acutely aware of his crooked shins and eschewed the company of the opposite sex. As we all must, he died some years ago, in his late eighties.

It was in Butterbiggins Road that I saw my first talking picture. I was allowed to go to the cinema once a week, and went usually to the Majestic, a simple barn-like structure in Inglefield Street just round the corner from our shop . I watched and enjoyed cowboy pictures with stars like Tom Mix and Buck Jones and Hoot Gibson, all silent films of course, and I remember films with Harold Lloyd and Mary Pickford. One film which came back to the Majestic time and time again and which I went to see many times was *The Black Pirate* with Douglas Fairbanks, and I loved the sequence where he abseils down the sails of the pirate ship, slitting them with a dagger, thus rendering them useless and bringing the ship to a halt.

Then, in the early thirties, the talkies came to Glasgow, to the Coliseum in Eglinton Street, and people queued up for hours to hear Al Jolson sing in *The Jazz Singer*. I was dying to see and hear this new marvel, but the Coliseum was too far away for me to go there alone, and besides it cost sixpence for the cheapest seat, which for me was out of the question. The matinee at the Majestic, which I frequented every Saturday, was only a penny for children. After a year or so the talkies finally came to the BB Cinerama, a big cinema at the corner of Butterbiggins Road and Victoria Road. To this day I don't know what the initials BB stood for. There the matinee tickets for children were only threepence and there I saw my first talkie, *The Hounds of Zaroff,* with an actor called Leslie Banks. I must have gone back to see it a dozen times, so fascinated was I at hearing voices and background music coming from the screen.

When I was about thirteen years of age, disaster struck the family. My father took ill. Years of hard and unrelenting work had taken their toll, and he collapsed behind the shop counter during a busy Friday night session. The doctor was called in. I remember him vividly, a kind and gentle Dr Easterman who routinely attended the family during the not uncommon bout of measles, chicken pox and other such childhood ailments. For his visits a lace doily would be set on the kitchen table, on it a glass of Vermouth with an amaretto or some such delicacy. Beside the glass some money would have been discreetly placed; five shillings or so, to be pocketed by the doctor with a polite cough and acknowledging nod before partaking of the refreshment. Dr Easterman carefully examined my father and prescribed a long rest in some place with clean air and wholesome food. As the one who as yet did not contribute anything to the maintenance of the family, it was my duty to accompany my father for a year's stay in Bacchionero, where he could recover the health lost in the past years of strain and worry and hard work. I still had about a year's compulsory schooling left before I would have joined my brother behind the counter in the family shop, but schooling was not important; it was my duty to accompany my father. What was important was that the breadwinner should recover his health so as to take his proper place at the head of the family.

For a whole year I lived and worked and played amongst the magnificent chestnut trees of those valleys high above the town of Barga. With my two older cousins I helped tend the sheep and milk the goats and the two cows which Bacchionero boasted of, and helped to thresh wheat with a primitive contraption consisting of two pieces of wood, one long, one short. The two pieces were joined by a leather strap, with the short piece serving as a handle for swinging the long one hard down onto the wheat stalks laid out on the stone slabs in front of the church. The threshing done, stalks and grains would be spread out on a circular hand-held sieve, and tossed up into the wind, thus allowing the chaff to be blown away, with the heavier grain remaining. Then I would watch as the grains were ground by a water-driven millstone at the Carletti croft, where my aunt and some cousins lived, and there I would help to load the landlord Bertacchi's share on to the mules of his agents.

I still have clear memories of the small army of crofters and their families who came to Bacchionero at chestnut harvesting time. I remember the songs they sang in the evening around the fires as they roasted and ate the freshly gathered chestnuts, and I can still see them in my mind's eye afterwards, wending their way home to the valleys below, laden with huge loads of chestnut flour.

Sundays were special days in Bacchionero. On that day, the priest from the little village of Renaio, far down the valley, said Mass in the little chapel for the benefit of the neighboring crofters. Whole families would come from miles around for the ceremony, and since the church could accommodate no more than fifty persons or so, the congregation was made up almost exclusively of women. The menfolk stood in the little piazza in front during the ceremony and paid scant attention to the proceedings. However, they observed a dutiful silence and genuflected, together with a quick sign of the cross, when the tinkling of the Eucharist bell was heard from within. I was given the job of hand pumping the bellows to feed air into a little organ set high on a tiny balcony. The organ was played by my cousin Chiara, and I remember vividly the high-pitched penetrating voices of the women as they joined in the singing of the hyms, so like the singing I remembered from the Italian masses celebrated from time to time in Glasgow. After Mass, my uncle Peppino would open up a makeshift bar in one of the barns for the dispensing of refreshments to those willing to part with a few centesimi for the taste of my aunt Casilda's *necci*, a hot thin chestnut flour pancake liberally spread with soft ricotta cheese and washed down with a glass or two of rich red wine. Since no vines grew at Bacchionero's altitude, as likely as not the wine would have been brought there by the visitors as barter for some sacks of the Carani family's renowned chestnut flour.

There were times too when I helped my cousins to char the logs of wood which would be sold in winter to heat the houses of the rich people in Lucca many kilometres away. The wood was prepared by slowly baking the green, freshly-cut logs over a slow fire, and to this day the smell of burning wood evokes in me the memories of those days. I once nearly killed myself by taking a ride on one of these bundles of charred wood which the *carbonari* (charcoal makers) sent to the valley below on a rickety funicular, and I clung on in terror as the load went whizzing down the cable until gravity brought it to a stop about a mile away and about 300 feet lower than the point of departure. For my foolhardiness I was given a sound thrashing by my father, a sure sign that he was rapidly recovering his health.

I enjoyed every minute of my carefree stay in those hills, possibly because I knew that I did not have to live the rest of my life there and would eventually be going back to what had become my home. For, strangely enough, I had become as much an outsider in my place of birth as I was in Glasgow. There I was the wee Tally; here in Bacchionero and the surrounding hamlets I was '*Lo Scozzesino*', the wee Scots boy.

With my father now fully recovered, we returned to Glasgow, where for a year my mother and my brother of barely seventeen years of age had kept the family shop going and had earned enough to pay the rent and put a few shillings aside for the future. It is hard to visualize what life must have been like for them, a woman and a boy in his teens without the head of the family to fall back on; the hard unremitting drudgery of going to the fish market in the morning, the washing and cleaning of hundredweights of potatoes and several stones of fish each day, the preparations and the serving of the finished article to a clientele, a small percentage of whom were sometimes only too prone to address you with sneers and insults. It was during my time in Bacchionero that I began to mature mentally, and started out on the long road to understanding just what emigration meant in terms of psychological adjustment, and came to realize what a culture-shock it must have been for my mother to leave the clean air and simple life of her birthplace for the dark, soot-blackened tenements of the Gorbals.

❧ 2 ❧

The Savoy Days

At the end of the Butterbiggins Road lease, the family moved to Auchinleck, a small mining town in Ayrshire, where a shop was available for hire. The shop offered to my father belonged to Primo Togneri of Troon, who had married a Pieri and who owned the well-known Tog's Café in the sea-side resort. Although I was about fourteen at the time, the move to Auchinleck spelled the end of my school days, for I didn't bother to register at any school there, and I went straight to work.

In the great majority of Italian immigrant families in those days it was expected that the sons would follow in the father's footsteps and help in the family business, and since Ralph had already been serving behind a counter for several years now, I took it for granted that I would be leaving school as soon as possible to work beside him in the shop. Besides, although I had been fairly good at most subjects, I was struggling a bit at school. I had missed a whole year when in Bacchionero with my father, and was finding it difficult to catch up with subjects when I returned to St Mungo's. English and history and geography and suchlike subjects I could cope with, but to this day I remember the feeling of helplessness when I attended my first Maths class on my return. The class was already well advanced into the subject, so I hadn't a clue what the teacher was talking about, and the xs and the ys on the board did not mean a thing to me.

The shop in Auchinleck was on the main road at the side of a sloping path leading up to the railway station. The shop had two entrances, one leading into the fish and chip side of the business and the other into the ice cream café side of the shop. Every morning at seven o' clock either Ralph or I would wheel a trolley up into the station to await the arrival of the goods train which carried fish for us from the Glasgow market. The fish and potatoes were prepared in a yard behind the shop. That was our work, Ralph's and mine, and since the yard was in the open, with only a corrugated iron roof to give shelter from rain, hands and fingers soon became numb with cold. Pails of hot water were always on hand for us to dip them into. The shop was extremely busy and at night would be packed with the working population of the town. Although my father called them *I Pollachi* (the Poles), these were mainly miners from Lithuania, a rough and noisy bunch, and at first I was terrified of their demeanour and rough speech, but they were in the main a harmless lot, and a word from my mother would suffice to calm any rough behaviour. We had been advised to have a woman act as peacemaker if any fighting should break out amongst them. The intervention of a man would have resulted in a fracas directed at the intruder, but none of the miners would ever even think of laying hands on a woman. The café boasted a radiogram, the first I had ever seen, and Ralph and I would spend hours playing gramophone records, listening amazed at the sound produced by electrical amplification, so much clearer and louder than the sounds produced by the old horn-equipped gramophone of the McMeighans in Butterbiggins Road.

During our time in Auchinleck we received a visit from our aunt and uncle from Minnesota, who after thirty years in America were returning to their native Italy to spend their old age in the Barga of their birth. I remember my Uncle Paolo well. He was a jolly little man who was overjoyed at finding himself in a country where alcoholic drinks could be bought and consumed openly without fear of arrest. Those were the years of prohibition in the USA, the years when all alcoholic drink was banned and all drinking had to be done in illicit speakeasies where one could never be sure of the composition of the drinks served, and where one not only ran the risk of being arrested whilst in the middle of enjoying a glass of beer but also of being slowly poisoned by the moonshine liquor usually served in such places. During the month my uncle spent with us in Auchinleck, he made up for all the lost drinking time of his past years in Minnesota and went on a four weeks' crawl of all the pubs in Auchinleck area, of which there were many. I was given the job of minder and of making sure that he did not get lost in his new environment as his alcoholic haze increased, and I spent many a half hour waiting patiently outside pub after pub as he consumed pint after pint and chasers of whisky. At my age, fourteen or so, I was of course not allowed through the doors of any of these pubs, despite the risk of catching pneumonia on the cold pavements outside as I waited patiently for Uncle Paolo to emerge.

Our relatives had brought presents for myself and Ralph from America. I forget what his was, but mine was a five years subscription to a new American publication, *Time*, a weekly news magazine in its first years of publication and which did not as yet appear on the British news-stands. Although I was barely 14 I had by this time become a voracious reader of anything I could lay my hands on. There was a library only a few yards away from the shop and I would borrow any book that was of interest to me. I used to read these books behind the shop counter and the library attendants sometimes complained that the returned books smelled of fish and chips. Mr McMeighan, of our Butterbiggins Road days, had deeply held left-wing political beliefs and had introduced me to the socialist writers of that era. I read pamphlets by Guy Aldred, a political radical of the day, and other books issued by his Strickland Press. I went through books by Aldous

17

Huxley, by JB Priestley, by AJ Cronin. A great favourite of mine was his *Hatter's Castle*, which I occasionally browse through even now. I devoured the writings of Sinclair Lewis, John Dos Passos and Upton Sinclair, and my breast seethed with righteous anger as the exploitation of the American workers was graphically described in his novels *Jungle* and *Oil*. Not that I fully understood at that age the arguments set out in these books, but as each word new to me appeared I immediately sought its meaning in my by now well-thumbed dictionary and my understanding of the issues presented in these books slowly grew.

I welcomed my uncle's gift of this new *Time* magazine, for it opened up new horizons to me, the world of America and how the world was seen through American eyes. Each week for five years the postman would deliver a copy to our door, and when finally the subscription ended I was able to renew it in the UK with the international edition which had now appeared on the scene. I was not to know then that my aunt's present was to have unexpected and far-reaching effects on my life in the years to come. I should have been alerted as early as 1935 that the Home Office in London was keeping an eye on the magazine. In that year copies of *Time* were being delivered to me with several pages cut out of the foreign news section each week. I wrote to the magazine, at that time published in Chicago, complaining about this, and a few weeks later, in a plain envelope, I received the missing pages, which had been cut from the magazine by the British censor. The pages dealt with the affair between King Edward and Mrs Simpson, news of which had been kept from the British public. The whole world knew of the affair, apart from the people of Britain, who were kept in the dark for many months by their own government. Years after the war, as I shall recount later, I was to learn that a dossier was kept by the police on all Aliens, and on mine was underlined the fact that I was a subscriber to *Time* magazine. The powers that be considered *Time* to be an extreme right-wing publication of a fascist nature, therefore I too must have had fascist leanings! A conclusion that was to contribute to my being arrested at the outbreak of war with Italy.

I was about fourteen years of age when we took over the Savoy. Towards the end of our year in Auchinleck, word came through that the lease on the Savoy, where my father had first worked on his arrival in Glasgow, was up for sale. The asking price was £250. My father did not have that amount of money, so he went to the owner of the shop, Vincenzo Napolitano, with a proposal. He would give him £50 now, and would pay a further £250 over two years, thus bringing the selling price up to £300. Although the Savoy was a busy shop and worth every penny of the £250 asked, it was not an easy shop to sell. Although it did a roaring trade, so difficult was it to run that during the ten years of its existence the Savoy had gone through five owners, and had acquired a notorious reputation amongst the Italians of Glasgow. The place was just too difficult to control. Set at the edge of the city centre it was flanked at the rear by pubs and drinking dens, and the street corner on which it stood served as bus terminal for the mining towns on the outskirts of Glasgow. Given the trading potential for their wares, the area was a stamping ground for the hordes of prostitutes who plied their trade the length of Hope Street, from the Central Station to the Cowcaddens, and at night the Savoy was a focal point for all this low-life. It did a roaring trade, but drunks, prostitutes and toughs abounded, fights and disturbances were nightly occurrences, so small wonder that the shop had changed hands so many times in so few years; each owner put up with the dreadful place for a short time for the sake of the money to be made, but then would move on, nerves frayed and courage exhausted. But my father had seen the amount of business done there and was well aware of the still greater potential of the place if properly run, and realised that this was his chance to acquire a business the family could build on.

Vincent Napolitano had run the place for two years or so, and wanted no more of it. The shop had been up for sale for many weeks now, but no buyer had come forward. He had made a substantial amount of money during his tenure, but he had had enough of the nightly fights and disturbances and insults of his customers. He could stand it no longer, he wanted out, so he accepted my father's offer. The Savoy, the fish and chip shop which by the late thirties was to become something of an institution in the district, stood at the southern edge of the Cowcaddens, on the corner of Renfrew Street and Hope Street. It was situated at the edge of cinema and theatreland, and surrounded by a sea of public houses which ranged from the posh Guy's and Lauder's, down through the less elaborate Atholl Arms and Glen Afton to the many drinking dens frequented by the less savoury elements of the Cowcaddens. It drew its custom from the richly variegated spectrum of humanity attracted to the area by all these amenities, and profited also from the custom provided by the inhabitants of the densely populated tenements behind it, whose staple diet seemed to consist largely of fish suppers, pies and chips and black puddings.

In 1933, the year our family took over the Savoy, it was no better than many of the drinking dens in the district and every bit as rough, and needed the use of a very strong arm to carry on business there. But my father, now about fifty-three years of age and fully recovered from his bout of ill-health, was made of stern stuff and was well able to cope. He could see the potential of the place if a better class of customer could be attracted, so he began the slow process of weeding out the riff-raff and of making the Savoy a place which decent people could frequent. In this he was helped by three things. Firstly, his physical strength and courage. Although only about five feet four inches in height, he was as strong as a bull and more than capable of dealing with the toughs and drunks who came about the place; there was never a fight started nor a disturbance created that my father could not handle. Secondly, a bus terminal was built some distance from the shop which siphoned the drunken miners and most of the prostitutes away from the immediate area, and the third very important factor was police sergeant Black Alec McCrae. Black Alec was an old friend of my father. During the First World War, several Scottish regiments had been sent to the northern Italian front to help stem the Austrian advance after the debacle at Caporetto, and there the two had met, fighting side by side in a mixed regiment in the bitter battles on the Piave, where they formed a friendship which was to be continued in later years. For to my father's delight, on taking over his new shop he discovered that his wartime companion was now a sergeant in the police, and patrolled the Savoy beat. Black Alec too was happy to renew the friendship.

'That's a bloody rough place you've landed yourself with, Frank, but if you want to sort it out, I'll back you up. The first thing you've got to do is bar all the whores, they bring nothing but trouble; then clean out the neds and riff raff. Don't kill anybody, but hit 'em hard and I'll run 'em in.'

And so the place was cleaned up. The prostitutes were told in no uncertain terms to go elsewhere and take their customers with them, and the toughs and troublemakers were given short shrift. If necessary they felt the heavy weight of my father's fists, then were subjected to a much more merciless hammering by Black Alec and his squad before spending a night in the cells. In a very short time the Savoy was transformed; word quickly spread amongst the troglodytes of the district: don't go near that place, you'll get a tanking if you do. At first business suffered; instead of the unruly mass of drunks and low life who frequented the place originally, in the evening very few tables were occupied, but as word of the good service and relative tranquillity to be found there spread, new customers were attracted, and soon even a greater volume of business than before was being done. Lots of drunks and semi-drunks came in as customers of course; there were very few about the streets then at night who were not frequenters of pubs, but the rougher elements to be found in the Savoy six months before had been eliminated and money once more began flowing steadily into the till.

We had to work hard in the new family shop, but we didn't mind that. The Savoy was ours, it was not a hired shop belonging to others, and the work we were doing was for our own benefit and for nobody else's. We closed on Sundays, but the remaining six days of the week demanded unremitting hard work. The day started at six o'clock in the morning, when I accompanied my father to the fishmarket in the Briggate, as early as possible so as to select and buy the best of the fish on offer. The boxes chosen would be marked with the buyer's particular sign, usually his shop street number, and then, once having seen them loaded onto the carrier's horse-drawn cart, they became the carter's responsibility. Then, a visit to Cooper's coffee room in Howard Street for a coffee and a chat with one's fellow nationals was mandatory. The way from the fishmarket to Cooper's could have been found blindfolded, all one had to do was to follow the enticing odour of roasting coffee beans wafting from the coffee grinding and roasting machine in Cooper's shop window. On the way there, along Clyde Street, a stop would often be made at Fazzi's famous delicatessen at the Clyde suspension bridge for the purchase of some Italian food delicacy or some particular design of chip frying basket, various types of which hung suspended behind the counter. Then, a cup of coffee or so later, enjoyed in front of a welcoming coal fire always alight in the coffee room at Cooper's, back to the shop to start the real work of the day. The electrically powered potato washing and chip cutting machines which were beginning to appear on the market had as yet been installed in only a handful of fish and chip shops in Scotland, and all the preparation in the Savoy had to be done manually. A few hundredweight of potatoes had to be washed, peeled and cut into chips, either by hand with a knife or by means of a heavy guillotine-type potato cutter which required considerable strength and stamina to operate. Then the preparation of the fish, which by now the carter would have delivered to the shop premises, would begin. The fish used in most shops was usually haddock. Some of the shops in the poorer districts served whiting, a much cheaper fish which could lower the price of a fish supper from the sixpence charged in the better shops down to fourpence, or even less.

The fish, once freed from their bed of chipped ice in the boxes, would be headed, gutted and filletted, often by hand with no recourse to a knife. Winter or summer, this required a pail of hot water to revive one's hands and fingers, numb with cold from the ice-cold fish. My father was of the opinion that a fish with its bone extracted by the fingers, which left it with a rough-textured flesh rather than with the smooth surface imparted by a filletting knife, made for a far tastier fish. He maintained that the roughness left in the fish by tearing away the bone by hand trapped the tasty batter in which the fish was fried and gave it a better flavour. The smooth flesh left by a filleting knife, he claimed, allowed the batter mix to swell up on the surface of the fish, thus allowing grease to enter. Whatever the truth of his opinion, this was the way he wanted the fish prepared and the filleting process could go on till midday or after. The morning's work finished, a hearty meal would follow, almost always some traditional Italian dish prepared by our mother. After this we had a few free hours until the shop opened for business at 4.30pm, and so fifteen minutes before this deadline, down we went to the shop to start the fires and prepare for the night's business. In those far-off pre-war days there was no lunchtime potential for our type of restaurant. The working man almost invariably lived in the tenements built close to his place of work and could go home for his lunchtime break, or else could carry his lunch box with him. The busiest day of the week, as far as the carry-out section of the Savoy was concerned, was a Friday. One third of the population of Glasgow was Catholic, mainly from the Irish flow of immigration in earlier years of the century, and since Friday was a day of abstinence in the Catholic calendar, then on that day meat should not be eaten. The result was a long queue at the local fish and chip shop on Fridays at tea-time. We can only speculate as to what the pious had to eat on days of abstinence before the coming of fish and chips.

Religious discrimination was at a very high pitch then, and because of this Catholics found it difficult in those days of high unemployment to find work in the shipyards or in heavy industry in general. When some lucky ones did land a job, their religious affiliation was made obvious to their fellow workers on the first Friday of their employment. They were the only ones not to have a meat item of some sort in their lunchbox 'pieces', and the ubiquitous cheese or sardine sandwiches gave their Catholicism away. This almost always resulted in some mishap befalling them personally, or their tools would be made to vanish, thus effectively terminating their employment, leaving their job to be filled by someone of a religious persuasion acceptable to the management and the rest of the workers.

As far as the sitting area of the Savoy was concerned, because of the hordes of shoppers who thronged Sauchiehall Street and the crowds who queued up to see the latest movies at the nearby cinemas, Saturday was by far the busiest day. On Saturdays we opened from morning till night to serve a seemingly never-ending stream of hungry customers. At the peak of the Savoy's trading life, in the decade between 1950 and 1960 or thereabouts, at a time when there was as yet little or no competition in that area, on Saturdays we could go through a ton of potatoes and about 20 stone of fish, not to mention a crate of eggs and 100 steaks, each steak of four ounces weight and specially cut by Roger's butcher shop in the Cowcaddens. If, as was the case every second week, Rangers were playing at home at Ibrox, the hundreds of supporters making their way to and from the football ground to Buchanan Street Station passed our doors and a good proportion of them stopped to buy a fish supper. But by then we were employing a staff of fifteen workers or so, and we could cope well with such a flood of trade.

Ralph and I revelled in the hard work, for that and the long hours we spent behind the counter were beginning to pay dividends. My father paid me two pounds a week in wages, which was really pocket money, since I had no living expenses, and on my weekly day off I could jingle a few half crowns in my pocket and could treat myself to a good seat in the pictures. We were surrounded by picture houses. Directly across the road was the Savoy cinema, just round the corner in Sauchiehall Street the Gaumont cinema had its entrance, and directly across the road from it stood the La Scala. A few yards further west the Regal was to be found, and still further west at Charing Cross was the Kings, with the Norwood, one of the legendary entrepreneur Pickard's cinemas, close by. Round the corner in Renfield Street there was the Regent and the newly opened, state-of-the-art Paramount cinema, whose neon-lit frontage, with the first neon illuminations to be seen in Glasgow, drew large crowds to see this marvel of modernity. I remember the opening film, a Bing Crosby musical *We're Not Dressing* with Carol Lombard as his co-star.

Many of the staff of these cinemas were frequenters of the Savoy, and I got to know most of them. Often I would be allowed in without a ticket, and in winter I popped in and out of the cinema on an almost daily basis, sometimes only for the hour or so which I had free in the afternoon. This meant that I could almost never see a film in its entirety at the one sitting, but had to return on several occasions at different times if I wanted to see the whole of the production. My friendship with the cinema staff at times brought me into possession of "Trade Show" tickets. These tickets were for members of the trade to view films in the forenoon, months before they were made available to the public and if I was prepared to get up a few hours earlier than usual so as to finish my preparation work in the shop, I could attend these trade shows and allow myself the luxury of viewing a film all the way through. I am not ashamed to say that I learned more English listening to the good quality early talkies than I ever learned at school.

Those were the days when the big American dance and swing bands were becoming well-known in Britain through the medium of gramophone records and the newly invented talkies, or sound cinema. The names of Duke Ellington, Louis Armstrong, Paul Whiteman, Rudy Vallee, Hoagy Carmichael, the Dorsey Brothers, Fletcher Henderson, Sydney Bechet, Don Redman and such like were now becoming well known to jazz music fans here, and through the efforts of Johnny McMeighan, who played and replayed their recordings to me, I had grown to be as enthusiastic as he was about this great new music that was being created in America. He took to identifying the various instruments for me, he guided me time and time again through some of the intricate arrangements of Ellington and Fletcher Henderson and of Benny Carter. He pointed out the virtuosity of some of the soloists, the incredible range and innovation of Louis Armstrong in those early days before the demands of commercialism had spoiled his extraordinary talent. Johnny played his recording of *West End Blues* over and over, until I, like him, marvelled at the trumpeter's skill. Johnny claimed that Armstrong's last chorus on that recording was the purest piece of jazz music ever recorded, or ever likely to be. I still have Johnny's analysis of that chorus written down in an old diary, though God knows how it has managed to survive the seventy and more years since he wrote it down for me:

> *He opens with a high B-flat. He holds it for four bars and lets*
> *the tension build up. Then when the tension is at its peak, he*
> *plays a harmonically complex figure five times. This sequence*
> *has the sound of a series of despairing cries, an effect he enhances*
> *by delaying the second note and advancing fractionally the one*

> *that follows. Then he begins to wind down into a mood of sad-*
> *ness with a dramatic run-up to a B-flat, followed by a quick*
> *tailing off, which is rhythmically very complex.*

I now have a digitally remastered CD of *West End Blues*, infinitely superior in its clarity to the scratchy old waxy 78 we listened to in those days. I play it occasionally and think of the Johnny McMeighan who opened up and explained the world of jazz music to me.

Then round about 1933 or so, many of those legendary orchestras began to cross the Atlantic for a tour of the UK, starting with appearances at the London Palladium, and when Duke Ellington finally came to Glasgow to appear at the Empire, I was beside myself to go and see and hear his orchestra. Ralph, who had also been introduced to the joys of jazz by Johnny, and who also had fallen under its spell, was every bit as enthusiastic as I was, and we could barely wait until the great day of Ellington's visit. There was a problem however. Given that I was only fifteen, father would not allow me to be out alone late at night, and since one of us had always to be in the shop, Ralph and I could not have the same night off. Father volunteering to accompany me to the theatre solved the problem. When the great night arrived I sat in the stalls of the Empire hypnotised by the waves of syncopated sound and rhythm that flowed from the stage. The difference between the thin sound of the old gramophones of those days and the reality of the music was incredible and I sat transfixed for the two hours or so of the performance. I don't think father was as appreciative of the music as I was, for he sat and fidgeted during the whole time and probably would have dozed off if the waves of sound from the stage had permitted.

My cup of joy spilled over on the Saturday night of that week. After the theatre performance Ellington was to give a concert in the Green's Playhouse ballroom, and Johnny got my father's permission to have Ralph and I accompany him there. That father should have assented without demur was a remarkable thing, since it meant being out until 3am, an unheard-of occurrence as far as our family was concerned. That night I spent two or three of the most memorable hours I have ever had, seated no more than a few yards away from the musicians of the legendary Ellington orchestra. Their names will probably mean nothing to many who might read this book, but they were giants of the big band era. Cootie Williams on trumpet, John Hodges on tenor sax, the legendary clarinettist Barney Bigard and the singer Ivie Anderson whose rendition of a popular blues song of the day, 'Stormy Weather' was asked for again and again. To cap it all off, some of the Ellington musicians took their meals in the Savoy during their stay in Glasgow, and since black Americans were rarely seen in the streets of the city then, they invoked curious but polite stares from our other customers.

In those days, in order to keep myself fit, I was a frequent visitor to Johnny McMillan's Gym in Sauchiehall Street, near the Regal Cinema. The gym, run by the Scottish boxing lightweight champion, was a mecca for those who wanted to rub shoulders with the boxing greats of that era. Boxing then was a much followed sport and still carried the name of 'The noble art of self defence'. Those were hard times and they produced hard people, and boxing offered a chance to anyone with the necessary physical attributes to escape from the soul-destroying deprivation of the slums of the cities, and names like Elky Clark, Tommy Milligan, Johnny McMillan, Sandy McKenzie, Johnny McManus and Jim Campbell were known in every household in the land. Scotland had more than its share of great boxers in those days, and none were greater than Glasgow's own Benny Lynch, who in 1935 rose to international fame by becoming world flyweight champion. One of the attractions of Johnny McMillan's gym was the fact that Benny Lynch could be seen there almost every day, sometimes training, sometimes just lounging and basking in the adulation of his fans.

Many of the above named were frequenters of the Savoy, Sandy McKenzie particularly so, for he lived just a few closes down from us in Renfrew Street, and never a day passed but Sandy could be found in the Savoy tucking in to a plate of something or other. Although he trained every day at the gym he was no longer the force in boxing that he had been a year or so ago, for he had never recovered from a beating in the ring administered by Tommy Loughran, the American light-heavyweight champion of the world whom he had fought for the championship in New York some years before. Although the fight went the full fourteen rounds, Sandy never stood a chance, and in the process absorbed so many blows that he was never the same again. When frequenting the Savoy he always sat at a window seat where he could observe the world go by.

Given that from there they could see the police box which stood at the side entrance, the back shop of the Savoy was a favourite oasis for the police constables who operated out of the Northern Police station just a few yards away in Maitland Street. These police boxes were the only means of communication between constables and the local division headquarters, and they were surmounted by a blue light which flashed intermittently if a policeman's attention was required. One day the shop door was thrown open and an agitated woman came in shouting repeatedly 'Call a policeman! There's a maniac out here!' A young constable who happened to be in the back shop, a rookie by the name of John McArthur, rose to his feet, came into the front shop and went out to the pavement, where he stopped in his tracks.

On the pavement at the other side of the street, in front of the Savoy Cinema ticket booth, stood the figure of a man stabbing at the air around him with a large kitchen knife. He swayed from side to side, with unintelligible shouts coming from his lips as he threatened passers-by with the slashing blade. The crowd waiting to buy tickets for the cinema had scattered away from the menace of the knife, and although no one seemed as yet to have been hurt, the girl attendant in the ticket booth was screaming hysterically, and panic was spreading in the tightly packed crowd as people tried to escape the threat of the lunging knife. John McArthur drew his baton and stepped out to confront the man. Sandy McKenzie's meal had been rudely interrupted by the shouting and the commotion, and he followed the policeman on to the pavement, flicking crumbs of food from his lips as he observed the proceedings. He watched with interest as the young policeman advanced slowly towards the shouting man, then strode out, pushed the constable to one side and went forward to confront the knife. A target identified, the knife wielder advanced towards Sandy, the flicking blade indicating his intention. Sandy dropped into a boxer's stance and went forward with a light springy step. The armed man paused for a moment, then made a vicious lunge at him with the knife. Sandy timed his move to perfection. He ducked under the slashing blade and hit the man with a powerful hooking left-handed blow to the stomach. Gasping for breath, the man dropped his knife, and was finished off with a pounding right-handed blow to the jaw. He dropped silently to the pavement. Sandy picked up the knife, handed it to an astounded John McArthur and returned without a word to his unfinished meal.

Despite my frequent visits to John McMillan's gym, I had no great interest in boxing. Although I had a powerful enough physique and was very fit, I was very far short of the quickness of movement necessary for that sport, and I had no desire to acquire a possible broken nose or cauliflower ear by participating. But I was interested in keeping strong and fit, and I exercised a lot with the bar-bells and weights provided by the gym. I did not mix much with the other frequenters of the place, but I was on nodding acquaintance with a customer of ours, Gus Hart, who was Benny Lynch's current manager. Gus Hart's real name was Giuseppe Passarelli, and he had ran away from home at an early age to join a circus. There he was befriended by a family by the name of Hart, and elected to be known by that name for the rest of his life. He met up with Benny Lynch and towards the twilight of the boxer's career he took up the management of the ex-world champion. One night he and Benny Lynch were involved in a car crash, and although not badly injured, both were taken to hospital and kept in overnight for observation. On reading of the accident in a newspaper, Benny, who did not know Hart's real name, wanted to know where the third passenger by the name of Passarelli had come from!

One day in the gym I was going through my usual routine with the weights, watched by Gus Hart as he balanced against the wall on two legs of a chair. Benny Lynch was shadow-boxing in the ring, alone. Gus waved at me.

'Hello there Joe. How about giving Benny a couple of rounds? You've got the build for it.'

'No way,' I replied 'I can't box.'

'Aw, come on, just spar around for a few rounds, Benny wont hurt you. Just throw a few punches at him to give him some practice.'

I thought for a moment. I weighed a good two and a half stones more than Benny. The champion was a skinny eight stones and had a placid enough appearance. What the hell, why not?

Gus put a large well-worn set of gloves on my hands and we sparred around for a few minutes, Benny weaving in and out, throwing light punches at me. I began to enjoy the experience, and threw some punches of my own, all of them wide of the mark. Benny fell into a clinch, and as we broke I hit him as hard as I could with a punch to the chest. The blow knocked Benny off his feet, his eyes seemed to glaze over, and he jumped off the floor of the ring and proceeded to bombard me with a flurry of lightning fast blows to the head. I did my best to protect myself, but to no avail. The speed and ferocity of my skinny opponent was unstoppable, and I was saved from serious injury only by the intervention of Gus, who had leapt into the ring immediately to pacify his enraged boxer. Benny at once calmed down, and as I staggered dazed around the ring he patted me affectionately on the back of the head.

'Sorry about that, ah lost the heid fur a minit. Ye shouldnay huv hit me so hard. Ye made me lose the place,' and proceeded to wipe the blood from my nose with a sweaty towel. I did not regain my usual appearance for a week, the time it took for my two black eyes to regain their natural colour and for my nose, fortunately unbroken, to regain its natural shape. From then on I stuck rigidly to my weight-lifting routine.

The war intervened. In 1940 I was interned, and five years later returned to take up my work in the family shop. A favourite item on the Savoy menu for our late night drunken diners was our tripe supper, which consisted of boiled tripe soaked in a cornflour sauce and served with mashed potatoes, to be consumed by them in the belief that it helped the sobering up process. Two or three times each week a bloated drink-sodden figure would appear in the shop, go unsteadily to a table and order up a tripe supper. He would pay for it on delivery, always leaving a few coppers for a tip, then sit apathetically with closed eyes until closing time. He spoke to no one and bothered no one. At closing time I would go up to him, help him to his feet and guide him to the door, to leave him propped up against an outside wall. As I wished him good night, I often wondered if he knew me and if the memory of our brief encounter in Johnny McMillan's gym one day in 1935 lay dormant somewhere in Benny Lynch's drink-sodden brain. One night in August 1946 he seemed to be more comatose than ever as I escorted him to the door of the Savoy. Two days later I read in the *Evening Citizen* that Benny Lynch had died in the Southern General Hospital.

In the Savoy the ebb and flow of all types of humanity could be observed. The place was frequented by a very broad cross-section of the population of the Cowcaddens and the city centre. Theatre and cinema-goers, theatre artistes, shoppers, workers, prostitutes, drunken pub-crawlers, bookies and men of the cloth, all such types crossed our threshold in the course of a day's business. At the top end of Renfrew Street, the Garnethill area was dotted with dozens of good quality bed and breakfast homes, and these were in constant use by many of the artistes who appeared on a regular basis at the Pavilion and Empire Theatres. On their way to these theatres they had to pass in front of our Savoy, and many of them became regular customers during their visits to Glasgow. Dave Willis and Jack Anthony popped in often for a fish tea, as did Jack Radcliffe and Jack Milroy, and Max Miller was a regular visitor during his many appearances at the Glasgow Empire. GH Elliot, the 'Chocolate Coloured Coon' of Lily of Laguna fame (now, sixty and more years on, such a stage name would be considered racist and could not be used), was a regular for breakfast; two poached eggs and a pot of strong tea every morning. A secluded corner table was reserved for him during his visits. Not that anyone would have recognised him without his coloured make-up.

The story I like most to tell about one of our customers relates to a certain Johnny Myers, a runner and minder for Joe Docherty, the Weymss Street bookie. You might be justified in thinking that the young Johnny had been specially genetically bred for the job of hard man and minder. Short and squat in build, he had the physique and strength of an ox. A bullet head sat squarely on massive shoulders with no visible neckline, and powerful arms terminated in thick fingers that could form themselves into rock-hard, intimidating fists when clenched. Nature, however, had been less generous in the allocation of brain cells, and his fearsome physical attributes were by no means matched by his intellectual powers, which were exactly in inverse proportion to his brawn. But he was perfect for the part of hard man bookie's runner; give him an order, zip up the back of his head, and Johnny could be relied on to carry out his duties to the letter. If he was on your side, you always felt safe with Johnny around.

Johnny Myers ate often in the Savoy, and although he often did not pay for his fish and chips, I overlooked such slight lapses on his part, since his frequent presence in the shop was a disincentive to any potential troublemakers, of whom at night there were many. One night Johnny was standing eating a fish supper, and I watched him as he shovelled pieces of fish into his mouth with none too clean hands. As I was doing so, I noticed a flurry of movement behind him as two men moved quickly behind his back. One of the men had a shiny object in his hand and as he passed behind the runner struck him a blow to the back of his head with it. Johnny spat out a mouthful of half-chewed food, roared out an oath, turned as quick as a flash and knocked his assailant to the ground with a blow from his massive fist. Then with a bellow of pain and rage he turned to his assailant's companion who was running out of the door, and kicked him with all his strength in the small of the back. The man bounced off the wall into an unconscious heap.

Johnny turned to me

'What did they do to the back of ma heid?'

My mouth fell open in amazement, for there, embedded in the back of Johnny's skull was a tableknife, the tip well embedded into the bone.

'Pull the fuckin' thing oot !'

I did as I was told, and had to exert a fair amount of strength to release the knife, embedded a full quarter of an inch into the skull.

The police were summoned and the two men were identified by Johnny as hooligans who had wanted to pay off an old score. I confirmed that the runner was blameless in the matter, so the two, bleeding profusely and still semi-conscious, were promptly bundled off under arrest. Johnny refused to go for medical attention, and after I had washed and disinfected the wound to the best of my ability, still not able to believe the incident I had just witnessed, he went home to sleep it all off. The next day he appeared at his bookies pitch as usual, none the worse for wear, complaining only of a stiff neck and a bit of a sore head.

About thirty-five years after these events this story had a sequel. I was by this time retired and living part of the year in Majorca. One night, as my wife Mary and I were leaving the entrance to a five-star hotel after having enjoyed a meal and a cabaret there, a large black Mercedes limousine drew up and disgorged four passengers, two youths and two heavily painted Spanish-looking ladies. The two young men, who spoke with a distinct Glasgow accent, noticed as Mary and I paused to let them pass. The front door of the limo opened, and from the seat next to the driver there emerged slowly the squat bulky figure of a man. Features could not be made out in the dim light, but the shape with its bull neck seemed oddly familiar, and as the man came into the brighter light of the foyer recognition was complete.

'My God, it's Johnny Myers!'

It was indeed, older and greyer of course, but still rock solid and as powerful as ever. The squat figure turned.

'Jesus! It's Joe!' and I was almost knocked out by an affectionate pat on the back. I was then caught up in a bear hug and left with feet dangling off the ground as Johnny expressed his delight in seeing his old friend again after all those years.

'Hey Joe, day ye remember the night those bastards stuck a knife in ma heid? Aye, we hud sum great times in they days!' and in order to explain his presence: 'Ah'm here tae look aifter these two boys fur a pal back in Glasgow.'

Introductions were made as Johnny kept pounding me on the back.

'You tell 'um Joe, you tell 'um aboot the auld days in the Savoy. You tell 'um aboot the night they bastards stuck a knife in ma heid.' So I told them the story and admonished them.

'You're a couple of lucky fellas having Johnny to look after you. Treat him well, he's the best in the business.'

In the years before the war I became interested in golf and took it up as my main pastime. The Savoy was frequented by most of the policemen who operated out of the Northern Police Station in Maitland Street, situated about 500 yards from the shop, and one of them, John Clapperton, was a keen golfer. He used to leave his clubs in our back shop to be picked up at the end of his night shift, and off we would go for a round as soon as I had finished the morning's work. Glasgow then was well supplied with some first class and well maintained municipal courses; there was Littlehill in Auchinairn and Linn Park at the opposite end of town, and there was Knightswood, a nine-hole course at the edge of the new housing estate just north of Anniesland Cross. Available too for a modest green fee, we had the Clober course at Milngavie, run by the Lyle family, who were to become famous in years to come through the achievements of Sandy, Masters and Open winner of later years. At first I went just to keep him company, but Clapperton would let me hit a few balls with one of his clubs, and when I found that I could hit a niblick just as far, although not quite as straight as he could, I bought myself a second-hand set of wooden-shafted clubs at the Crown salesrooms in Sauchiehall Street for a few shillings, and promptly became a golf addict.

The problem was finding the time to play. Apart from the one full afternoon and night off from the shop, there was only Sunday free, and although I had long since been released from saying the rosary after Sunday lunch, there was no way I could get out of going to Mass in the morning without mother taking a stick to me. That left Sunday afternoons, when in summer the municipal courses would be packed, with a long wait for a tee-off time, or a few hours each afternoon in between lunch time and teatime, when I had enough time to play only nine holes, which meant of course that I had to give up my quick visits to the cinema. Travelling time had to be taken into consideration as well. Very few had motor cars in those days, certainly none of our family had even dreamt of owning one, so the corporation trams and buses had to be used and the time spent in waiting at bus and tram stops had to be subtracted from the time available for playing. I became quite a good golfer. My handicap was about eight or so, with hickory shafts, and I began to dream of the possibility of getting down to two, which would have enabled me to fulfil my newly acquired dream of entering the qualifying rounds of the Scottish amateur championship.

I played a lot with John Clapperton, who was an orphan and lived alone with no family ties. For convenience, since it could be reached by tram in fifteen minutes from Renfrew Street, we played a lot on the Ruchill course, a nine-hole midden of a place set anachronistically in the middle of a rather rough housing scheme in Maryhill by the side of the canal. The first hole was a par three with the tee shot hit blind over the brow of a hill, and nobody played it, for a ball hit out of sight over the hill would be nicked by the young hooligans who lurked on the other side of the slope, ready to pinch anything that came over. Nobody ever holed out on any of the greens, for the same young hooligans used the holes there to piss in, and you were never sure if the ever-present liquid in them was rainwater or urine. You had to be a really dedicated golfer with no other place to play on to have wanted to play the Ruchill course.

But in general, considering the number of feet that tramped the fairways each and every day, together with the variety of divots cut up by inefficiently wielded clubs, the Glasgow Corporation golf courses were in remarkably good condition. The greens and fairways were carefully tended, both by the greenkeeping staff and by the players, who in the main replaced their divots and took care not to damage the well-trodden greens. These courses were, after all, our golf clubs, the citizens of Glasgow's clubs, provided cheaply by a civic administration for the benefit of the working classes of the city. The possibility of belonging to and playing on the dozens of private courses close to the city was not within reach of the masses, since even for those lucky enough to be in work, wages did not stretch very far beyond providing the bare necessities of life. So, in addition to the many fine public parks available to the citizens of Glasgow, the Corporation had provided half a dozen or so golf courses within the confines of the city for their benefit, at a price well affordable to all but the very poorest. Sixpence was the charge for eighteen holes of golf, and at such prices no one complained about the heavy traffic on these Corporation courses and the consequent slowness of play.

So as to broaden our choice of courses Johnny managed to get hold of an ancient bull-nosed Morris Oxford which solved our transport problem, when it ran, that is, for as often as not the 1929 vintage car would develop all sorts of mechanical problems and would force us back on to public transport. It was understood that I pay for the petrol, and since petrol was only about a shilling a gallon then, I was only too pleased at the arrangement. When it ran Johnny's car expanded our golfing horizons. These now could extend as far as Prestwick, where I renewed a family relationship with Johnny Moscardini of the Lake Café at Prestwick Cross.

Johnny Moscardini was a second generation Italian born in Falkirk a few months after his parents' arrival in Scotland, and was a footballer of international renown. He played for Falkirk for a spell, then went to live in Italy for some years, where he played for the Italian national team which won the World Cup in Czechoslovakia in 1934. He came back to Prestwick to take over the family business, the Lake Café, and had made some friends on the staff at one of the hallowed links of the game, the Old Prestwick course. Without connections, a lowly Glasgow policeman and his Tally friend would have stood no chance of setting foot on the fairways there, but Johnny arranged matters so that we could have the occasional game on the links. Those were moments to be treasured, those games played on one of the finest courses in Scotland.

One year, 1936, I was able to take some time off from the shop, and Johnny and I went down to Prestwick for a week's holiday. We stayed at the Auchencoyle Hotel, a small family-run place just facing the Old Prestwick clubhouse, and were able to have a full week of playing golf, thirty-six holes a day and more if we wanted, since it was summer and daylight lasted until very late in the evening. There was a young American staying at the same hotel. He had come over to compete in the British amateur championship at Prestwick and was putting in some practice on the course before the tournament, to be played there in a few weeks time. He introduced himself. Lawson Little was his name, and since Johnny and I knew the course well he joined up with us on our rounds. He was a great companion and a marvellous golfer, who went on to win the British Amateur Championship at Prestwick a few weeks later, to which he added the American Amateur Crown later in the year. It was the first time I had seen a golfer of that standard play, and the several rounds we played with him cured me of any notion I may have had of achieving golfing greatness. The difference in the quality of play of a top class golfer such as he was and my own game was just too great ever to be bridged. He could have given Johnny and I a stroke and more at each hole and still beat us. We were fascinated both by the quality of his golf and by his clubs. These were the new steel-shafted variety which had appeared some years before and which were now beginning to be seen on the golf courses of Scotland. Johnny set his heart on getting a set. The hire-purchase method of buying goods had just recently been introduced, and he promptly put down the deposit for a set of Tommy Armour steel-shafted clubs. Beautifully made by Forgan, famous clubmakers of that time, the clubs had an oval grip and cost him about £30, as I remember, an absolute fortune at a time when the average wage was about £5 a week or so. The oval grip on clubs was declared illegal by the R & A some years later, as I remember it. I wanted to buy a set in the same way, but my father would not hear of it. You will buy nothing on tick, he said. Save your money and buy your clubs when you have the cash and not before. In those days a father's word was law, so I continued to play with my outmoded hickories, never imagining that the day would come in the not too distant future when I would become the owner of Johnny Clapperton's oval gripped steel-shafted Tommy Armour clubs.

Play on the Prestwick course was frequently interrupted by the roar of fighter airplanes taking off from the adjoining RAF field, flying in tight formation and performing all sorts of aerial acrobatics as they did so. These were the Spitfire single-seater fighters which were to play such an important role in the Battle of Britain of a few years later. An orphan and bachelor with no ties, Johnny joined the Auxiliary Air Force, and found that he had to do much of his training at the Prestwick airfield. The aircrew there had the run of the Old Prestwick course if they wished, and in the years immediately preceding the war we could play there as often as we wanted without having to depend on Johnny Moscardini's connections.

On the outbreak of war in 1939, Johnny Clapperton was immediately called up for service. He entrusted his beloved clubs to me for safekeeping. On his first patrol over the Rhineland he and his plane failed to return to base, shot down by German flak. After the war I used Johnny's clubs for a time, and now, nearly seventy years later, I still have one in my possession, a spoon, or three wood as that fairway wood is called now. I have not played golf for several years, time has taken its toll on me, but I still occasionally heft Johnny Clapperton's beautifully balanced club and think of him and of those golden, nostalgic, carefree days we spent together on the Old Prestwick links.

In those pre-war days my chums were exclusively Scottish. There were no Italians near us. The Italian colony was scattered throughout Glasgow, with no national enclave such as existed in the Clerkenwell and Soho districts of London, and if you wanted to meet other Italians you had to go to La Casa Del Fascio, later to be called Casa d'Italia in Park Circus. This club had been set up by the Italian government in the early thirties as a show piece for the new Italian Fascist regime, and was intended to serve the social needs of the Italian community. It was frequented by many Italian families on Sundays as a place where one could meet one's fellow nationals and where one's children, if born in Scotland, could properly be taught the language of their fathers.

Some families shunned the club however, because of the fascist connotation. Many Italians abroad were anti-fascist, and would not go near the place, and my own father, who was a socialist and would probably have been given a dose of castor oil in Italy for his political views if he had dared express them there, expressly forbade me to go near La Casa del Fascio, or Casa D'Italia, as some preferred to call it. A massive forced dose of castor oil was the punishment meted out by the fascists in Italy to anyone who dared criticize the regime. A pint of the liquid poured forcibly down a person's throat ensured that the unfortunate would remain incapacitated for a long period, and not likely to offend a second time once recovered. The fact that La Casa del Fascio was put out of bounds did not in the least bother me, for I had many Scottish friends and had no desire to seek out any other. Moreover, although I had developed a sense of pride in some of the achievements of the new Italy: the Schneider Trophy victories; the mass transatlantic flight of Italo Balbo from Rome to the World Fair in Chicago, and back, which had involved building twenty-five flying boats and flying in formation over the western part of Europe, then over the Atlantic and the Eastern part of the US at a time when such a feat had been deemed impossible; Italy's victory in the 1934 football World Cup, and so on, but I also found plenty to criticize in the posturings of Mussolini, and I doubt whether I would have been made welcome in La Casa del Fascio. On the subject of the Schneider Trophy races, in the main square of the town of Sirmione, at the southern end of Lake Maggiore, there is a huge bronze sculpture depicting a streamlined female figure with wings soaring into the sky, erected to commemorate the Schneider Trophy races, two of which had Lake Maggiore as their venue.

Francy Traynor had by this time found work in the Central Hotel kitchens a few hundred yards from us at the bottom end of Hope Street, and he spent much of his spare time in our Savoy, as did Johnny McMeighan the violinist, who used the shop as a meeting place for himself and his fellow musicians, many of whom, including Johnny himself, played in the pit orchestras of either the Empire or the Pavilion theatres. By this time I had made a new friend and golfing companion in the form of Joe Docherty, a bookie from round the corner in Wemyss Street who was a low handicap golfer and also friendly with Johnny Clapperton. Joe, as befitted a bookie, had a car, a good one which never seemed to break down, unlike Johnny's old bull-nosed Morris, and would often take us to his course at Cawder in Bishopbriggs for a game. Johnny and I enjoyed playing with him alone, but always opted out if any of his betting fraternity joined us. Alone with Johnny and me, Joe would play for the pleasure of it, with a few pennies a hole for a little competition, but with his bookie friends the stakes would rise to ten shillings a hole and more, sums which were far removed from what Johnny and I could afford to play for. This period, from 1935 or so until 1940, was probably the only period in my life that I felt completely integrated into my Scottish environment and gave no thought to my origins or to my place in a Scottish environment. To my often drunken customers I was still a 'Tally', but the word meant nothing to me, it was just another form of address. As far as my friends were concerned I was simply one of them, with no mention ever made of my Italian background.

By the year 1938 the family had attained a modest level of success. Ralph and I had become the driving forces in the business, the shop had been expanded in size and was doing excellent trade. We were only a stone's throw away from the Pavilion and Empire Theatres, and on the other side of us the Garnethill district served as a bed and breakfast zone for many of the artistes who regularly performed there. The most glamorous and desirable of all these theatrical customers to me were the luscious Bluebell chorus girls who stopped at the shop for carry-out suppers on the way to their lodging houses. The most attractive of the girls as far as I was concerned was Dorothy Dickinson, a beautiful young dancer from Preston, and during the Christmas panto seasons and yearly summer shows, which between them took up about three months of the year, Dorothy and I began to see a lot of one another. She had rehearsals in the morning, and apart from the matinee days of Wednesday and Saturday, was free in the afternoons, a timetable which suited me nicely, since I too worked in the morning and at night. We spent our afternoons together, going for long walks if the weather was good, or smooched in the back seat of a cinema if it was bad and where we didn't pay a great deal of attention to the screen, no matter how good the film. We began to drift euphorically towards the idea of marriage, to the unconcealed dismay of our respective families.

'Sure Joe, Dorothy's a nice girl, but why don't you find a nice Italian girl for yourself?' This, in Italian of course, and then my mother would go into the familiar hand-wringing bout of lamentation about local girls, a criticism which had not changed throughout the years.

'And not even a Scottish girl...but English!'

Ralph, my American-born brother, had by this time married and had set up house with his wife, Teresa Nicoletti, the daughter of a Glasgow-Italian family from North Street. The idea of a liaison with any except an Italian girl was anathema to Italian families, and our mother would shake her head in deep disapproval on hearing of a marriage of an Italian to anyone else except his or her own kind. There would be a heavenward rolling of eyeballs and a solemn wringing of hands if such marriages were mentioned. Such a union could lead only to disaster, she would intone, and no good could ever come of such a marriage. In parallel fashion, but with English reserve, Dorothy's family was politely frigid when I was introduced to them during a visit to their home in Preston.

'Oh yes, Dorothy...he's a nice chap, but he's an Italian!'

By the age of twenty-one, driven by a constant thirst for knowledge, I was still reading everything I could lay hands on, and my ongoing subscription to *Time* magazine kept me well informed of world events. I followed the unfolding international scene with great interest, and I was well aware of my position as a foreigner in this country and as a possible future enemy alien. All the indications seemed to point to war between Germany and Britain, with Italy as an ally of Hitler. Since the time we had moved to Renfrew Street my lifestyle had been almost purely Scottish, apart from my daily contact with my parents, to whom I always spoke in Italian, but each day I was forced to remember that I was a 'Tally', an Italian, and somehow different from the people I lived amongst. The 1930s had been a period of political turmoil in Europe. Italy's invasion of Abyssinia and Mussolini's intervention in the Spanish Civil War had created a wave of ill feeling against Italy in the general population. The childhood taunts of 'dirty wee Tally' had given way to more frequent, forceful and insulting remarks about my nationality from some of the more drunken and belligerent types who made up a good percentage of our night-time clientele. 'Dirty wee Tally' had given way to 'Tally bastard'. Not that these people knew me or anything about my background, I could just as easily have been Scottish, or French or any one of a dozen different nationalities. But I had a chip shop. Only Italians had chip shops, ergo I must have been an Italian. These remarks did not bother me much, they were part and parcel of my environment, but nevertheless they served to remind me that I was not one of them.

I encountered more discreet and polite discrimination at the other end of the social spectrum. A foreign name could guarantee blackballing from a club membership, and even the better educated of my acquaintances, with absolutely no malice intended, could make the odd remark which would place me firmly in an Italian context.

'Are you going home to Italy for your holidays, Joe?'

'Do you think you'll ever go back to live in Italy, Joe?'

The Savoy went through substantial quantities of merchandise, and our custom would be much sought after by the various suppliers.

'Must have you and Ralph out for a meal sometime, Joe.'

'Must have you out for a round of golf at the club, Joe.'

Empty phrases, all for the sake of doing some business. The golf clubs many of them belonged to had never been trodden by Jewish, Italian or, for that matter, Catholic feet, and I never saw the inside of any of their houses. This type of xenophobia pricked the skin a little, where the 'Tally bastard' variety did not.

We are what we are because of two factors: genetic inheritance and environmental influence, and the latter in my formative years had gone to creating in me a sense of detachment from the society in which I was living. The Jesuits used to say that if you gave them a child to educate for seven years he would be a Jesuit for the rest of his life. I used to apply that dictum to my own formative years. I was born in Italy, my family upbringing in Glasgow was that of an Italian child, the language I learned at my mother's knee was Italian and to that extent I was Italian. But Glasgow was my home; this was the place I had grown up in, where I had gone to school, and this was the place where I earned a living and where my friends were. I understood all of this, and was learning to cope with the dichotomy that had grown within me, for even in the land of my birth the people there did not accept me as one of themselves. In Glasgow I was 'the Tally'. In Barga I was *'lo Scozzese'*, the Scotsman. The lines from *The Lay of the Last Minstrel* by Sir Walter Scott could well have been written for the likes of me:

Breathes there the man, with soul so dead,
Who never to himself hath said,
This is my own, my native land!

It was clear that if war did come, Italy would be on the side of Germany against Britain, and it troubled me to think that my cousins there might one day have to bear arms against my many friends here. The sight of my many Scottish companions now in uniform also troubled me somewhat, for peer pressure plays a large part in one's behaviour, but they did not seem to mind that I was still a civilian, with some of them voicing the opinion that as an Italian I was lucky to be exempt from conscription. But then came Germany's invasion of Poland, followed by Britain's declaration of war, so I began to worry about what would happen if Italy were to join in. Weeks went by and I reasoned that the danger had passed. If Mussolini had wanted war he would have joined in from the beginning, I said to myself. Besides, nothing would happen to me in any event; I had no political connections, and I had no dealings with La Casa del Fascio, the Fascist social club in Park Circus. Some of my older Scottish acquaintances spoke of the internment of Germans during the 1914-18 war, but I discounted that possibility as being just inconceivable in my case. So I applied myself single-mindedly to the business, bothered no-one, and kept my head firmly buried in the sand.

In the few months since the beginning of the war in 1939, life had changed dramatically for the people of Glasgow. There was an air of tension all around. A complete blackout had been imposed during the hours of darkness, and no chink of light was allowed to escape from the heavily curtained shops and houses. Cars were fitted with headlamp covers so that they emitted only a thin sliver of light, tramcars in complete darkness inched their way on their tracks along the pitch-black streets, and during the long, dark and often fog-bound winter nights, the city would grind to a standstill. Strange and disturbing incidents could happen on the dark and completely unlit streets. One night as I walked slowly and gingerly along Sauchiehall Street, through the murk I could make out the figure of a woman walking ahead of me, even more slowly than I was. As she went to step down off the pavement to cross an intersecting road she slipped and fell, and her handbag fell from her arm. I bent down to pick her up, and as I touched her she began screaming hysterically at the top of her voice, probably thinking that she had been pushed and that her handbag was being stolen. I bent to reassure her, but she became more and more hysterical, shrieking and shouting for help at the top of her voice. In answer to her cries, police whistles began to blow nearby, and I could see pencils of light from shaded police torches approaching. I took off as quickly as I could, with heart thumping, and panic-stricken at the thought of being arrested by some stranger of a policeman, and once safely at my destination it took several minutes for my heartbeats to return to normal.

Several nights later, during the hours of blackout, the presence of three policemen, very possibly the same ones I had fled from several nights before, saved
me from what could have been a serious assault and robbery. I was in the process
of shutting up shop, and was standing by the darkened door to allow the last of
our late night customers to exit. I closed the door behind the last of them, but
as I turned the key, there came a knock at the door. Thinking that perhaps one
of the customers had forgotten something, I opened it slightly, only to have it
explode open in my face. I was thrown to the ground as three men burst in over
me and into the shop, bent on God only knows what mayhem. Fortunately,
three of the local police were enjoying a plate of chips in the back shop, and at
the sound of the crashing door and my shout they came storming out, batons at
the ready. A short rammy ensued, with the quick and efficient handcuffing of
the by now completely subdued would-be robbers.

Gas masks had been issued to everyone, air raid shelters were signposted,
and parks and private gardens were equipped with Anderson shelters (named
after Sir John Anderson, the Home Secretary at that time). These were arched,
corrugated-iron structures dug into the ground and protected by sandbags, to
serve as civilian shelters in the event of air raids. To protect against incendiary
bombs, huge static water tanks had been installed in every street. Military con-
voys rumbled occasionally through the city. Fat balloon barrages, one of which
was anchored in the back yard of our shop, wallowed over tenement roofs,
presumably to protect from an attack by low-flying aircraft. Strange uniforms
were to be seen and strange languages were to be heard in the Glasgow streets:
English soldiers with accents incomprehensible to Glasgow ears, French sailors
with red pom-poms on their blue berets; French mountain regiments, the Chas-
seurs Alpins with their floppy black berets; Algerian Goums with baggy white
trousers, fierce dark faces and red fez-type hats. All these and more thronged
the Glasgow streets, pubs, cinemas and restaurants. The city throbbed with an
excitement and a glamour never before experienced by its inhabitants. War is
always good for trade. Money flowed freely, the Savoy cash register worked
overtime, the slump and misery of the 1930s had vanished and life seemed
somehow to be sharper and more vital, more purposeful and exciting. The war
fronts on the continent seemed unreal and far away, as if taking place on some
cinema screen, and Germany and the Allies were safely ensconced behind their
respective Siegfried and Maginot lines.

> *We're gonna hang out our washing on the Siegfried Line*
> *Have you any dirty washing mother dear,*

went the popular song of the day, with the lyrics reflecting the almost frivolous
mood of the general public. I, too, was caught up in this atmosphere. Business

boomed, and money flowed into the till as never before. I no longer worried about my position as an Italian. The German invasion of Poland would soon be forgotten, the affair would fizzle out with some kind of international agreement and life would go on as before, or so I naively believed.

Then suddenly, on 4 June 1940, just as France was about to fall to the Germans and Britain was evacuating her army from Dunkerque, Mussolini declared war on what he thought was a beaten nation.

❧ 3 ❧

War and Internment

O ne day in the summer of 1974 my wife Mary and I were seated in a taxi in Montreal, on our way from our hotel in Sainte Catherine Street, to an island in the middle of the St Lawrence river, L'Isle Ste Helene. We were going to visit a museum there. This museum, dedicated to the military history of Quebec, was housed in a building built some 300 years before by Champlain, the governor of French Canada, to serve as a fortress guarding the river approaches to the city. The island was named after his new bride, Helene. The building is a grim, stark edifice of two storeys built of rough stone blocks and encompasses on three sides a narrow courtyard facing out to the river. On the far side of the river lies the main area of Montreal city, which slopes up gently to the imposing heights of Mount Royal. There, in the centre of a little square, dominating the entire city, stands a huge stone crucifix. The crucifix is edged with a neon strip and makes a magnificent sight when lit up at night. The approach to the island from Montreal is by the massive Jacques Cartier bridge which spans the St Lawrence river from the city to the suburb of Trois Rivieres on the southern bank. One of the bridge's pylons stands just a few feet away from the northern wall of the fortress.

As the taxi turned on to the slip road leading down to the island some sixty feet or so below, the grey structure came into view, and a few moments later, having paid the entrance fee, we were standing inside the courtyard of the museum. The exhibits in the interior, although not very well laid out, it must be said, are of an interesting nature, and consist of displays portraying the military history of the fort during the wars against the Indians and later against the British. These displays are labelled in English and French. At the end of one of the long and narrow second floor rooms, incongruously set amongst some military exhibits, are three wooden prison cells with iron barred doors. They are small and cramped, measuring about five feet by nine feet, and affixed to one of them is a plaque with the following inscription:

> 'During the Second World War this fortress served as a prison camp for Nazi and Fascist prisoners. These are the punishment cells used for the more dangerous of them.'

An inscription which goes to show the truth of the saying that the first casualty in war is truth.

After the passing of thirty years I had come back with Mary to visit the place where I had spent three years of my life, and to the cells where I had spent thirty days of those three years.

On the long plane journey from Prestwick to Montreal I had dozed occasionally, and my thoughts had drifted back to the day when my life was disrupted for ever, June 10th, 1940. The day had dawned warm and sunny and I had gone about my affairs listlessly. For many days business had been bad; the soldiers who had thronged the streets of Glasgow during the past months seemed to have vanished, and after working hours people were rushing home to their wireless sets to keep abreast of the constantly unfolding news from the war fronts. The news was unremittingly bad. The German army had broken through the supposedly impregnable Maginot Line, the French army had been well nigh destroyed and what remained of the British Army had its back to the sea at Dunkerque. The BBC announcer's voice broke into my reveries and echoed through the shop, unusually empty of customers, and I heard the words, 'and so a state of war now exists between Britain and Italy'. As I stood blankly, trying to digest the meaning of the announcement, the tall figure of a policeman appeared at the door.

'Hello Joe, you'll have heard the news?'

It was father's old friend Black Alex. I nodded and he continued.

'I suppose I shouldn't be telling you this and I'm sorry about it, but you're up for arrest during the night.'

I looked at him in astonishment. 'Arrest? What for?'

'For internment, that's what's for. There's a big list of you people posted up in the office. I think you had better close up right away, there's a lot of nasty neds about and you never know what's going to happen.'

He wished me luck, shook my hand and left. I immediately closed the door behind him, dismissed the staff, shut off all electricity and gas points and went upstairs to our tenement flat one floor up from the restaurant. As I came out on to the pavement I could not help but notice how unusually empty of pedestrians and of traffic the streets were. I was alone in the flat, for father and mother had gone off to Rothesay for a few days to enjoy the brilliant weather, and Ralph, whose day off it was, had now married and set up a home of his own some distance away. Very few people had phones then, we certainly didn't, and much as I felt the need to, there was no way I could get in touch either with him or with my parents. As I sat helplessly awaiting events I heard a commotion from the street below and, suddenly afraid, went to the window to investigate. A crowd of about a hundred shouting and gesticulating hooligans, pushing in front of them a handcart loaded with stones and bricks, were gathering in front of the shop. 'There's a Tally place...do it in!', came the shout, and a barrage of missiles came flying through the air, smashing into the glass frontage of the shop. Peering fearfully through the lace curtains, I watched as the doors of the shop were forced open, the windows smashed and as the contents of the looted shop were distributed to the milling, shouting mob. After a time the crowd dispersed, the street went quiet and evening dragged on into night. I lay on the bed fully dressed and slept fitfully until jerked awake by a loud knock at the door. Standing there were two policemen come to arrest me. Since I had been forewarned, I had packed a few belongings into a case, so without a word I picked it up then was escorted down to a waiting Black Maria. 'You must have been expecting us,' said one. I gave no answer, but as I climbed up the steps to the inside of the police vehicle, I paused to look behind me at the ruins of the family shop, too numb to feel any emotion at the sight of the smashed windows and doors and the glimpse of the shattered and looted interior. As I was to learn afterwards, there were few, if any, Italian shops in Scotland left unvandalised and unlooted by bands of hooligans on the night of Italy's declaration of war.

On the morning of Italy's declaration of war, the question of the internment of Italians had come up during a meeting of the British War Cabinet, and the problem of separating the obviously harmless from the potentially dangerous had been discussed. At the end of the meeting Churchill is reported to have issued the following short sharp order: 'Collar the lot!' An order had gone out to all police stations in Great Britain that all male Italians between the age of 16 and 70 should be arrested immediately and interned, and so, just a few hours after I had heard of the declaration of war, I found myself seated in a cell in the Northern Police station in the company of four other Italians of my own age.

I remained in the cell for another two days, and then, together with my fellow prisoners, a Black Maria, the black transport van used by the police to move prisoners, took us to Maryhill barracks, which was already packed with arrested Italians. It would have been hard to imagine a more motley bunch. Their ages ranged from the very young to bent old men, with the only common denominator being the possession of an Italian name. Some were second generation Italians who could speak only English; some complained loudly about their arrest; some shouted to the soldiers that they had served in the British army during the First World War; some proclaimed to anyone who would listen that they had relatives now serving in the army, and one elderly weeping grey-beard, Antonio Santangeli, declared to all and sundry that his son was a sergeant serving with the British forces in France.

On the morning of the fourth day at the barracks, after a breakfast of strong tea, bread, margarine and jam, we were told to get all our belongings together, and were marched out under heavy guard into the street. Word of the imminent appearance of the prisoners had spread and the pavements were lined with hundreds of curiosity seekers straining to get a view of the marching men. I tried to keep in some sort of step with my companions and keep my head held high. I'm not going to show any fear or despondency to these people, I thought, with the events of that first night still vivid in my mind. But the crowds lining the streets were strangely muted, in sharp contrast to the mobs which had taken to the streets on the night of the arrests, and although a few jeers were shouted at the prisoners, very few voices could be heard above the sound of scuffling feet.

Our destination was a railway siding some 500 yards from the barracks gates in Garrioch Road, and with the short walk soon completed, we were made to assemble on the station platform to await the next leg of our journey. The day was hot and sunny as we sat and waited, and the bright sun seemed to engender a mood of euphoria in us. We chattered and joked amongst ourselves and the guards relaxed with us, offering us cigarettes and chocolates. On the station platform was a ticket office manned by a solitary, elderly railway employee who stood watching the proceedings. He paused for a while, then came out to the platform, offering a few cigarettes to the waiting prisoners with the words, 'Good luck to you wherever you're going. We're all Jock Tamson's bairns.'

I cannot say whether the thanks directed to him was for the cigarettes or the words of comfort, but the prisoners were profuse in their acknowledgement.

The train from Maryhill unloaded us at Milton Bridge, a small village a few miles south of Edinburgh. We were surrounded by armed guards with bayonets at the ready, and in answer to shouted commands began to march raggedly out of the station. It was hot. Some of the older men became visibly distressed and had to be helped along by their younger companions. So we slowed the pace as much as possible, and ignored the commands and none too gentle shoves of the soldiers. After about an hour's march we finally came to a halt. A makeshift tented camp had been pitched in a grassy field surrounded with barbed-wire fencing about seven feet high, enclosing scores of tents erected in neat orderly rows. Hundreds of men lay sunning themselves in the spaces between tents and lazily stood up to observe our arrival.

We shuffled in through the gates one at a time, giving our name to an officer as we passed through. We were then escorted in groups of six to a tent, given blankets and groundsheets and left to our own resources. The slabs of bread and cheese issued on departure from the barracks that morning had long since been eaten, and we tried to bed down for the night with the pangs of hunger added to our general discomfort. An incident then took place which manifested the unselfishness and generosity which was often to show itself among the prisoners in the years to come. With us in the tent was a young man, Dino Orsi, who had a fish and chip shop in Grove Street in the Maryhill district of Glasgow. Without a word being said he pulled from his pocket four bars of Kit Kat chocolate biscuits which he proceeded to share out amongst us. This was a generous gesture, for he could well have consumed the biscuits himself without anyone being the wiser.

The next morning we were awakened by the sound of a bugle. The wire gate lay open, giving access to a long row of tables set down immediately outside the barbed wire fence. On these tables were piled stack upon stack of slabs of bread liberally coated with margarine, and large urns of steaming hot tea. Under heavily-armed guard we filed out for our share of food, to be eaten whilst seated outside our respective tents. Hunger satisfied, I began an exploration of our surroundings and turned my attention to the men already in the camp on our arrival. They were Italian, spoke no English, and did not conform to the Glasgow-Italian types of my experience, nor to the Italians I had known in the hills around Barga. I had difficulty in understanding them. Their dialects and accents were those of Sardinia, Naples, Calabria and Sicily, and it was not until I approached and spoke to one of their officers, a Captain Bonorino, who came from Genoa and who spoke a proper and understandable Italian, that their presence there was explained. These were the crews of five Italian tramp steamers seized while at anchor in Scottish waters and taken to Woodhouselea, the nearest available detention point. This explained the overcrowding at the camp and the lack of adequate rations. What had been originally intended as a camp for a few hundred civilians was now accommodating about 200 more unexpected guests.

On the morning of the eighth day at Woodhouselea we were made to gather our belongings and were split into two groups, with married men in the one and sailors and single men in the other. With the division completed, I found myself in a group composed of an equal number of merchant seamen and civilians. Until now I had made very little contact with the sailors, who had eyed us civilians from the time of our arrival with suspicion and reserve.

Who were these so-called Italians, some of whom spoke only English, some of whom spoke Italian only if forced to do so, and some who spoke freely with the guards in English, the sailors were asking themselves, and we civilians looked askance at our strangely dressed companions with their almost incomprehensible accents and dialects and wondered who and what they were. No explanation for the separation into two groups had been given, so in order to stay with friends and relatives, many men had simply lied with their feet. Married men had professed to be single, and single men had declared themselves married. Such simple acts would lead to dire consequences. What none of us knew at the time was that the married men were to be taken to the Isle of Man for a relatively comfortable and uneventful internment, whilst the single men, many of them boys in their teens, were to be shipped abroad in prison ships, and that many of them would lose their lives in the process.

From Woodhouselea we were taken to a disused cotton mill in Bury, a few miles from Liverpool. The mill was a disintegrating wreck from the industrial revolution. Built in the early 19th century to meet the demands of the developing cotton trade, the mill had long fallen into disuse and had lain dank and derelict during the long depression of the 1930s. Stripped of its machinery, the stone floor was greasy and oily with disintegrating cotton rags everywhere. A fine dust hung in the air. There was no electricity: the only illumination was the daylight which filtered through the dirty cracked windows and glass panels which formed part of the roof. Into this Dickensian scene were packed about 3,000 internees. The stench was well nigh unbearable. The original lavatory facilities, blackened and stained by long years of disuse, were inadequate and had been augmented by hastily dug latrines. Forty cold-water taps were available to meet the needs of the prisoners and the simple act of washing one's hands required long periods of queuing. A double fence of barbed wire about seven feet high, constantly patrolled by armed guards, had been erected around the perimeter and hundreds of men stood, sat or squatted as near to it as possible, preferring the open air to the squalor of the interior. At least the camp at Woodhouselea had provided a clean environment with plenty of fresh air, but at Warth Mills it was as though the portals of Dante's inferno had opened up. The sights, sounds and smells of the place were dreadful.

On arrival each prisoner was issued with a mattress and a blanket and made his bed wherever a piece of vacant dry ground could be found. Sleep was impossible amidst the noise of coughing, moaning and weeping while in the pitch darkness of night the squeaking and scampering of rats added a further dimension of terror. At the time of the arrival of our Woodhouselea contingent, the inhabitants of the camp consisted of German and Italian internees and Jewish refugees fleeing the advance of Hitler's armies. All age groups were represented, from a boy of 15, named Arturo Vivante, to elderly men well into their seventies, for whom, lacking the resilience and adaptability of youth, the conditions must have been absolutely unbearable. The commandant of the camp was a Major Baybrook, who addressed the new arrivals, assuring us that all this was purely temporary, that soon we would be leaving for new destinations and that everyone should cooperate fully both with the authorities and with one another. Each morning a list was read out for that day's departure, but I had to wait for a whole week until I heard my name called. That morning the departure list was read out by Captain Vinden, an officer who was to remain with our group for some months. We were not told of our destination, but this became apparent from the name 'Liverpool' written on the station signs as we drew in. After a short while the carriages stopped at a dockside loading area, and as we stepped down we were made to walk a short distance onto a long quay to join groups of prisoners already assembled there. Running the length of the pier and towering over the loading sheds, a large gray-painted ship lay at anchor. We faced the stern of the vessel and on the rear deck, above the name *Arandora Star,* I could see what seemed to be coils of wire with the outline of a large cannon behind them. Packed tightly on the quayside in front of us were thousands of men lined up the full length of the ship, some standing, some squatting and leaning against each other, some young, some old, all strangely silent. Rows of armed soldiers stood guard around us. After what seemed to be an interminable time, the crowd stirred slowly in answer to orders and began moving onto a gangway leading up to the ship, urged on by the soldiers. The loading of the ship proved to be a slow and lengthy process, but when the distance between myself and the *Arandora Star* had been reduced to about 200 men, the gangway was withdrawn, and the ship drew away slowly from the quay.

By this time our group had been joined by several hundreds of other prisoners. They all wore military uniforms which immediately identified them as German soldiers. Some were in Luftwaffe uniform, some wore the dark blue outfits of marine commandos and all looked tired and weary. Most seemed unhurt, but some who wore bandages seemed incapable of standing upright and sat on the ground, leaning against the legs of their compatriots. We learned subsequently that there were 900 of them. Some were Luftwaffe personnel shot down over Southern England and France, with the majority of them marines captured at the time of the British raids on Stavanger and Narvik in Norway.

We sat and waited and watched as the *Arandora Star* drew away, and wondered what our fate was to be. Some time later another ship was manoeuvred alongside the quay. This ship bore the name *Ettrick* and seemed to be somewhat smaller than the first vessel, but it too was painted a dull grey, had coils of wire visible on the deck, and also had a gun mounted at the stern. A gangway was run up to the deck, and orders to move up rang out. An army lorry was stationed at the entrance to the gangway, and as we shuffled past, each of us was thrown a paper bag full of hard-tack biscuits. The group from Warth Mills, about 400 of us, had remained intact, and as I moved up the gangway I looked behind to see that we were being followed up by the German POWs. The deck area seemed to be completely sealed off with barbed wire, behind which stood members of the crew curiously watching the proceedings. But we had little time to examine our surroundings, for no sooner had we taken a few steps along the deck, than we were made to descend into the bowels of the ship, urged on by a choleric little sergeant who stood at the top of a flight of stairs.

The accommodation in which we found ourselves was small and cramped, and consisted of four large hold-like areas connected by a narrow passage. The space was completely devoid of furnishings and afforded barely enough space for everyone to lie down at the same time. A row of portholes on one side was sealed up and the sole illumination consisted of a few bulkhead lights high on the ceiling. Ventilation was through gratings on the wall, and although the place seemed clean enough, the space available was totally inadequate for the 400 men crammed in there. At 6am the next morning the *Ettrick* set sail. As soon as she left the dock the guards were withdrawn and a group of us hurried out on deck, or the tiny part of it accessible to us. The implication of what we saw there did not immediately sink in. A section of the deck about twenty feet long and a few feet wide had been caged off with barbed wire stretching from the deck to the roof above it, which sealed off the area completely. This left a passage to the section which contained the German POWs, some of whom were already on deck. A barbed wire gate to the open deck was heavily padlocked and was guarded on the outside by two armed soldiers. The two groups of prisoners, Italian internees in one hold and the German POWs in the other, nearly a thousand men all told, were effectively sealed off from the rest of the ship, with a heavily padlocked wire gate as the only point of exit in the event of an emergency.

The *Arandora Star* had left Liverpool about twenty-four hours before us on the afternoon of 1 July and had taken a route which had brought her north past the Isle of Man, through the North Channel between the Mull of Kintyre and Northern Ireland, past Malin Head, then due west into the open Atlantic. At approximately 1.30am on 2 July, Gunther Prien, a German U-boat commander, caught sight of the vessel in his periscope. Gunther Prien was the same commander who, on 14 October, 1939, during the very first weeks of the war, had breached the supposedly impregnable defences at Scapa Flow in the Orkney islands and had sunk the battleship *Royal Oak* there. As his log book later was to show, he was returning to base from a tour of duty in the North Atlantic, with just one torpedo remaining in the boat's arsenal. He examined the *Arandora Star* through his periscope, and noted that the unmarked British vessel carried armaments fore and aft. He launched his last torpedo at her.

It struck in the boiler-room area in the aft region of the ship, and within thirty minutes the *Arandora Star* had sunk to the bottom of the sea, taking about 720 souls with her. The full extent of the losses will never be known because the haphazard method of loading did not make for accuracy of count. However, as far as the records go, she was carrying 1600 persons on board, of which 374 were British, made up of soldiers and crew, 478 were German, consisting of the crews of two captured merchant ships, German nationals living in Britain and German-Jewish refugees. 712 were Italians, all civilians living in the UK and broadly representative of the Italian immigrants there. The official casualty list showed that 486 Italians, 156 Germans and 79 Britons died.

To the prisoners on the *Ettrick*, even though we knew nothing of the fate that had befallen the *Arandora Star*, the danger of our situation was only too apparent. Imprisoned as we were in the hold behind the fences of barbed wire, in the event of an emergency we would be caught in a trap and would perish without the slightest hope of escape. The only consolation was that if the Isle of Man was our destination, as many of us still believed, our confinement would last for only a few hours.

I decided to stay for as long as possible on the deck area as I had no desire to go back into the cramped and badly-lit hold. At least I could breathe some fresh air. The soldier guards on the other side of the wire seemed friendly enough, so I attempted to make conversation with them. At the sound of my Scottish accent they responded freely enough, and expressed amazement at the nationality of their prisoners. They had been told that all the men behind the wire were German POWs and to be extremely careful when approaching them. Names and places of origin were exchanged. One of the soldiers hailed from Glasgow, knew our Savoy well and he promised me that on his return to Scotland he would get in touch with my parents with news of my whereabouts. Years later I was to learn that the soldier had indeed kept his promise, much to the relief of my parents who had thought that I might have perished in the sinking of the *Arandora Star*. The news of the sinking of that ship, with heavy internee casualties, had been released in the UK to the consternation of those Italian families who thought that their relatives might have been on board.

A chance remark from one of the guards revealed that the ship's destination was Canada and not the Isle of Man, as had been generally supposed. The information spread like wildfire through the prisoners, creating panic amongst us. To cross the Atlantic under such conditions, caged in like animals? How long would the journey take? It was just not possible, said some, and many of the prisoners refused to believe the guard's remark. As the hours passed, however, it became plain that the Isle of Man was being left far behind and the realisation that Canada was the destination descended on us. There was one among us, however, who refused to believe that Canada was our destination. Roberto Tagiuri was a young lawyer specializing in international law, and he spent his days proclaiming to all and sundry, including a stone-faced Captain Vinden when he showed his face at the other side of the wire, that the transportation of civilian internees across war zones where they could be at risk, was illegal. It was just not conceivable that Britain could be in violation of international law as laid down by the Geneva Convention, and therefore Canada could not possibly be our destination!

Fortunately no one on board then knew the fate that had befallen the *Arandora Star* some hours before. As it was, the fear of an Atlantic crossing and the prospect of some unknown fate in far-off Canada only increased the misery of the men packed into the claustrophobic confines of the hold. Had the *Ettrick* been torpedoed and sunk there is no question that all the prisoners on board would have gone down with her, given the manner of their confinement. The ship was crammed to overflowing with a total of 3,500 men. Of these, 385 comprised the British crew and soldiers, commanded by a Captain Howell. The prisoners consisted of 900 German POWs of all ranks, about 1,800 Jewish refugees and German civilians and 407 Italians, 257 of them civilians and 150 merchant seamen. There were more men on the *Ettrick* than on the *Arandora Star*, which was a far bigger ship. The *Ettrick*, however, was a purpose-built troop carrier and was designed to accommodate 2,800 men, though not in conditions such as we were in. The presence of 900 highly-trained German soldiers who might have been a threat to crew and guards was probably the reason for the proliferation of barbed wire and tight security. However, given the conditions into which the prisoners had been crammed and the padlocked barbed wire doors which blocked every exit, the *Ettrick* was nothing less than a floating coffin.

The weather, which had been warm and sunny for weeks, now worsened. The wind rose to gale force and the heavy seas brought to us the added misery of seasickness. There was hardly a man unaffected by the heaving motion of the ship, and the smell of vomit and sickness lay heavy in the cramped confines of the hold. The bad weather brought one benefit: it made us forget our constant yearning for proper food. Our rations each day consisted solely of bully beef and hard biscuits, masses of which were dumped each morning at the wire gate for distribution amongst us. No eating utensils were provided, apart from a tin mug for each man which could be filled at will from large tea urns set with their spouts turned inside the wire. One prisoner with some medical knowledge was heard to wonder how long it would be before we developed scurvy on such a diet! Although the *Ettrick* had been designed as a troop ship, with adequate toilet facilities in normal circumstances, the latrines had been unable to cope with a combination of overcrowding and seasickness. Buckets were provided for emergency use. When full, these had to be emptied over the side by the prisoners, and because hours would sometimes pass before a guard was provided as escort, the stench in the hold was indescribable.

On the morning of 15 July, twelve days after setting sail from Liverpool, a shout of excitement rang out from the deck. Land was sighted and with it came the prospect of an end to our misery. What in fact had been sighted was the southern shore of Newfoundland, and our journey was to last another day as the *Ettrick* moved slowly through the Cabot Straits, into the Gulf of St Lawrence, and then into the wide estuary of the river. On the morning of the 14th the ship docked at the city of Quebec and the prisoners were unloaded at the docks by the old citadel in the shadow of the Chateau Frontenac.

Clutching our belongings, all 407 of us stumbled awkwardly down the gangplank. Those who had never moved from the confines of the hold were half-blinded by the unaccustomed sunlight, but those who could gazed around in wonder at our new surroundings, and the scent of flowers and shrubs and fresh air was in stark contrast to the fetid atmosphere of the hold we had lived in for the past twelve days. As we came down the gangplank, one by one, our names were taken by Captain Vinden, and we then assembled on the quayside, tightly ringed by armed soldiers and military vehicles. We presented a sorry sight. For a month now we had lived and slept in the same clothes, and only the most rudimentary hygiene had been possible. Many had not shaved for weeks, and as we stood in clothes stained with vomit and excrement, lice-ridden and scratching, a more unkempt and dirty bunch would have been hard to imagine.

We sat and waited on the dock for some time, and as our eyes became accustomed to the brightness of the sun, took in the magnificent vistas of the St Lawrence and of the city of Quebec and the Chateau Frontenac above us. Then, in response to the orders of Captain Vinden, we began to shuffle out of the dock area through a gauntlet of soldiers. Orders were given in an almost incomprehensible English-French patois, the meaning of which was plain enough when accompanied with a push by the butt-end of a rifle. A huge Canadian Pacific train had got up steam by the dockside, and we climbed into it as our suitcases and belongings were snatched away unceremoniously in the process. As we got on each man was issued with a large brown paper bag which, to our delight, contained a welcome and unexpected surprise. Inside was the whitest of white bread, cheese, fruit, tins of tuna fish, little pats of butter and miniature jars of jam and marmalade. Whoops of joy greeted the discovery, and an almost hysterical elation spread contagiously throughout us. We reacted like children who had just been given surprise bags of sweets.

Holding on tightly to our precious food parcels, we each of us found a seat in the carriages, laughing and joking amongst ourselves and shouting pleasantries at the impassive guards around us. The train set off to the sound of song and merriment. Having eaten and enjoyed some of the food, for my appetite was now beginning to return, I settled back comfortably to enjoy the unfolding majesty of the Canadian scenery. The train puffed steadily through villages and hamlets with strange-sounding French names: Pont Rouge, Deshamboult, Trois Rivières, and as the day went on speculation mounted as to our possible destination. Night had fallen when the train drew up in what was obviously a large city, and the name Montreal spread rapidly through the carriages. A small fleet of buses and military vehicles had drawn up beside the train, and we were given orders to move out by the guards who stood with rifles and bayonets at the ready at the exit to each compartment. Chattering excitedly to my companions and holding my food parcel firmly, I jumped up the few steps onto one of the buses. In the back were three guards. When twenty men were loaded into each vehicle three more guards were positioned at the exit and the doors closed. In all there were twenty buses, and all were being loaded in the same manner. The fleet of vehicles then moved off, proceeded by some sort of military half-track with a machine-gun mounted on the rear. Glancing back, I could see a similar armoured car making up the rear of the convoy.

The vehicles made their way along the brightly-lit streets of the city, with policemen at each intersection ensuring an unhindered passage for the convoy. We carried on through quieter streets until we reached the massive spans of a huge steel-girdered bridge. Looking down from above, a cluster of intense bright lights under the far end of the bridge, a hundred yards or so away, caught my eye. The buses slowed to a crawl and I could see about eighty feet below us a small rectangular area flooded in the glare of powerful searchlights. There were uniformed figures moving around in front of a long, low, building and as the buses reached the end of the bridge to begin a slow descent, the lights disappeared from view, leaving only a bright glow in the sky. Slowly, the convoy moved on, and finally came to a halt in front of a set of iron gates flanked on either side by the pillars of a massive stone archway. The leading armoured car slowly preceded the first bus through the gates, followed by the second bus, then, after a short interval, by the third.

It was then our turn, and the bus jerked forward and stopped after a few yards. A blinding light shone into the interior, the door flew open, the three guards at the front jumped out, and a blast of sound erupted into the bus.

'*Heraus! Heraus! Schnell!*' The shouts were in German, and suddenly frightened, we descended from the bus, urged on by the three guards at the rear. I paused at the top of the step, blinded by the dazzling light in my eyes. A hand reached out, grabbed the lapel of my jacket and pulled me roughly to the ground. Another set of hands pulled at my food parcel. Instinctively I held on and pulled back, but the bag was torn from my hand. Dazed and shaken, I was pushed forward by two soldiers shouting at me in German.

'*Schnell! Schnell!*'

I moved several steps forward, then, exhorted by shouts of '*Sitzen! Sitzen!*' was made to sit cross-legged on the ground. This procedure was repeated as each unsuspecting prisoner stepped down from their bus. Some fared better than others, but everyone had their food parcels ripped from their hands and all were roughly pushed around and forced down to a squatting position while the guards continued their verbal tirade in what seemed to be a mixture of German, French and English. The priests among us fared worse of all, for the sight of their priestly habit seemed to spur the guards to even greater effort and the unfortunate prelates were pushed around roughly and their clothes all but torn from their backs. As each bus entered, the focus of attention was drawn further away from our group and I sat rigid with fear, trying to summon up enough courage to inconspicuously angle my head slightly to observe our surroundings. There were three groups of prisoners before ours already sitting on the ground, each with four soldiers standing over them menacingly. Clearly each group had been greeted in the same way as ours, for they all sat silent and cowed, some with torn clothes hanging from their backs. We were sitting in a kind of courtyard, and, as my eyes became accustomed to the glare of the searchlights, I made out the outline of the long, low, building in the background. Curious as I was to see behind me, I did not dare move my head for fear of another blow, but from the corner of my eye I could make out a high wooden platform. On it was a machine-gun manned by a soldier. My stomach grew cold with fear. Armed soldiers paraded up and down in front of us, and paused occasionally to fire shots into the air. Half a dozen huge Alsatian dogs roamed in and out of the squatting men, sniffing and barking furiously and adding to the general air of intimidation. If all this had been meant to cow and frighten, then the plan had succeeded very well indeed, for we sat petrified with terror, and the thought passed through my mind that this could very well be our last moment on earth. Some in the group were crying quietly, some were repeating Hail Marys under their breath, some were cursing quietly. Jimmy Berretti, a tall quiet youngster from Ayr, was shivering uncontrollably despite the warmth of the night, and I could feel nausea and panic begin to well up inside me. Sitting cross-legged in front of me was Ronnie Girasole, my cellmate at the time of my arrest. One of the marauding dogs stopped beside him and peed on his leg. 'Fuckin' bastards...fuckin' bastards!' was his angry whisper, at which my growing panic turned into a semi-hysterical giggle. Yet even in such moments a sense of humour can show itself. Aldo Magris, head waiter from Quaglino's famous London restaurant, sat massaging a painful spot on his ribs where an enthusiastic guard had urged him on with a painful shove from a rifle butt. As he stroked the sore spot he came across a long forgotten pocket in his tattered jacket, from which he surreptitiously extracted a packet of condoms. Glancing around carefully to be sure of escaping detection, he proceeded to blow one up, gave it a sharp tap, and the resulting balloon floated gently up into the warm night air. This was followed by two more, until Aldo was discovered and given a cuff on the head to match the pain in his ribs.

The unloading and manhandling took the better part of two hours or so, and when completed we had been sorted out into twenty groups of twenty frightened men sitting on the ground, fearfully and passively awaiting whatever else might be in store for us. A Canadian officer approached the first group and began to shout at them in a staccato flow of German. Enraged at the lack of response, he repeated himself even louder, and poked his stick at one of the prisoners in front of him. Ralph Taglione, one side of his face swollen from a blow, raised a hesitant hand and spoke in a cultivated English accent.

'Please sir...nobody here speaks German.'

The officer looked at him blankly. 'What do you mean you don't speak German? What bloody language do you speak?'

'Please sir, everybody here speaks English.'

'English?', the officer seemed confused. 'What do you mean English? Where do you come from?'

'Please sir, in this group we are all Italians from London.'

The officer's jaw sagged slightly. He looked oddly at Taglione, then turned on his heels to confer with a major standing close by. The major motioned to Taglione who stood up and hobbled over to the him, barely able to walk. He questioned Taglione closely, and I could see him listening intently to the Londoner's answers. These were long and fluent, punctuated by a series of gestures which ended with a characteristic arms half-raised, palms upturned, hunched shoulders pose which spoke volumes.

It will probably never be possible to discover the combination of events which brought 407 Italian internees to a camp obviously prepared for high-risk Nazis, and the truth of the matter will probably remain unknown forever to those who suffered that night. Was the sinking of the *Arandora Star* a factor? Had the camp been prepared for the Germans who sailed on *that* ship? But the Germans on the *Arandora Star* were all Jewish or political refugees, who no more merited the treatment of that first night than we Italians did. Were the priests singled out for special treatment because it was thought that they were spies disguised as priests? Why were the soldiers' commands given in German? Why were all the notices in the compound written in that language? The camp had obviously been specifically prepared for an intake of high-risk German POWs such as the *Ettrick* had carried. Could there have been a mix up at Quebec, with our group sent off to the wrong destination?

But Captain Vinden knew the truth about the men whose names he had read out in Warth Mills some two weeks before. He certainly knew their nationality, so why had the colonel in charge of the reception of the prisoners who was obviously convinced that he was dealing with Germans, not been informed of their true identity? What is certain is that no one, least of all a bunch of hapless internees consisting of boys, old men, shopkeepers, waiters, chefs, doctors, refugees and deckhands, should have been subjected to the calculated brutalities of that night. And all for having committed the crime of being born an Italian or possessing an Italian name. That no one was seriously injured is remarkable, and the memory of the first night at Camp S will long remain in the minds of those who experienced it.

After the questioning of Taglione the attitude of the soldiers changed dramatically. Orders were now given in English, and although the voices were as rough as before, no more hands were laid on and the marauding dogs were withdrawn from the compound. The first group of men was made to stand and strip off all their clothes, then ordered naked into a dimly-lit room furnished with two rows of showers. Before entering the showers, all body hair was sheared off by a group of soldiers wielding electric hair clippers, then, issued with a bar of soap, each man was ordered into the showers. Hot and heavily disinfected water streamed out of the first row of showers, and then, after a cold rinse in the second row, the first group of men were paraded dripping wet to stand in front of a bored medical officer. From a safe distance behind a plain wooden table, his examination consisted of a prod with a swagger stick and a quick glance at the front and back of each prisoner. Although all use of excessive force had stopped, we were still being manhandled, the soldiers emphasising their verbal commands with shoves and pushes.

As I was in the fourth group waiting to be stripped, shorn, showered and examined, I had ample time to notice that as each man undressed, all pockets were emptied out and rings, bracelets, watches, pens and anything of any value was confiscated by the guards. A Scots-Italian in our group, Peter Nesti, had a small mother-of-pearl fountain pen in his pocket. When he saw what was happening, he hid it by surreptitiously inserting it into his anus as he squatted on the ground. I wore a gold crucifix ring of a type fashionable in those days in Glasgow-Italian families, which had been given to me many years before by my mother. This had great sentimental value for me, and I had no wish for it to be stolen. I flattened the ring as best I could and placed it between my toes, where it remained safely hidden during the shearing and washing procedures. George Martinez wore a handsome gold ring gifted to him a few months before in Naples by his newly-acquired fiancée. He saved this by tying it into the sleeve of his shirt before being stripped and searched, then popping it into his mouth before throwing his discarded clothes into the growing heap. For many days afterwards gleeful prisoners exchanged stories about the various ways in which they had managed to save cherished objects. These tales, sometimes embellished, raised morale amongst the men. In our situation such little acts of defiance could be considered victories against our captors.

It was soon my turn to undergo the cleaning procedure. I was quickly rid of a month's accumulation of grime and dirt, after which I was issued with a large towel and a bundle of clothes. Vastly relieved that orders were now being given less forcefully, I followed the shouted instructions of the guards and ran up some wooden steps into a long, low and dimly-lit vaulted room. The only furnishings were two rows of double-tiered metal bunks, separated by a passage no more than three feet wide, and each supplied with a mattress and folded blankets. A sergeant stood by, directing each of us to a bunk and, barely dry, utterly drained and exhausted by the events of the day, I fell instantly asleep.

The next morning dawned to a completely changed atmosphere in the camp. As we woke up and cautiously poked our faces out of the dormitories, no military presence was to be seen, and soon the compound was full of men taking in the details of our new accommodation. A long three-sided building of three floors, surmounted by a gently sloping roof, the structure was made of stone blocks about two feet thick. Access to the ground floor was by means of two large doors in the centre section, whilst the upper floors could be reached both by internal wooden stairs and from the outside by means of sets of stone steps leading directly up from the compound. The floors of the upper sections were of rough wood, and the ground floor was paved with large flagstones. The rear of the fortress was an unbroken stone wall, and at the front of the building, regularly spaced window apertures gave light and ventilation. Across the front of the building a seven-foot-high, double barbed-wire fence had been erected to form a courtyard about 100ft wide by 350ft long. At either end of the fence stood an elevated wooden tower, each equipped with a heavy machine-gun manned by three soldiers. The whole structure ran parallel to the river and was separated from it by some fifty yards of gently sloping ground. Across the river lay the city of Montreal, surmounted by a huge neon illuminated crucifix on the heights of Mount Royal beyond. Dominating the scene was the impressive structure of the Jacques Cartier bridge as it passed over the northern end of the building, with one of its giant concrete pylons almost touching the perimeter fence of the compound. We were to learn afterwards that we were being held on Ste Helene's island in the St Lawrence river in an old fortress built some two hundred years before by Champlain, the French governor of Quebec.

News of the arrival of the prisoners had evidently filtered through to the population of Montreal, for the bridge high above us was thronged with curiosity seekers strolling along, stopping whenever possible to stare at the packed compound below them. Soldiers posted on the bridge kept the pedestrians on the move. These soldiers, together with the machine-gun crews on the towers, were the only military personnel in sight. We had now donned the clothes given to us the night before, which consisted of a blue shirt with a large red circle on the back, trousers with a broad red stripe running down the side of the leg, and a blue jacket, also with a large red circle on the back. As the morning wore on without any sign of guards appearing inside the compound, we gained in confidence, and soon the courtyard was packed with a milling mass of blue-clad red-striped prisoners. Although the space available was very limited, after the claustrophobia of the *Ettrick* the men revelled in the luxury of freedom of movement, and strolled around exchanging experiences of the night before, comparing cuts and bruises.

After some time the gates of the camp opened and some soldiers entered. The officer who had interrogated Ralph Taglione the night before began to address us from the top of some stone steps set into the wall of the fortress. He introduced himself as Major O'Donohoe, the Camp Commandant, and with no reference to the events of the night before, informed us that this was to be our permanent camp. He then presented to us a Captain Pitblado, who was to instruct us in the routine of the camp. The captain was a jolly-looking, rotund little man approaching middle age, with the face and manner of an avuncular WC Fields. He smiled broadly, waved a hand as if in greeting, then proceeded to address the assembled prisoners in the manner of a boy scout leader exhorting his adolescent charges. This was to be our home for the foreseeable future, he said, so everyone had to cooperate to make it comfortable for all. Each group of twenty had now to choose a leader, who in turn would elect a Camp Leader, who would be in daily contact with the military to ensure the smooth running of the camp. Provisions would now be arriving, and the first task of the prisoners would be the selection of their own kitchen personnel. He beamed cheerfully at us and gave a little wave with a plump hand. He then concluded his address with a little homily by which he was to be forever remembered, and which was to become the catchphrase of the camp.

'Now lads, now that we know one another we've got to play ball together. You play ball with me and I'll play ball with you.'

At this, there were a number of blistering *sotto voce* comments from the prisoners, most of whom were still nursing the bruises of the night before. Then, flanked by two massively-built sergeants, both of whom had been noticed acting with great enthusiasm and vigour at the reception of the previous night, the little captain began a tour of the compound. He nodded pleasantly to all and sundry, his manner that of a paternal schoolmaster making himself acquainted with his pupils. He stopped from time to time to speak to individual prisoners, always finishing the conversation with his catchphrase.

'You play ball with me and I'll play ball with you.'

Pitblado's manner and walkabout amongst the prisoners served the purpose of creating a much more relaxed and less fearful atmosphere in the camp. Moreover, the promise of the arrival of provisions and the prospect of good and regular meals boosted our morale and pushed into the background the memory of the previous night's reception. Then, some weeks later, to the great delight of the prisoners, a weekly cinema show was introduced to the camp. This was an Army entertainment unit consisting of a 16mm projector with a supply of all the latest Hollywood productions, obtained for the camp through the good offices of the International Red Cross. Permission was given by the Camp Commandant for films to be shown once a week in the recreation hut, subject to the good behaviour of the prisoners.

The recreation hut bulged at the seams on the occasion of the first film, *Captains Courageous* with Spencer Tracy and Freddie Bartholomew. The audience, packed tightly into every available inch, sat and stood enraptured for a short two hours, with the reality of their surroundings forgotten. The non-English-speaking section of the camp were not happy however, for the dialogue was meaningless to them, so I began the challenging and satisfying undertaking of doing a simultaneous translation of the films for the sailors. On the *Ettrick* I had struck up a friendship with a little Sicilian sailor, Pasquale Nardo, and he approached me on the crews' behalf. At their request I drew up a petition asking for a second showing of each film for the benefit of the merchant seamen. This was agreed to, and I sat surrounded by scores of sailors listening eagerly to my translation of the dialogue. I took considerable pride in these translations. I tried to convey accurately in Italian the meaning of the dialogue as it unfolded and I found great satisfaction in the knowledge that I was doing the translations well. At that time Hollywood was producing many films of worth: screen versions of some of Dickens' novels such as *David Copperfield*; biographies of great men of history such as *Abe Lincoln* and *Juarez*; period films such as *The Hunchback of Notre Dame* and romances of the *Lost Horizon* type, all of which gave excellent practice in simultaneous translation from good English into Italian. The pot-boilers of the day, the gangster films, the westerns and the musicals, were all very trite stuff, with dialogue so repetitive and banal that I could actually finish the actor's words before they did. So I became proficient in the art of simultaneous translation, and would reflect wryly on the fact that much of my education had come and was still coming to me by means of a medium meant for entertainment and not for learning.

There was no official compulsion on the prisoners to take part in any form of organised work, and it would have been very easy for us to sink into a routine of slothful apathy. Many did, in fact, and performed only the most basic of tasks which consisted of eating, sleeping, and allowing themselves to be counted twice a day. But most men instinctively need activity, and so every day most of us tried to keep active in some way in an attempt to ignore the unpleasant reality of our camp existence. By the summer of 1941 various kinds of work had been made available to the prisoners. About a quarter of a mile from the camp there stood an old stone building called *la poudrière* (the powderhouse), presumably because at one time it served as a munitions store for the fortress. This was put into use as a joinery shop and provided work for about thirty men who made wooden packing cases and simple articles of furniture. A small workshop for the packaging of Red Cross bandages had been erected inside the compound and this also provided work for a dozen or so prisoners. A place in the Powderhouse work party was much sought after. To work there meant leaving the confines of the barbed wire and a change of surroundings. The march out of the fortress, although the work party was under heavily armed guard, was in itself a tonic. To be able to walk in a straight line for more than a few hundred feet; to be away from the milling mass of men in the compound; to see and smell the leafy perfume of shrubs and trees, that was pleasure indeed.

The setting up of these two workplaces gave rise to bitter controversy in the camp. The fascist element labeled as traitors anyone participating in what they claimed was work calculated to help the enemy. A visit to the camp was made by Red Cross officials who quoted from their well-worn copy of the Geneva Convention. They assured the prisoners that such work was permitted by the regulations, but their assurance was to no avail, and the Fascists remained firmly opposed. To their chagrin, a vote was held on the matter by the prisoners, who came down solidly in favour of the proposed work, but this decision created further tensions in the camp, for the Fascists then claimed that since no voting was allowed in Italy, such a procedure had no place in an Italian camp! It was significant that a high proportion of the sailors were strongly and openly in favour of the projects, which showed that they were beginning to think for themselves in these matters.

The authorities were asked to provide yet more work, and so the island cleaning parties were formed. These consisted of groups of twenty prisoners or so, armed with an assortment of wheelbarrows, shovels, brooms and rakes. They were taken out to all parts of the island under guard to tidy up the many roads and pathways criss-crossing it. This work also was much sought after, since it too gave the possibility of spending time outside the wire. In the winter months so-called snow parties were formed. Brooms and rakes were exchanged for long-handled snow shovels and the men were put to clearing roads blocked by the frequent heavy falls of snow. But work on the snow parties was not very popular, because it entailed working in sub-zero temperatures with the thermometer showing as much as ten or twenty degrees below zero. At these temperatures a man's breath would literally freeze at his nostrils, with beads of ice forming around nose and lips. Moreover, although the winter uniforms were of thick felt material with heavy ear-muffed caps, layers of underclothing had to be worn to protect against the intense cold. The exertion of wielding the shovels heavy with snow would make the men break sweat, which would then chill on the skin, making it almost impossible to remain warm.Care too had to be taken to urinate before setting out in such low temperatures. Peeing in such conditions was a risky and complicated procedure. Some with a perverse sense of humour would return from the snow party carrying slivers of amber-coloured ice to throw at their comrades back in the warm dormitories of the fort, a practice not surprisingly stamped out on the grounds of hygiene.

Occasionally, after exceptionally heavy snow falls had swamped the Montreal street-cleaning facilities, volunteers would be asked for and then escorted into the city under heavy guard to help clear the streets. In the winter months these groups wearing blue uniforms with red discs on the back and red stripes on the trousers became a familiar sight to the citizens of Montreal. The heavy guard was there not only to prevent a possible escape but mainly to prevent fraternization with the people of Montreal. Many French-Canadians were politically hostile to the English and would attempt to talk to the prisoners, sympathising with their lot and offering gifts of chocolates and cigarettes. This work was never very popular, even though the participants could be sure of returning to the camp laden with goodies, because many considered it a humiliation to be paraded thus in full view of the local population.

The political hostility to the English was evidently shared by some Canadian politicians, for in the summer of 1942 the camp was graced for a short time by the presence of Mayor Houde of Montreal. He was an advocate of an independent Quebec, and had been removed from office and arrested for his persistent speeches in criticism of the English and his exhortation to French Canadians to resist conscription into the Canadian army. He was kept in the camp for about a month, then placed under house arrest for the remainder of the war. Politically, his arrest proved to be of no embarrassment whatsoever. On his release after the war he was re-elected mayor of Montreal with a thumping majority.

To a great extent our way of life in the camp depended on the whims of the commanding officer and the nature of the soldiers in direct contact with us. The ones who had been so enthusiastic and vigorous on our reception night belonged to an English-Canadian regiment, and although no further violence was delivered, they rigidly enforced discipline. Orders were barked at us in best parade-ground fashion, and any slowness or reluctance on our part was dealt with none-too-gentle pushes and nudges with rifle butts. A few months later they were relieved by ageing French-Canadian home guard types, who were friendly enough, and not nearly as strict as their predecessors. The guards were changed every few months or so, and we soon learned to adapt to differing degrees of discipline, or the lack of it. We always cheered the arrival of French-Canadian units. Given the strong anti-English secessionist movement in Quebec, the Quebecois soldiers looked upon us as more sinned against than sinning. Life under them was relatively easy, discipline was lax, and the work parties were not made to break sweat.

Sometime in 1942, Bosco became an inmate of the camp. One day an island work party returned to base followed by a large, bedraggled, emaciated and flea-ridden sheep dog. Obviously a stray, it had hung around the prisoners all day, hungrily wolfing down the scraps thrown at it during meal breaks. Next morning the dog was still at the gates. It followed the work group all day long, devoured the scraps thrown at it, and again bedded down for the night at the camp gates. Captain Pitblado was approached. Would he kindly ask the Camp Commandant for permission to take the dog in, delouse it, and keep it as a camp mascot? Permission was given, the dog was scrubbed, disinfected, and given the name Bosco. Regular and plentiful food fattened him up, and after a few weeks the camp had a large, handsome and affectionate sheep dog as a mascot. He ambled around all day, occasionally went out with the work parties, and became as much part of the camp as we were. Each morning at roll-call he learned to stand at attention with our Camp Leader, sometimes to be given a pat on the head by the officer of the day as the count was begun.

Then, an amazing discovery of a Pavlovian nature was made. Every time a piece of raw onion was placed on his nose, Bosco would defecate on the spot! This remarkable and hilarious reaction was at once put to good use. Next morning Bosco was in his accustomed place at the gate awaiting the entrance of the officer of the day for roll-call, but with one difference. He now faced backwards, bushy tail where his nose ought to have been. The gate opened, and in marched Pitblado with his escort of five soldiers, ready to start the count. A slice of onion was quickly administered to Bosco's nose, and on cue and with a rather fruity whump, a large soft turd hit the ground directly in front of the startled captain. An epidemic of laughter broke out and the men struggled to keep faces straight. The contagion spread to the five soldiers, who had to wipe away tears of silent mirth as they accompanied the red-faced Pitblado on the rest of his round. Once could have been an accident, but when the same thing happened the next morning, with an even fruitier turd deposited at Pitblado's feet, poor Bosco was banned from the compound at future roll-calls. Some wag remarked that he had been lucky to escape a period in the cells.

Because of my fluency in Italian and English, I was given the job of interpreter in the internal camp office, and towards the end of 1941 I was requested to type out an order of the day for the notice board. This was an enquiry as to whether there were any fluent German and English speakers among the prisoners who might wish to apply for a position as an interpreter in those languages. In a few months Camp S, henceforth to be known as Camp 43, was to become a transit camp for German Officers and NCOs captured in North Africa until their transfer to camps further west.

The request went unanswered, for no one in the camp had any knowledge of German. So I volunteered for the job, despite the fact that I knew not a single word of that language. I announced myself to the authorities as a fluent, although somewhat rusty, German speaker. I was on perfectly safe ground, for there was no one to put me to the test, so in the absence of any other applicants I was given the job and immediately set to work. Declaring myself in need of practice and revision I asked for a dictionary, a grammar and a reader, all of which were unquestioningly supplied, and for the next two months I devoted every spare hour of the day to concentrated study. Declensions, genders and verb forms were committed to memory by a process of constant repetition. Each day I added ten new words and all their forms to my vocabulary. The reading book provided was a German translation of *Salammbo*, a novel by Flaubert, which dealt with the semi-fictional adventures of a Libyan prince at the time of Hamilcar, the father of Hannibal. I laboriously translated the first page of the book, and the form of each verb and noun, until the meaning of the sentences became clear. At the end of ten weeks of feverishly intensive work I had acquired a vocabulary of some 1000 words, and was able to read and translate the rest of the pages without a great deal of difficulty. There was one very big problem though. Apart from the contact with the German POWs on the *Ettrick*, I had never heard a word of conversational German spoken in my life, so I awaited with more than a touch of apprehension the arrival of the first contingent of prisoners. That day duly arrived, and I stood at the side of Colonel O'Donohue ready to put my newly-acquired knowledge to the test.

Preceded by a jeep armed with a rear-mounted machine-gun, an army lorry rolled into the courtyard. It stopped, the tailgate slammed down and the six occupants jumped out at the prompting of their guards. Still in their sand-stained uniforms of the Afrika Korps, with characteristic peaked caps on their heads, the German officers stood stretching their limbs, turning their heads with curiosity to take stock of their surroundings. Prompted by O'Donohue, I nervously stepped forward, cleared my throat, and proceeded to deliver my well-rehearsed speech, pronouncing my words in my best Conrad Veidt accent.

'*Sie sind jetzt*...you are now in Camp 43 in Montreal. This is a transit camp where you will remain until transportation is ready to take you to your permanent camp further west.'

The senior officer, a young captain, looked at me and and let loose a rapid stream of words. I did not understand a single word of it. I swallowed nervously, and ignoring the Colonel's enquiring glance, said slowly in German.

'*Bitte, sprechen Sie langsam*...please speak slowly, I am an Italian internee and I have never heard German spoken. Please speak slowly and clearly.'

The astonished captain looked at me with open mouth, and with relief I understood my first spoken German words.

'*Mein Gott, Er spricht wie ein Buch.*' 'My God, he speaks like a book!'

In a very short time, by dint of spending as much time as possible with the German POWs, and a continuing intensive study of the language, I became as fluent in German as I had originally claimed to be, and I eagerly awaited every new German arrival so as to put my newly-acquired skill to use. I revelled in my duties, happy at the acquisition of a new language, and I took intense interest in my conversations with these German soldiers who had actually fought in the battles which were constantly talked about and which had an important bearing on the length of time we might have to remain as prisoners.

I tried not to waste my time in the camp. The International Red Cross had supplied us with a broad variety of text books, and classes were set up by those in the camp who had the education and expertise to pass on their knowledge to any who cared to attend them. There were many university graduates and academics among us. Romeo Capitanio, a quiet and studious Venetian who had lived many years in London as an employee in the Credit Lyonnais, a French Bank, had a string of qualifications after his name, and organized classes in French and Italian. George Martinez, a young Neapolitan with a BSc in engineering from Cambridge, set up a class in mathematics. Father Rofinella, a Jesuit priest, also a Cambridge graduate, held classes in English and Italian Literature, and Emilio Barocas, an assistant to the Astronomer Royal in Greenwich, gave interesting

talks on Astronomy. Apart from the mathematics class, a subject I knew absolutely nothing about, I attended them all, absorbed all the information I could
from them, and in later years I used to refer to my time spent on Ste Helene's
Island as my years in college.

The journey to Montreal in 1974 was the first of the many trips Mary and I
were to make to Canada in subsequent years. The country itself fascinated me:
its size, the diversity of its peoples, the awesome beauty of the Rocky Mountains
and the National Parks, the still and peaceful timelessness of the mountain lakes,
culminating in what must be the most beautiful natural view on Earth, the vista
along the length of Lake Louise in Banff National Park. All these things alone
were worth repeated journeys, but there were other factors, human ones, which
motivated our many visits. Mary's old childhood friend, Carol, the girl who had
grown up with Mary in Maitland Street and who had shared the first date with
my future wife, now lived permanently in Niagara on the Lake, a picturesque
little town on the banks of the Niagara river, the boundary between Canada
and the USA. As chance would have it, Carol too had ended up with marriage
to an Italian, Rudy Valiani from London, whose parents also hailed from the
Barga region and whose childhood had been spent in circumstances similar to
my own. Almost ten years younger than I, he had escaped internment and had
taken up a career in hotel management which had ended with his retirement as
the manager of a Marriot hotel in Toronto. He and Carol had acquired Canadian
nationality and had elected to spend their retirement in the picture postcard pret-
tiness of Niagara on the Lake, and it was from there that we started our Canadian
holidays. Rudy was a mine of information on the history of that part of Canada,
and took us on many a descriptive tour of Ontario and the northern bank of the
Niagara river. Then off we would go across the continent to Calgary, the place
we used as a springboard for our tours of the Rockies. In Calgary we always
paid a visit to Michael Hannigan, a schoolmate of our son Lorenzo, who had
qualified as a vet, and had taken up a lucrative career in that western Canadian
city. Michael was a keen golfer and a member of the Glencoe Country Club, a
leisure complex built around a spectacular golf course, where he treated me to
many a game of golf. I would then reciprocate with games on the Banff Springs
golf courses about fifty miles west of Calgary. These consisted of three nine-
hole courses built around the Banff Springs Hotel, the hotel which Mary and I
used as a base for the exploration of the national parks. These courses were of
varying degrees of difficulty, and a round on them could be mixed to make for
as difficult or as easy a round as one desired. Michael, by now well accustomed
to the vast open spaces of Alberta, thought nothing of doing a round trip of a
hundred miles for a round of golf, and so came to play at Banff Springs several
times. During one holiday Mary and I stayed at the Château Lake Louise Hotel,
which, like Calgary, was about fifty miles from the Banff courses, although on

the western side, and we met up for a game at Banff, which meant that both of us had to drive a round trip of 100 miles, an experience I vowed never to repeat. We had stretched the game to twenty-seven holes, and after the drive back I had a gin and tonic, showered, then, with Mary, went down to the hotel dining room for a meal. As we walked to our table, I became aware of a weird sensation which felt for all the world as if I were walking on a water bed, and became possessed of a curiously unreal, detached feeling which was to last for the rest of the night. A night's sleep did much to make me feel better, but Mary insisted that I consult the hotel doctor. His diagnosis was that at sixty-seven years of age, as I was then, I had no business playing twenty-seven holes of golf on a golf course several thousand feet above sea level, then to follow it with a fifty mile drive and a stiff gin and tonic before showering. The exertion in the thinner air had lowered my blood pressure, an effect heightened by the intake of alcohol, all of which had given rise to the weird and somewhat frightening sensations of the night before.

Each trip to Canada would include a mandatory visit to Montreal, not only to visit my old camp, but also to renew my friendship with O'Connor Lynch. I had first met O'Connor in the winter of 1941, at the time of his appointment as civilian interpreter to the camp. At that time part of my work in the camp consisted of preparing notices in Italian and English for posting up as orders of the day, so I came into contact with him on a daily basis, and slowly a cautious friendship developed between us. This was fuelled by a common interest in art and literature, subjects in which I had become interested after reading the many books sent to the camp by the International Red Cross and of attending classes run by some of the academics we had there as prisoners. Himself an artist, O'Connor had lived for three years in Rome, spoke fluent Italian and in his travels in Europe had acquired some German books on the technical aspects of Italian paintings of the Renaissance. On learning that I was about to become the interpreter for the camp in German, he asked me to translate them for him. The dictionary I had did not stretch to coping with the work he had asked me to do, so he obtained another larger one, with the German in gothic script. This I used in the successful translation of his books, a work which took me the best part of two years to complete, and which, I was to learn later, he had properly printed and bound, then placed in the McGill University of Montreal's library, and which, for all I know, might still be there to this day. I still have the dictionary he gave me, but it now serves no useful purpose; for forty years now I have neither spoken nor read any German, besides which my eyes can no longer decipher the somewhat intricate gothic script. At the war's end O'Connor set up an art studio in Montreal, where I made a point of dropping in to renew an old relationship each time we went for a holiday to Canada. One year we spent a week in Quebec city, a fascinating old French anachronism on the edge of an

English-speaking continent, and stayed at the Chateau Frontenac high above the port where fifty or so years before I had been unloaded as a prisoner. As I looked down at the railway siding where the train had been waiting to take us to St Helene's Island, I could not help but wonder what turn my life would have taken had I accepted the work offered to me by the Canadian authorities on my release half a century ago in 1943.

❧ 4 ❧
Aftermath

A t long last, in July of 1943, I was called to the commandant's office to be informed that my release had come through from the Home Office in London, and that a group of forty of us from the camp were to be sent back to Britain on the first available convoy. An alternative offer was made to me. At that time the newly formed United Nations Organisation was being set up in San Francisco, and there was a need for translators who could undertake simultaneous translations in various languages. In those days there were not many who could fit the bill, and I had acquired a reputation for quick and accurate interpretation in any combination of English, Italian and German. The colonel was empowered to offer me an initial one-year contract with immediate release and transportation to San Francisco. I was sorely tempted. A whole new world could have been opened up for me. The USA was a melting pot of nationalities where your surname did not matter, and where the word 'Tally' was unknown, or so I believed. What would I find back in Glasgow after a war in which I had been labeled an enemy alien? How could I stand behind a shop counter and serve customers with the mark of Cain on my forehead? It was a hard decision to make and I almost wished that my present cosseted and confined circumstances, where all decisions were made for me, could continue. But my parents back in Glasgow were now old; both had struggled and worked and sacrificed to keep the family shop open for a few hours each week so that their two sons would have something to come back to after the war. Such is the faith of the religious and the elderly; they had not even considered the possibility of any other end to the troubles of the past four years. Their two sons would survive, Ralph would come back safely from his service in the British army, I would come back from my internment and the family would be reunited to work together. There was therefore no question of my going to the UN, no matter how enticing the prospect and how easy the road ahead. I owed my parents too much. I regretfully turned down the offer and elected to take my place in the group to be returned to Britain.

At the same time Pasquale Nardo, my little Sicilian sailor friend, came to me with an item of news that could well have affected our return to the UK. I had met Pasquale Nardo some three years before on the docks at Liverpool, where

we had been squatting for hours together with thousands of other prisoners awaiting embarkation on one of the two prison ships at anchor there. He was a short
stocky youth in his middle twenties, with short curly dark brown hair and a face
that reminded me of a smaller Gilbert Roland, a film actor of the day. He told
me about his capture a few weeks before just off the coast at Trapani, a fishing
port on the west coast of Sicily. On the day of the declaration of war he and his
three companions were going about their business a few miles out at sea, and as
their little fishing smack emerged from a dense fog bank they rammed the side
of a British submarine which had just surfaced. Presumably to keep his position
secret, the British captain promptly took them on board as prisoners and sank
their craft. Two days or so later, at Malta, they were transferred to a ship bound
for Liverpool, where they joined up with the contingent who eventually finished
up on the St Helene's island camp. The captain of the submarine must have
been a very humane man, for he could just as easily have sunk the four without
trace along with their craft. Pasquale spoke Italian with a thick Sicilian accent,
which I at first found difficult to understand, and he was amazed at the fact that
I could speak both English and Italian. He plied me with questions. Where was
I from? Why could I speak English so fluently? I had lived all my life in a place
called Scotland? Where was this place? Was it near America? He had an uncle
in America, he said. Why was I a prisoner like himself? What kind of work did
I do in this place Scotland? What were the people there like? These conversations continued for the next twelve days in the cramped hold of the ship that
was taking us to Canada, and a bond of friendship was formed between the two
of us, one a Scots-Italian from Glasgow and the other a Sicilian fisherman.

A few months into the life of the camp Pasquale decided to put his full trust
in me. Post had begun to arrive through the International Red Cross, and the
little Sicilian had received a letter from his father in Trapani, written on the old
man's behalf by the local priest, for his father could not read or write. Pasquale
too was illiterate, in common with many southern Italians in the Italy of 70 years
ago. Other illiterate sailors from the merchant ships as a matter of course went to
their officers to have their letters from home read out, but Pasquale did not trust
these officers. Most were Northerners, and all were *fascisti*. Pasquale had a deep
hatred of the *fascisti*; too many of his friends had been arrested by them and sent
into exile on the Lipari Islands of fearsome repute. So he approached me and
asked me to read his letter, and listened attentively to the words of his father as
set down by the village priest and read to him by his new friend from Scotland.
I wrote an answer as Pasquale dictated, and was deeply touched by the simple
words of love and affection from a son to his father. To read and write a man's
intimate mail with a parent is to see into that man's soul, and so I, as a mark of
my appreciation of the trust that Pasquale had put in me, would occasionally
read out my own family letters to him. He would listen to these intently, asking

me all sorts of questions about life in Glasgow, and could not understand why my brother Ralph was now a soldier in the British army whilst I was a prisoner like he was. But I did more. Despite my own comparative lack of schooling, slowly and painstakingly I taught Pasquale to read and then to write. He had a keenly intelligent and retentive mind, and after hours spent with heads together over what Italian books were available in the camp, at the end of the first year of captivity Pasquale was writing his own letters to his father in Trapani and reading the priest's replies. He read everything he could get his hands on, and thanks to the generosity of the Red Cross there was no lack of material to choose from. New horizons had been opened up to him and he was slowly but surely emerging into a new world of literacy and understanding.

He found out that a small group of die-hard fascists, even at this late stage in the war, when half of Italy was occupied by Allied troops and it was obvious that Mussolini was finished, had decided on one last gesture of defiance and had started on an ambitious plan for an escape from the camp. Their plan consisted of building a tunnel between the recreation hut and the wire perimeter of the camp. The tunnel passed under a service road, which bisected the camp compound, and was to emerge outside the barbed wire fence on a slope which led down to the St Lawrence river. Apart from causing the authorities the maximum possible inconvenience, it was difficult to see what the undertaking could have achieved, for such an exodus would have simply been a pointless escape to nowhere. Only one man, Baron Von Werra, a Luftwaffe pilot, had ever escaped from a Canadian POW camp, and that had been in January of 1941, when the USA was still neutral and had provided him with a safe haven. Von Werra's was a remarkable feat. He had escaped while in transit from Halifax to a camp in Ontario, then had made his way in the bitter cold to the US border, crossing the frozen St Lawrence in the process. He was discovered half dead in the snow by an American frontier guard and handed over to the German consul in New York, pending an extradition warrant from the Canadian government. He disappeared from his house arrest and made his way back to Germany via Yokohama in Japan and then via the trans-Siberian railway to Russia, both of which countries were as yet not involved in the war. The Von Werra saga ended in December 1941, when he was shot down and killed over Moscow. His story was made into a Hollywood film in 1957, *The One That Got Away*.

Work on the tunnel had been a closely guarded secret known only to the half dozen or so men actively engaged in digging, but there was little that went on in the camp without Pasquale being aware of it. I thanked him for the information and realized immediately that an incident of that nature would be disastrous for myself and for the thirty-nine others who were awaiting their freedom. A mass escape from the camp could put our departure in jeopardy, for were it to happen before our departure, a quarantine would almost certainly be imposed on the camp until the escaped prisoners had all been recaptured and the matter investigated. I broke the news to two of my companions also awaiting transportation back to the UK: Joe Guidi, the owner of the Alhambra Restaurant in Argyle Street, and John Agostini, a hard-as-nails type from the east end of London. They were in agreement that something had to be done about it. A direct betrayal of the tunnel to the authorities was absolutely ruled out. The idea of informing on fellow prisoners was dismissed out of hand, for Agostini, who had a London gangland background and carried the scars of a score of gang fights on his body to prove it, had no time for narks. Joe Guidi came up with a thought. How would it be if the authorities discovered the tunnel by themselves, in a manner which would implicate and harm no one? We listened to his idea. After lights out that night and with all the camp asleep, my two companions and I crept into the recreation hut. In the reflected lights of the perimeter searchlights we followed Pasquale's instructions and found the hidden trapdoor leading to the tunnel. Leaving Guidi on guard, Agostini and I lowered ourselves into the space beneath.

The tunnel had been very skillfully dug out, was about two feet high and broad enough to allow a man to wriggle his way forward. A few wooden props sustained the roof, and at the point where it passed under the service road which ran the length of the compound, the props were arranged closely together to compensate for the weight of any passing vehicle. Working as quickly as possible in the cramped space, Agostini and I stripped away the majority of the wooden supports, leaving a 10-foot section under the road practically unsupported. We replaced the trapdoor, retraced our steps and the three of us went back to our bunks to sleep fitfully and to await the arrival of daylight. At exactly 6.30am, half an hour before reveille, a large army truck, heavily-laden with provisions, rolled slowly through the gates, and as the wheels crunched over the unsupported tunnel, the service road collapsed, leaving the truck with its front wheels embedded in the ground. The tunnel now discovered, reaction was swift. The recreation hut was put under armed guard while a swarm of soldiers searched the building until the trapdoor with the entrance to the tunnel was discovered.

Colonel O'Donohue, the camp commandant at that time, inspected the entrance to the tunnel personally, then listened with interest to the report of the sergeant who had examined the whole of it. The lorry was pulled out of the hole and the exposed part of the tunnel also inspected. The contented officer summoned the Camp Leader, a Joe Crolla of Edinburgh, to his office. Crolla, who had known nothing of the proposed escape, was informed that, in the light of all the circumstances, the discovery of the tunnel and the foiling of the escape plan was satisfaction enough for the Colonel, and no further investigation or action would be necessary. Furious arguments broke out amongst the conspirators as they sought to apportion blame for the fiasco, and when it came to repairing the section of road where the lorry had come to grief, it became obvious to the planners of the tunnel that their work had been tampered with. They vowed vengeance on the traitors, as they called them, who had sabotaged their plan. Unknown to us, the absence of my two companions and myself from the dormitory that night had been noted by some of the prisoners and this information got back to the conspirators, who now had clear evidence as to who the saboteurs were.

Down through the camp grapevine came the threat: those three are going to be dealt with. This was no idle menace. There had been several stabbings in the camp, none of them fatal, but two serious enough to have required the hospitalisation of the victims in a Montreal hospital. Although the assailants had never been officially identified, it was common knowledge in the camp that they belonged to a hard core of Fascist activists in the merchant seamen group. These were the same ones who had been building the tunnel, and they were threatening vengeance on myself and my two friends. For the next few days we went in fear of our lives, sleeping in shifts with one of us always on guard for a possible attack, and never separating during the day. It was then that little Pasquale Nardo approached me once again.

'I think you are in trouble, Giuseppe,' he said. 'I want to repay you for your goodness to me in these past years. I want you and your two friends to meet with me and Captain Bonorino and some others tonight.' Bonorino was the captain of one of the merchant ships' crew and a man universally respected throughout the camp.

That evening a small group assembled in the recreation hall: Guidi, Agostini and I, Captain Bonorino, Pasquale and seven seamen, all of them from Calabria, and all of them involved in the digging of the tunnel. Pasquale began to speak, slowly and in Sicilian-accented Italian. His words were accompanied by expansive gestures.

'I am a friend of friends in Trapani, and Giuseppe and his two companions are now my friends. They have harmed no one here. No-one has been named and no-one has been dishonoured. The war is lost and we all want to go home in peace to our families. There are bad people here and to them I say this. If any harm comes to Giuseppe and his two friends through anyone in this camp, I am sworn to seek vengeance for them. If I cannot, then my friends in Trapani will. *È ora di farla finita con queste scemate.*' 'It's time to make an end of these stupidities.'

He stood for a moment, then with an outstretched hand and pointing finger he gestured theatrically towards his silent audience of seven seamen, who slowly rose, passed and bowed their heads to him, saluted Captain Bonorino, then quietly left the room. Pasquale turned and said to me:

'You don't have to worry now. Nobody will dare to touch you or your friends, for they know that they will certainly pay for it one day if they do. If I cannot make them pay, then my friends and family will and the captain here is my witness.'

The three of us looked on in amazement, and I translated for the benefit of Agostini, who, since he did not speak Italian, had not understood a word. Captain Bonorino explained:

'I don't pretend to understand the mentality of these *meridionali* (southerners), but I think that you have just seen the power of the Sicilian Mafia. It's good to have one as a friend, but nobody wants one as an enemy. I don't think anyone will dare to harm you or your friends now, for if anyone does they will pay dearly for it, no matter how long it will take.'

He paused, put a fatherly hand on my shoulder and said, 'Go home to your family in Scotland, Giuseppe; you are fortunate, for God alone only knows what awaits us after the war in Italy.'

I used to think a lot about this incident in the years after the war, and brought to bear upon it the mass of information I had subsequently acquired about the phenomenon of the Sicilian Mafia and of the psychology of men like my friend Pasquale, born and raised in an environment of vendetta and fierce loyalties. Indeed, some years ago I wrote a book, which did not find a publisher, entitled *Men of Honour* which deals with the history of the Sicilian Mafia and attempts to show the grip that the Mafia has on the south of Italy and how to a large extent it controls the politics of the whole country. In it I used this quote by Enzo Biagi, a contemporary Italian writer:

> *The Mafia started out centuries ago as a system of reciprocal protection and defence against invaders and corrupt and venal authorities in their midst, but over the years slowly degenerated into a system of crime, delinquency and self-interest. There is now no law in Sicily, there is only the need for survival, and all the actions of an individual are motivated by this instinct. A good deed will be remembered and repaid, a slight or an insult will never be forgotten, and a friendship will never be betrayed. Make a friend of a Sicilian and you have one for life, make an enemy of one and your life could well be forfeit.*

I had made a friend of Pasquale, and he had repaid me in the only way he knew how, by instilling the fear of death and retribution into those who would have harmed his friend. But then I sometimes thought further: what if the tunnel builders had themselves been Mafiosi? What then would have been our fate? Then I realized the stupidity of such a conjecture. A Mafioso will carry out an act if there is a matter of honour or of vendetta attached to it, or if a profit to be made from such an act. The digging of the escape tunnel was pointless. It served no purpose other than that of nuisance value. There was no profit or personal honour, in the Sicilian sense of the word, attached to it. Therefore no one of the Mafia would have been associated with it.

Three weeks later, and without further incident, forty of us shook the dust of the compound from our feet for the last time. I took emotional leave of the many friends I had made over the last three years, with a special embrace for Pasquale Nardo. Then I watched the gates of the camp and three years of my life close behind me as I started on the first leg of the journey back to eventual freedom. Unlike our journey to Canada three years before, the journey back across the Atlantic was swift and uneventful. We sailed on the *Queen Elizabeth*, the sister ship of the *Queen Mary*, launched just a few weeks before the outbreak of war. The liner was unescorted, her speed more than sufficient protection against U-boat attack. Fitted out as a troopship, she could carry 15,000 men and their equipment across the Atlantic in just over three days and was a marvel of organisation on board. The men slept in cabins from which all furniture had been removed, and each of which could accommodate forty men in hammocks. To facilitate movement, all doors had been taken away too, and during emergency drill the sleeping quarters could be evacuated in a matter of minutes. The feeding of such a mass of humanity was a masterpiece of logistics. Each area was allocated a number, and the day would start with a call over the tannoy system. 'Zone 1, first call for chow' and the first group would form a queue to move towards the galley area, there to be issued with a metal tray of food to be eaten when seated in any available space on deck. Then a queue formed for the use of the huge tanks of soapy water used to wash the utensils, followed by another queue for rinsing. Five hours later the process was repeated. Latrine requirements had been attended to by the erection of a row of wooden toilet seats over the side of the ship round the complete circumference of the lower deck, providing hundreds of sea-going equivalents of dry lavatories. It was while seated on one of these on the afternoon of 27 July, with my bottom exposed to the cold Atlantic spray, that I heard over the tannoy of the downfall of Mussolini and of Italy's surrender to the Allies. The new head of the Italian government, Marshal Badoglio, had immediately joined with the Allies in the fight against the Germans. We Italians were now no longer enemy aliens, but Allies. The next day the *Queen Elizabeth* docked at Greenock. Our group disembarked, and still under the supervision of our corporal, mounted a train which took us south to Liverpool, there to stand on the same quay from which we had climbed on to the *Ettrick* three long years ago. There we boarded a ferry for the short crossing to the Isle of Man.

My release had been conditional on taking up some form of work of national importance. Farming and any other form of food production came under this category, and having opted for work of this type, I had the choice of having a work-place found for me by my parents near home. While awaiting my release papers to come through from the Home Office I spent some 6 weeks on the Isle of Man. The contrast between Camp 43 and the camps there could not have been greater. On the Isle of Man internment zones had been formed by wiring off areas of terraced houses and small hotels and designating them as camps. Two or three men shared each bedroom, and toilet facilities and living accommodation were more than adequate. There was space in abundance. We were assigned to the Onchan Camp, and to us 'Canadians', as we were immediately christened by the internees there, the place had the appearance and the amenities of a holiday camp!

A man could live as a human being in Onchan Camp. You wore your own civilian clothes, not a prisoner's uniform. You slept in a civilised bedroom and ate in a proper dining room. You did not have to share a cramped and stuffy dungeon-like dormitory with a hundred farting, coughing, swearing and often unwashed companions, and you did not have to share a latrine with twenty other men. You had sitting-rooms to lounge in, with newspapers and books to read and a radio to listen to. There were no machine-gun towers to menace your every move. You could find privacy if desired and did not have to rub shoulders constantly with persons you disliked and yet could not avoid. You could go to work on one of the many farms on the island and be left alone there all day, and not be herded into closely guarded work parties to serve as objects of curiosity for the local inhabitants. And most important of all, you could have visitors and see and talk with your loved ones.

The only inferior aspect of life on the Isle of Man was the food. Compared to the cornucopia of all good things we had to eat in Camp 43, rations there were plain and not overabundant, but in this the internees fared no worse than the general population of Britain in wartime. There was no doubt in my mind, however, that after my experiences in Camp 43 I would have preferred a three year diet of bread and cheese and water on the Isle of Man than a three year stay in Camp 43 with its superabundance of good food. The short stay in Onchan Camp was sheer luxury for me. I shared a room with two other 'Canadians', and we never ceased to marvel at the difference of life in the two camps. There was no strict routine imposed on us. Roll-call consisted of a visit and a cursory inspection of the room by a sergeant, after which you were as free to do as you pleased within the confines of the camp. If you felt like some work in the fresh air you presented yourself at the gate in the morning after breakfast, to be picked up by a lorry and left for a day's work at one of the hundreds of farms which dotted the island. This work would be supervised only by the local farmer, and we were treated at all times in a friendly and pleasant manner. The day's work over, the lorry did its rounds of the farms and returned the day workers to the camp. No fuss, no armed guards, no shouted orders, no push and shove with a rifle butt. The contrast with life in the St Helene's camp could not have been greater.

Time passed quickly and some weeks later, on 9 November 1943, to be precise, I was a completely free man, standing alone in a Liverpool railway station with travel permit in pocket, waiting for the Glasgow train. For the first time in three years I was not under some form of military constraint or other. I had been left completely to my own resources and free to move about as I pleased. The sensation was a strange and frightening one. I could feel anxiety and apprehension well up inside me, and for a brief moment I almost wished I were back in the compound of Camp 43 surrounded by all the well-known and now strangely desirable elements of that environment.

Sudden release from captivity can be almost as traumatic as the shock of arrest. The suddenness of my imprisonment had cut me off without warning from my family and friends and the environment I had always known. As a prisoner, the routine duties of having to earn a living and making a way for myself in life had stopped. Life was organised forcibly for me and I no longer needed to take responsibility for myself. Existence was merely a long round of killing time and waiting for an uncertain future, with my destiny no longer in my own hands. I simply had to obey orders and do exactly as I was told; I had become effectively depersonalised. With my release, the tensely wound psychological spring which had enabled me to come to terms with my captivity seemed to have suddenly snapped loose. I was free and had to depend purely on my own resources. There was no one there to tell me what to do or how to do it, no one to pull me by the arm or give me a nudge with a rifle, no armed soldier to order me brusquely on to a train.

With a tight knot in my stomach I looked around at the others waiting with me on the platform. These were people who for the last three years had looked upon me as a dangerous enemy. What would their reaction be if they knew who and what I was? I longed for the sight of a familiar face, of a familiar figure to turn and talk to. There were a few civilians standing about, but in the main the waiting passengers were military personnel of both sexes, weighed down by their kit, either going or returning from leave. They stood in groups chatting and laughing, their camaraderie evident, and I felt a complete outsider, an outlaw, afraid to engage in conversation in case my status be discovered and my identity as an ex-enemy alien made known to all.

In the packed train compartment I was the only one not in uniform and thus stuck out like a sore thumb, drawing curious stares from my fellow travellers. I politely refused the many offers of cigarettes and sandwiches from them and fended off their attempts at conversation as non-committally and as politely as I could. Then, so as not to have to participate in their exchange of introductions and small talk, I pretended to fall asleep. The pretence turned to reality and I did sleep, to be jolted awake by the jerking of the train as it drew into Glasgow's Central Station. It was dark on the platform as I stepped down from the compartment. I had forgotten about the blackout, and in the semi-darkness did not at first recognise the uniformed figure approaching alongside the train.

Slightly more grizzled and grayer than three years before, and now in a police inspector's uniform, was my father's old friend Alex McCrae. His hand reached out and shook mine.

'So you're back now, Joe. How's it going?'

I was put at ease by his friendly greeting, and as he escorted me out of the station I was surprised to see parked at the edge of the pavement a dark box-like Black Maria, of the type used in my arrest. Alex laughed at my look of surprise.

'We'll bring you back the same way we brought you in!'

But this time I sat in the front of the van beside Alex and the driver, and not as a prisoner locked up in the back. My parents had gone to live in Bearsden, on the outskirts of Glasgow, and as the van crawled its way along the blacked-out streets, following the barely visible tram tracks for direction, the slow journey gave me just a little idea of what life must have been like in the winter in wartime Glasgow. Alex kept on chatting, giving me news of old friends. Do you remember so-and-so? Well, he was shot down and killed over France. And so-and-so? He died on a torpedoed merchant ship. And so-and so? I heard he had been killed in Africa. The realisation dawned on me that I had been one of the lucky ones.

Slowly and tentatively I edged my way back into society. My parents were overjoyed to see me alive and well, with mother crying tears of happiness every day and saying rosary after rosary of thanks for the return of her son. Alex McRae had seen to the repair of the vandalized Savoy, and despite their advancing years they had managed to keep the shop going, opening for a few hours each week without help, paying the rent so that their sons could have something to come back to after war's end. They had nothing but praise for their neighbours, for despite their obvious Italian origin, no harsh words had ever been addressed to them and many were the stories they told me of the kindness and help they had received from all the locals.

I had been allocated a job on a farm in Summerston, near Glasgow, and enjoyed the hard but healthy work there. The owner, Tom McClymont, a dour, honest Scot, treated me no differently from the rest of his workers, most of whom were Land Army girls, and the months spent in that environment went a long way to easing the feeling of estrangement within me. Ironically, even on that farm there were times when I could almost feel myself back in Camp 43. At Garelochhead, near Glasgow, there was an Italian POW camp, and occasionally lorry-loads of prisoners were brought to the farm to help in the work. I would then take up my old role as interpreter, much to the delight of Tom McClymont, who was thereby relieved of the frustration of having to mime instructions to his Italian workers. I felt quite close to those POWs, for it hadn't been so long ago since I had been in the position they were in, and I could feel much sympathy for them.

In the course of time I began to make contact with old friends and acquaintances, a process which I did not hurry. For obvious reasons I preferred them to make the first approach, and all who did seemed genuinely glad to see me again. Not one harsh or insulting word did I hear, the one irritant being the constantly repeated enquiry as to how I had enjoyed my stay in Canada, as if I had been on holiday there. But then as I began to realise the sacrifices and suffering the population had undergone during those years of war, I could see that they might well consider me lucky in my experiences.

For many years after the war I kept in touch with my Sicilian friend Pasquale, the one who had saved my skin in the camp. On his release he had returned home to his native Trapani, where he found that his family had all been killed in the bombing of the town. He then went north to Naples, and in 1968, during one of our trips to Rome, Mary and I carried on further south to visit him in his Neapolitan home. He was now married with two children and had his own fishing boat in addition to a thriving fruit and vegetable stall. We spoke of the old times in the camp, but he was reticent about his return to Trapani and what he had found there. '*Erano tempi brutti. E' meglio dimenticarsi.*' Those were bad times, he said, better to forget them. I wondered if his old Mafia connections had been of any help to him in the building up of his business, but there was something in his newly acquired sophistication that made me hesitate to ask. He died in 1991.

❦ 5 ❦

Back to Work

The war ended. Although I was still obliged to continue in some form of 'nationally important' work, I began to think of taking some tentative steps back into the family business. Had I gone by the book and made representations through official channels, the necessary official permits would have been a long time in coming. I was now employed as a labourer at a piggery in Lambhill on the Balmore Road. After some months of rather unpleasant work collecting brock from a variety of restaurants and food shops in Glasgow and feeding swill to the pigs, I struck a very happy arrangement with the owner. Rather than have him pay me £3 per week for my labour, as he was doing, I paid him double that sum to present myself for a half hour each morning and then be allowed the rest of the day as a free agent to go about my own affairs. I could earn much more than £6 a week in our own shop, and my little deception did not worry me. I felt that I was doing more good all round by helping to feed a hungry populace rather than a herd of hungry pigs. I ran the shop from behind the scenes, as it were, without any personal contact with customers, and even when, a year or so later, I was given official permission to go back to work in the Savoy, I did not have the courage to face people across a counter, feeling as if internment had left a visible stigma attached to me.

Remarkably enough, when I did go back to serving the public face to face, I found that attitudes seemed to have been transformed. Complete strangers, ex-soldiers who had fought in the Italian campaigns and who correctly assumed that I was Italian, would regale me with their stories of war in Italy. Of how they were treated as liberators, of the hospitality received from Italian families, of the help given to escaped British prisoners and of the friendliness of the population in general. For whatever reason, the war seemed to have broadened attitudes and increased people's tolerance. Paradoxically, after all that had happened, for the first time in my life I began to feel welcome and part of the society in which I lived. At the end of 1945 my brother Ralph was demobbed, and together we applied ourselves to the family shop and the eventual expansion of the business, and the memory of the war began to fade a little. We gave the Savoy a lick of paint and a clean-up and carried on with business as though a world war had never intervened. Business had never been better, and we could sell all the food we could lay hands on, not an easy matter in the days of strict rationing.

By the year 1947 the memory of the war was slowly beginning to recede, demobbed soldiers in their thousands were returning to civilian life, their pockets swollen with well-earned gratuity pay, and business potential had never been so good. Industry was booming in an attempt to repair the ravages of the war years and money flowed as freely as it had during the early months of the war. Everyone seemed bent on an orgy of spending. The lifting of the wartime blackout had revitalised the night time entertainment trade in the city centre, with pubs, dance halls and cinemas doing unprecedented business. In those days there was no superabundance of fast food cafeterias and takeaways such as can be found in any city centre now, and the relatively few fish and chip shops were queued from morning until night by hungry patrons. Severe rationing of food was still in force, food coupons were required for delicacies such as eggs, butter and meat, and the only foods freely available were fish, potatoes and bread. The time was yet to come when, in the early fifties, these were also in short supply, as was coal. A critic of the new Labour post-war government was able to say with truth that only an organisational genius could have brought about a shortage of coal and fish on an island made of the one and completely surrounded by the other. The trouble was that although the raw materials needed for our business, i.e. fish and potatoes, were abundant, the materials used to fry them were not. Dripping was in very short supply and severely rationed, and cooking oils were well nigh unobtainable. Every fish and chip shop had a small allocation of dripping, the medium used to fry their product, and in all cases this ration, which was based loosely on pre-war consumption, went nowhere near to meeting demands, so many shops opened for a few days a week only. In our Savoy the allocation of cooking fats was such that we could not operate for a full week on our official ration, which meant that the amount of money to be earned was limited. This affected Ralph more than it did me. He was married, a daughter had appeared on the scene, and with a wife and family to keep, he obviously needed to maximise his earning power. Now that I was back, some way had to be found to increase the flow of cash over the counter, and I became the black-market scavenger for the family, the person whose job it was to scour the neighbourhood for black-market foods and cooking oils without which the flow of business could not be increased.

So, fish and chip shops such as ours opened only for a few hours each day or for three or four days each week. That is, the law-abiding ones did. Others, the great majority, sought supplies on the widespread black market in an attempt to increase the number of hours they could open. If you could keep your doors open you were guaranteed sales and you could make money. I could never understand why the powers that be did not simply allow market forces to have their way and allow free trading in all foodstuffs. The food was there, rationing simply encouraged the development of a flourishing black market. Prices in the shops could have been regulated and food coupons would have guaranteed food supplies to the population, and a free market allowed for all that remained. We ourselves could have done twice the trade we were doing if supplies could be found, so I searched around and was able to tap into some very rich seams of 'honest' black-market dripping. I use the word to differentiate from supplies which could well have been stolen from food warehouses or suchlike places. By 'honest black-market' I mean those supplies available from livestock farms on the outskirts of Glasgow which did a brisk but illegal trade in the clandestine killing of their own cattle and pigs, so that they could supply two branches of the food trade from stock undeclared to the government food offices. Butcher shops would buy the meats, and fish and chip shops and restaurants would buy the rendered-down fats for frying. I had acquired a long list of such farms, and to go round them all we bought a second-hand car. Second-hand cars were all you could find to buy in 1947. There were long waiting periods for a new one; six or nine months for a modest Austin 8 was quite a common waiting time, so the aspiring car owner had to make do with an old banger dating back to the years before the war. Such cars had almost all been laid up during those years, and lack of use and maintenance meant that they all suffered from a variety of defects. Ours was a 1936 vintage 1.5 litre Jaguar drop-head coupe, which looked great until the wheels started turning, at which point the driver and passengers could well have been in the boiler house of a steamship, so great was the variety of mechanical noises which came from the car once in motion.

In anticipation of spillages to come, I hammered flat some biscuit tins and covered the boot of the car with the metal so as not to allow grease to percolate. My weekends were spent doing a tour of the farms on my list and filling the boot of the car with various grades of cooking fats to be used the following week for frying fish and chips. During these trips the days of the general strike in 1926 came back to mind, and I would remember the scavenging trips made with father's horse and cart along the self-same roads. Some farmers actually made more profit on the black market than was made in legitimate trading, with the added advantage of there being less work for them to do. No records to keep, no tax returns to make, and no tax to pay. The only disadvantage was in knowing what to do with the undeclared profits. Many farmers, relatively unsophisticated in the management of capital, could think no further than putting the pound notes under the floorboards. This procedure carried unexpected dangers; it was rumoured that one such had his entire hoard eaten up by mice! To my certain knowledge one pig breeder on the outskirts of Glasgow did not trust paper money, and kept his tax-free gains in the form of half crowns and two shilling pieces packed into milk churns and stored in remote barns. Ships docking at the busy Glasgow docks were also a prolific source of black-market goods. Coming as they did from more fortunate countries in the Americas which had escaped the ravages of war, goods were always in surplus, and it was not difficult to find the enterprising merchant ship's captain who would sell you a few hundred-weights or so of prime Argentine beef dripping plus a few ten-gallon drums of cooking oil.

All this had its element of danger, of course. If you were found in possession of black-market cooking fats a hefty fine could be levied by the local food office. If, as many times was the case, the dripping and oil had originally been stolen from somewhere, then the police were involved and criminal charges could follow. Despite the obvious fact that some shops were opening far longer than their allocation of materials allowed, possession of black-market goods had to be proved, and I had grown adept at sticking to 'honest' black-market sources, avoiding the criminal ones and outwitting the local food office. Moreover, many food offices were quite accommodating in turning a blind eye to the obvious. What harm was there in feeding a hungry public? None whatsoever, and this philosophy was shared by many a sympathetic food office inspector in the exercise of a quid pro quo. All of which went to foster my growing opinion that unwarranted and silly laws contribute to the corruption of society.

However, be that as it may, I was ever on the lookout for new sources of cooking fats, and one day I stumbled on to an unexpected discovery. Our mother was a devout woman who attended Mass every day, sometimes bringing gifts of candles and flowers to the local priest for the decoration of the altar. I looked in to her for a chat every day on the way home, and during a visit I noticed a large can of some kind of liquid on the kitchen table. I was informed that this was special oil sold in Catholic Truth Society shops for use in churches, where it was blessed by a priest, and then, as Holy Oil, would provide a floating base for candles, thus rendering them more potent as supplicatory objects. The Holy Oil was also used sparingly in the administration of some of the Sacraments of the Church, and mother made it a point to keep the local parish well supplied with this oil.

I pondered. Was this a possible new source? What harm was there in experimenting? After all, the oil was not holy until it was blessed by a priest, so I could not see why anyone or anything on the other side of the grave could possibly object to its use for the benefit of the living. So I sent old Ivo on an errand. Old Ivo was a fixture in the back shop of the Savoy. A man of sixty-five or so, he had no family, lived alone in a bleak tenement flat in the Cowcaddens and regarded the Savoy as both home and sanctuary. He had a set of keys for the shop and arrived at the crack of dawn each morning when he began to wash, peel and cut potatoes into chips and to gut and fillet fish, happily tending his machines, puffing on a foul pipe, listening to the wireless and running the occasional errand when asked to do so. He would stay on all day, in the summer going out for an occasional walk, and in the winter quite happy to sit in the warmth and comparative comfort of his work shop, puffing away at his ever-present pipe, cutting chips when required and keeping his machines spotlessly clean.

A few hundred yards along from the Savoy in Renfrew Street there was a Catholic Truth Society shop, and Ivo was dispatched there to purchase a gallon tin of church oil. I would have gone myself, but since I was known there as the owner of the Savoy and not particularly noted for my piety, a purchase of oil by me would have been looked on somewhat askance. On Ivo's return a half pint or so of the oil was poured into one of the three cooking pans of the fish range and thoroughly mixed into the existing quantity of dripping. A basket of chips was experimentally fried. I felt a surge of excitement. I had indeed struck oil! Up came the fried chips, golden brown and crisply dry, of a texture achieved only by the best fish friers using the very finest and rarest of cooking oils. The taste matched the appearance. Deliciously tasty, dry, and without the sometimes characteristic greasy texture of deep-fried potatoes, the chips were undoubtedly the best the Savoy had ever produced. A similar amount of oil was decanted into the remaining two pans, and for the rest of the day the Savoy's customers partook of some of the best fish and chips they had ever tasted.

However, a gallon of oil does not go far, even when used in small quantities, so after three days Ivo was dispatched once more for a further purchase, and once more the resultant mix produced magnificent results. When the second gallon was exhausted I sent Ivo further afield. It would not do to arouse suspicion by buying from one source only, so a list of Catholic supply shops was drawn up, and Ivo was dispatched by taxi to make the necessary purchases. Although Ivo was a man of very few words he was not devoid of intelligence, and he did remonstrate on one occasion with me when it became obvious to him what the church oil was being used for. Was it right to use holy oil to fry fish and chips? Ah, but! I replied, it's not holy till the priest blesses it! and with this answer Ivo was grudgingly but unconvincedly mollified. He was a loyal man, however, and the secret would be safe with him.

It has repeatedly been said that the Savoy was a busy shop, and to cope with the large volume of business the very best and latest fish frying range had recently been installed. This consisted of three large pans set in a stainless steel frame, with the pans fired by gas jets. The fumes from the burning gas and the steam from the cooking process were carried away by a powerful fan into a metal duct which passed underneath the cement floor. The duct appeared above floor level in the back shop where Ivo worked, passed through two heavy wooden partitions and then disappeared up the back of the tenement to eject all fumes above roof level. These wooden partitions formed two of the sides of a staff lavatory. The problem with the underground duct was that it was impossible to keep clean and free from accumulations of fat and grease. It was, however, self-cleansing in a primitive sort of way, for every now and then, at peak periods when the heat from the gas jets became intense, the duct caught fire. This served to burn out the accumulated grease, and the fire would then extinguish itself, its fuel exhausted. Since the fierce draught from the extraction fan kept the flames well away from the inflammable cooking fats there was no danger of the fire spreading to the pans above. The roar caused by these fires, which happened regularly two or three times a week, could be quite frightening and out of all proportion to their danger, so Ivo was well used to their occurrence and paid no heed.

One winter's day at lunch time the shop was particularly busy, and the gas jets were roaring to their full capacity. Ivo was seated comfortably on the staff lavatory seat, trousers off and hung on a hook behind the door, quite content to sit in the warmth of the little cubicle. He was reading the *Noon Record*, a betting sheet of that era, and this was draped over the warm duct which passed through the toilet. Suddenly there was a familiar roar and the duct under the cement floor caught fire. For some reason or other the fire was much more intense than usual, and in a few seconds the duct in the toilet glowed cherry red with the heat, and the Noon Record caught fire. A few seconds more and the wooden partition began to smoulder, and wisps of flame began to lick upwards from the by now red hot metal duct. From some hidden resource Ivo found the speed of youth, leapt to his feet, took no time to collect his trousers, flung open the back door and dashed into the backyard, trouserless. A heavy return spring slammed the door shut behind him. As was always the case, the fire burnt itself out, but I could smell smouldering wood and rushed into the back shop to investigate, just in time to throw water on the burning wooden partition, thereby averting what could have been a dangerous fire. I went back to the front shop to attend to customers, with never a thought for Ivo, but eventually I was attracted by a knocking at the back door. There, spindly legs purple with cold, stood Ivo, rendered more speechless than usual by his predicament

It was all the fault of the oil, grumbled the old man through his pipe and clenched teeth. It must have been the oil that caused such a bad fire. It was a sacrilege to use it, the fire was a warning of more drastic things to come and he was finished as far as buying it was concerned. A further problem arose. His trousers were badly scorched and ruined, so I had to by him another pair. They were not easy to replace, since coupons were required for the purchase of clothing and neither Ivo nor I had any, but the ubiquitous black market came into play, and next day I presented a much mollified Ivo with a brand new pair of trousers. That was the end of the holy oil experiment. There may well have been a latent streak of superstition in me, for Ivo's words about sacrilege did give me a little food for thought.

As I write this, nearly sixty years after the event, and with the wisdom that age brings, I look back at the incident and shudder when I think how foolhardy and stupid one can be when young. What was the nature of that 'Holy Oil'? What damage could it have done to those who consumed food fried in it? Just a few years ago scores of people died in Madrid and many hundreds were seriously injured in health by the consumption of olive oil of doubtful origin. Could my 'Holy Oil' experiment have damaged anyone? I can only say that I probably ate more fish and chips fried in that oil than any of my customers, as Ralph also did, and it caused us no harm.

Be that as it may, as one door closes another opens and a few days after the last of the holy oil had been used, the owner of the San Remo fish and chip shop paid us a visit. Mr Gennasi, an old friend of the family, was a widower, and on Sundays he would occasionally appear unannounced at our home in Bearsden to partake of some of mother's excellent cooking. He had entrusted the running of his shop to Gino Ferretti, a young Italian of my own age and with whom I used to work out at Johnny McMillan's gym in Sauchiehall Street. The San Remo, situated in Parliamentary Road, and the Savoy were reckoned to be probably the two busiest chip shops in Glasgow, and since they were far enough apart not to constitute competition to one another, Gino and I often made purchases at the fish market for each other, thus giving ourselves some extra free time in the mornings. After having consumed his usual heaped plates of pasta, washed down by several glasses of wine, Mr Gennasi informed us that through some contacts he had in the docks area he was in a position to buy a large quantity of Argentine beef dripping, ten large barrels of the stuff amounting to about forty hundredweights, two tons, to be precise. The dripping came from a perfectly legitimate black-market source, he said, the word legitimate indicating that it was not stolen merchandise, and he went on to explain that it had been brought over from Argentina, but since it was too large an amount for him to handle alone, would we be interested in sharing it with him? Such an amount of dripping would solve our cooking problems for many months. Storage was not a problem. The San Remo had two huge cellars underneath used for coal storage (in later years these cellars were to become Glasgow's first Italian trattoria, The Canasta) and it could be hidden there for use as required, well away from the prying eyes of any marauding food inspectors. So we hired two horses and carts and two trustworthy carters from Dunne, the transport people, and went down to the docks with them to load up the barrels of dripping. Although this was a perfectly 'honest' black-market operation in that the seller was the ship's captain who had bought the stuff in Buenos Aires for sale in Glasgow at a huge profit, care had to be taken that the load should not come to the attention of food office inspectors, who might not take a sufficiently broadminded view of the operation. We knew the right times to avoid the beat policemens' prying eyes, since they too might misunderstand, and after a short journey through the deserted night streets, duly unloaded the heavy barrels at the door of the San Remo, where they were then lowered into the cellars below. A substantial tip to the two drivers ensured their silence and full cooperation.

Every Monday morning I would go down to the San Remo cellars with Gino, break open a barrel and transfer chunks of the dripping into sacks, our share of which would be given to one of the carters for transportation to the Savoy. As has been said, there were forty hundredweights of dripping in those barrels, and months were to pass before we came to the end of the supply, by which time a substantial amount of coal dust had got mixed in with the contents of the barrels. We tried our best to sieve the fine coal from the dripping, but it was impossible to extract all the black dust from it, and for some time our customers were heard to complain of a gritty feeling in their teeth as they chewed on our fish and chips.

There was another problem. The Savoy was reverting to the tough reputation it had enjoyed at the beginning of our family's ownership. At night toughs abounded. Money flowed freely, and at pub closing time drunks roamed the pavements looking for a place to satisfy their alcohol-induced hunger and once again a heavy hand was required for control. We consulted Black Alec McCrae, now an inspector of police and on the verge of retirement, who this time advised the services of a doorman, and on his recommendation big Steve Campbell appeared on the scene. Steve was indeed a big man. About six feet two in height, his weight of sixteen stones was made up of solid bone and heavy muscle, with not an ounce of excess fat on his frame. His face seemed hewn out of solid granite, and his craggy features were set off by a bright red, almost skinless nose, the result of a mustard-gas burn received during a German gas attack on the Western front in the spring of 1918. When he came to us in 1948 he was about fifty years of age and worked as a coalman and carter, loading and delivering heavy bags of coal to households in the Cowcaddens district. As often as not these deliveries entailed the carrying of hundredweight sacks of coal up three floors, finally to be emptied into coalbunkers on each stair landing of the tenements. Such work was definitely not for the puny.

His wages for this backbreaking work was a princely five pounds a week, so the offer of two pounds plus a meal each night for standing at the Savoy door for two hours to keep out drunks and undesirables was wealth indeed. Provided with a peaked military style cap, he would take up his position in front of the door of the Savoy at 9.45pm each night, to stand there menacingly unmoveable until the 11pm closing time. Big Steve's wages were money well spent, for with his coming tranquillity reigned in the Savoy. Any would-be troublemaker would take one look at his massive frame and rock-like face with its scarred red nose and move on to likelier pastures, while drunks too far gone to be impressed by his appearance and seeking entrance to the warmth and comfort of the restaurant would be disdainfully repelled by a powerful shove, which if not at first successful, would be followed by a few well directed cuffs around the ears, which invariably were.

Occasionally however, disturbances would break out inside the dining area, and these would be quickly and efficiently dealt with by Big Steve. If the offender were standing, he would approach the man smilingly, lean over as if to impart a confidence, and then stamp the heavy heel of his boot with all his strength on the man's toes. The ensuing howls of anguish would then stop suddenly to be replaced by an assortment of gasping gargling noises as a heavy punch was delivered to the solar plexus zone, after which the culprit, now reduced from aggressiveness to an ineffective mass of jelly, would be deposited none too gently on the pavement.

If, however, the offender were seated and refused to go on request, Big Steve would carry out a simple but effective procedure. Standing behind the person concerned and leaning over the man's head, two hooked fingers would be inserted into his nostrils. One hand kept the body hard pressed into the chair; the nose was pulled backwards until the chair tilted back on two legs and the man would sit helpless as he was dragged by the nostrils to the nearest exit. Once on the pavement, the chair was kicked away, leaving the man suspended by the nose on two powerful fingers. He would be kept hanging thus for a few seconds, then suddenly released and helped on his way down by a sharp tap from Steve's heavy hand. Such tactics were fully condoned by the policemen on the beat, who as likely as not would have served in Percy Sillitoe's 'Heavy Squad' who had used even heavier tactics against hooligans in the immediate pre-war days.

In the middle 1930s, Percy Sillitoe had been appointed Chief Constable of Glasgow with orders to keep the hooligans and gangs off the streets, and he proceeded ruthlessly and efficiently to do so. His methods were, to say the least, very robust. He picked the roughest and toughest men in the force, formed them into so-called 'Heavy Squads', and gave them a completely free hand with whatever force they cared to use against street gangs and hooliganism. Fifty or so of these 'Heavies' would be quickly transported in plain vans to the scene of a street fight, where they were unmerciful in their use of fist and baton against the hooligans, always seeking out the leaders for special treatment, very often inflicting injuries serious enough to put them out of action for a very long time. There was no such thing as a Council for Civil Liberties then, and the punishment meted out by the Police more than suited the crime. Sillitoe brought order to the streets and remained as Chief Constable from 1931 to 1943, and was knighted for his services to the community. Although the organised gangs no longer existed, his methods were continued after the war in the treatment of the casual hooligan and criminal. From that time on, woe betide any hooligans, or 'neds', as they were called, who caused any trouble in the streets or in any public place. Summary justice would be handed out by 'The Polis' in the form of a series of heavy blows with fists, boots and batons, any resulting marks or scars on the prisoners being attributed to the resistance of arrest on the part of the wrongdoer, and so Steve's heavy-handed approach to the keeping of order in the Savoy met with the approval of the men on the beat.

The punishment meted out to offenders varied in severity according to Steve's prevailing mood. He had two great overriding passions in life, the first and most compelling of which was football. He was an ardent Celtic fan, and the success or lack of it of his beloved team determined his moods. Saturday night was the time of greatest activity at the Savoy. The pavements seethed with humanity anxious to spend the weekly pay-packet, there were drunks everywhere, and Big Steve was kept busy denying them entry. If his team had won that day, then fairly good-natured methods would be employed in sending them on their way, but if Celtic had fared badly, then woe betide anyone who crossed his path that night. Of special importance were the nights following a Celtic-Rangers encounter, and unfortunate indeed was the person who invoked his displeasure if Celtic had lost that day to their arch-rivals. Even innocent passers-by would feel his resentment. Every night just before pub closing time, which in those days was 10pm, I would go to the door and stand chatting for a few moments with Big Steve. On Saturdays the talk would invariably be of football, and one night after a rather bad defeat of Celtic by their Ibrox adversaries I stood commiserating with him. A small inoffensive man approached us. He wore a cloth cap, or bunnet, the trademark of the working man, and sported a blue and white scarf, an article of clothing which gave the clue to his team preference.

'Where's Killermont Street bus station?' he asked of the two of us standing side by side at the Savoy door. The bus station in question was about three minutes walk away. Big Steve looked down at the man, fixed a basilisk stare at the Rangers scarf, paused for a moment, then leaned down and barked at me from the side of his mouth.

'Tell the cunt nuthin'.' And gazed disdainfully into the distance over the enquirer's head.

There were several nights during the summer when Steve did not take up his stance at the Savoy door. July was the traditional marching month for the Orange Order, and the Billy Boys drum and flute band, playing rousing Orange airs and preceded by a prancing Pipe Major, would march past the Savoy to arrive at their marshalling point in the Orange Hall in Port Dundas. On the way up Hope Street they had to pass directly under McConnell's tenement building, which stands there to this day. This was a fortress-like tenement block tenanted solely by Catholics, who, having blocked off all doors and manned the roof, bombarded the marchers below with a variety of missiles. Bags of ordure, bricks and bottles, some empty, some filled with urine, would rain into the procession below, scattering the marchers and giving rise later to pitched battles in the streets. Any shop along the route of these marches was well advised to put up shutters for the occasion and Steve was given those evenings off. We often wondered what his reaction would have been to some of the provocative sectarian songs raucously shouted out by the marchers.

The second great passion in Steve's life, of all things, given his background, was the game of chess. He had learned to play in the trenches and had acquired a very considerable skill in the game, to the extent that only the very best could match him on the chessboard. Someone once said that chess was too serious to be a pastime and too frivolous to be an occupation, but Steve treated the game very seriously indeed. He was a member and champion of a local chess club, and since I had learned to play chess in the camp and was quite taken with the game, I went along to his club on several occasions to play. I was not a bad player by any manner of means, on the contrary, I considered myself to be better than most, but over the many scores of games played over the years, never once, to my great chagrin and to his intense satisfaction, was I able to beat him. So intense was my desire to do so, that on quiet nights I would set up a chessboard on the service counter and engage in a game with Steve. Despite the occasional inter-ruption when he was called away to throw out an obstreperous customer and the break in concentration thereby undergone, the game always finished with my pieces in a checkmate situation.

❧ 6 ❧
The Silver Lounge

purred on by the 'Holy Oil' incident, Ralph and I turned our thoughts to acquiring a less questionable source of added income. Next to the Savoy, in Renfrew Street, was a row of small shops, three of them owned by a well known office supply company, Harry Sarna Ltd. Harry was a customer of ours, and during one of his visits he mentioned his intention of putting his three shops up for sale. By this time Ralph and I were beginning to acquire a certain practical business expertise and we were now aware of how capital could be raised for business purposes. With this new knowledge we had already secured a loan, repayable over fifteen years, for the purchase of the Savoy building. We approached the lenders, the Paisley Building Society, who agreed on a further loan for the purchase of the Sarna shops. That particular building society had been introduced to us by our solicitors, Wright & Crawford of Paisley, who now acted as our lawyers. Back in 1932, when father had first purchased the lease of the Savoy from Vincent Napolitano, he did not have a solicitor who could act on his behalf in the drawing up of a contract, so Vincent introduced him to his own, a Mr Gilchrist, a partner in the Paisley firm of Wright & Crawford. Mr Gilchrist explained to my father that it was not usual for two opposing parties to be represented by the same lawyer, since a conflict of interest might one day arise, but he would be happy to do so if my father signed the necessary waiver. That was the beginning of a happy relationship that was to last for 50 years until the eventual dissolution of F. Pieri & Sons Ltd., as the company we had recently founded had been named. The person who handled our affairs over all those years was a young solicitor, Bob Martin, who came into the firm of Wright & Crawford straight from a wartime career in the Army, which had seen him earn several medals for bravery in action.

A loan was secured and the Sarna shops became the property of the newly formed company of F. Pieri & Sons Ltd., which had as shareholders and directors our father, Ralph and myself. Town Planning regulations had just been introduced in Glasgow, and since no-one was quite sure what the procedure was for opening up a café, rather than wait an interminable time for officialdom to get into gear we simply got hold of a joiner and painter and decorator, and without asking anyone's permission, started work. Within a few weeks our second shop proudly opened its doors. We had modelled it on the lines of Tog's café in Troon, which we had known since our Auchinleck days, although our Silver Lounge, as we named it, was only a rather pale copy of that famous café and lacked its sumptuous furnishings. The walls were panelled in hardboard and painted to resemble wood, and on the plaster frieze a series of pretty women's heads in bas-relief went round the entire shop. This last feature was much commented on by our appreciative customers, who were not to know that the idea was a direct steal from Tog's café, although I don't suppose that there is any copyright on such matters. The Silver Lounge fittings consisted simply of a counter and a gantry packed with boxes of chocolates and cigarettes, and the seating area had accommodation for about sixty persons, with elegant café tables and wicker wrap round chairs. Within a month or so of opening we had to extend the seating accommodation to an upstairs floor, which gave us an extra hundred seats in order to cope with the flood of customers. The big attraction of the Silver Lounge, which brought in customers in droves, was the background music we provided, an amenity completely unheard of in the somewhat austere traditional-type café to be found everywhere in Glasgow, although it was soon to be overtaken by the advent of the jukeboxes soon to be installed in cafés everywhere. We had incorporated loudspeakers into the wooden panelling, which gave out the music from records played on an old 78 turntable set up in a corner of the café's backshop. On each table was a menu, plus a numbered list of gramophone records which encompassed the spectrum of music from the jazz of Louis Armstrong and Duke Ellington through the crooning of Bing Crosby to classical concertos of Brahms and Beethoven and the voices of Caruso, Gigli and Tetrazzini. We had a selection of hundreds of such records, amassed during our long friendship with the musical McMeighans. The customer simply ordered a cup of coffee or suchlike from the waitress, plus the number of his chosen record, and sat back to enjoy his or her favourite piece of music. The danger was that the customers would linger too long over their coffee or ice-cream, so the waitresses had been well trained in the art of taking away empty cups and of polishing the table energetically as a hint that their time was up. It took a very thick-skinned customer indeed to resist this treatment. News of this fantastic innovation spread and customers literally queued up for seats in our new café.

Around this time, a mighty and unexpected blow had been delivered to the very roots of the English monarchy. The Stone of Scone, the historic Stone of Destiny of the Scottish people and the potent symbol of the authority of the English Crown over the long vanquished Scots, had been stolen from beneath the coronation chair in Westminster Abbey. The stone, which, as myth had it, was once Jacob's pillow and had served as seat for the crowning of one hundred and ten Scottish kings over the centuries, had been carried off to London by the conquering Edward I of England in 1296. There, in Westminster Abbey, it was placed under the coronation chair as a symbol of the subjugation of the Scots, and over it, for 650 years, English kings and queens were crowned, symbolically squatting over the very soul of the Scottish peoples. On Christmas Eve 1950, the five hundredweight mass of stone had vanished without trace, leaving behind a few splinters of wood where it had been torn from its fastenings. Scotland exulted and chortled at the daring of the perpetrators. England was outraged at this effrontery to the Crown and spoke of treason and vandalism. Scotland Yard went immediately into action, and a massive investigation, centred naturally around the Scottish Nationalists and other political dissidents north of the Border, swung into action.

There is a school of philosophy which claims that if a butterfly were to flutter its wings in the Gobi desert, the ripples of that event would eventually be felt thousands of miles distant. Had I known then of that particular theory, the manner in which the liberation of the Stone of Scone in Westminster was to touch my own life hundreds of miles away in the Silver Lounge café some days later, would have forced me to endorse it fully. I shall explain.

During the summer months on Saturdays and Sundays the upstairs room in the Silver Lounge was reserved exclusively for the use of a group of nature lovers and hill walkers who congregated there for their weekend meetings and discussions. They called themselves 'The Hikers', and the membership consisted almost exclusively of young Scottish Nationalists culled from all walks of life. There was a fair share of eccentrics amongst them, not least outlandish of whom was their leader, Wendy Wood, head of the Scottish Nationalist Party. Wendy Wood was a woman who had lived her life for the Scottish cause and who had done everything in her power to keep the flame of Scottish Nationalism alive during the years when other small matters, such as the war against Hitler, was keeping the nation otherwise occupied. In the immediate post-war years she had redoubled her efforts to have the Stone of Destiny returned to its rightful place, and to this end was frequently photographed in the Royal Mile in full Scottish regalia, sporting a sandwich board emblazoned with the words 'Where is the Stone of Destiny?' She presided regally over the weekly café meetings of 'The Hikers', sweeping majestically through the door of the Silver Lounge, clad in a tartan suit, acknowledging the deference of her acolytes with a gracious and queenly wave of the hand. Her every word was listened to by the audience as if it were gospel. Eccentric she may well have been in her dress and in her actions, but she had a case to state and did it eloquently and efficiently.

At the disappearance of the Stone of Destiny, police investigations north of the Border focused on Wendy and her group, and one night just before closing time, a young CID constable, Joe Beattie, whose acquaintance I had just recently made, came through the doors of the Silver Lounge to inform me that two of his superiors would like a word with me. Bells of warning began to tinkle in my ear. What had I done wrong? What crime had I committed to warrant the attention of high ranking police officers? Had they been trailing me on my black-market farming rounds? A few minutes later two imposing looking figures dressed in plain clothes entered. I immediately recognised one of them as Detective Inspector Kerr, an occasional visitor to the Silver Lounge. The inspector stepped forward and introduced his companion.

'Hello Joe. I want you to meet Mr Ferguson.'

The tinkling warning bells in my head reached a thunderous crescendo.

'Mr Robert Ferguson?' I asked, and the knot in my stomach tightened at the affirmative nod. The name was notorious in the Italian colony as belonging to the official who had so enthusiastically carried out Churchill's injunction to 'Collar the lot' at the outbreak of war. So enthusiastically indeed had Ferguson carried out the order, that it was joked that anyone who had ever eaten Italian ice-cream or an Italian fish supper was liable to be arrested and interned.

Ferguson's stone-like face cracked into the semblance of a smile.

'I hear good reports about you, Joe. You've settled in well after your trip to Canada, I see.' Referring, presumably, to my internment there five years before. 'How did you get on there?'

I mumbled something to the effect that I had enjoyed the experience thoroughly.

'I wonder if you could possibly do us a favour,' continued Ferguson, looking around at the arrangement of the café. 'I hear that Wendy Wood and her friends come here every weekend. Could I see where they meet?'

The knot in my stomach began to ease. Maybe this wasn't about anything I had done. The detectives stood in the upstairs room and looked around. Ferguson asked for explanations about the two large loudspeakers on the wall.

'Excellent.' He rubbed his hands briskly. 'Excellent, couldn't be better.' He placed an avuncular hand on my shoulder and proceeded to tell me what he was going to do, with my permission, of course. It was proposed that the two loudspeakers should be converted into microphones which would pick up conversation in the room and relay it to a suitable point on the premises, where it would be monitored and recorded by a police officer. It only remained for a hidden monitoring place to be chosen. The premises were examined, and only one suitable place could be found, an old disused outside lavatory at the back of the café, probably built towards the end of the last century and which had remained locked up for at least the past twenty years. Small and dark and damp and cramped and smelly, it could just about accommodate an officer and his equipment, and the triumphant Ferguson declared it perfect for the purpose. The police technicians worked all night. The speakers were converted to microphones, wires were led down the back of the building and into the old lavatory, where a wire recorder was set up (there were no tape recorders then), powered by a connection from the main fuse box, since there was no electricity in the old toilet.

Barga

The author's parents as newly-weds, about 1909

Mother as a young woman (about 1912)

About 1912: Mother and brother Ralph in a tenement in the Bronx, New York

Soldiers in the Italian army in 1917. In the centre is the author's father, Francesco Pieri

The author with his father, mother and older brother, Glasgow 1922

Mother as an older woman on the beach at Via Reggio—still wearing mourning for father, as was the custom for her generation

The author (front row, second from left) with a group of UK-Italians on the day of release from the internment camp at Ile Sainte Hélène, August 1943

With mother's family and relations at Bacchionero, 1950. The author is third from the left at the back (in hat).

Darkness at noon! Argyll Street in Glasgow taken by a street photographer, early 50s

Behind the counter in the Savoy—the author and Mary his wife about 1952

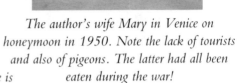

The author's wife Mary in Venice on honeymoon in 1950. Note the lack of tourists and also of pigeons. The latter had all been eaten during the war!

Mary, the author's future wife, on their first date. She is standing by his Jaguar, which was used on runs to access black-market supplies.

Mary with their daughters Luisa, Linda and Laura on the promenade at Viareggio

A 1904 Rolls Royce in front of the Silver Lounge. It was owned by a bookie, Jack McLean, who had it to show his clients that their money was safe in his hands!

Demolition of the Savoy in 1974

Next morning Mr. Ferguson returned, inspected the work and patted me on the back.

'This requires absolute discretion on everybody's part. It would be rather awkward for all concerned if it ever got out, wouldn't it?' I nodded frantically in agreement, and so began what was to be called 'The Shite House Shift' by the participating policemen.

Every Saturday and Sunday, from round about noon till closing time late at night, some unfortunate police officer sat for hours, cold and cramped, on a plank placed over the toilet seat in the old lavatory, headphones clamped on his ears, ready to switch on the recording mechanism at the first sound of conversation. Every hour another constable would pass to retrieve the recorded spool, which presumably was taken off for analysis somewhere. Every four hours the policeman in the lavatory was relieved, emerging stiff and blue with the cold (it was the middle of winter), to ask for a hot cup of coffee in the privacy of the back shop, and to curse the effing eejits who had thought the idea up.

Wendy Wood and her followers came and went and orated and conversed, but it is doubtful if any useful information came over the wires. The occasional word could be made out, but what emerged from the recordings was mainly a rumble of incomprehensible conversation. During all this time the Hikers occasionally asked for some favourite record to be played, and complained quite bitterly at the length of time it was taking to repair the loudspeaker system. Finally after four weeks, to the great relief of the participating policemen, the fruitless 'Shite House Shift' was called off, the wires were removed from the outside lavatory, the speakers were returned to their original condition and the upstairs customers could once more listen to the Silver Lounge music selection for their pleasure. During the period of the surveillance the Stone had been returned to Westminster by the perpetrator, Ian Hamilton, who was later to become an eminent QC. Whether Wendy Wood was involved at all in the affair has never been known.

A very popular yearly summer revue which appeared regularly for more than a decade at the Theatre Royal in the early post war years went by the name of 'The Half Past Eight Show'. One of the principals in the revue was a baritone, William Dickie, a fine singer who had studied in Italy under Beniamino Gigli and who had been declared by the famous tenor to be the best non-Italian singer of Italian opera he had ever heard. 'The Half Past Eight Show' ran each summer for about two months in Glasgow, and from the first arrival of the revue there William Dickie became a regular daily visitor to the Silver Lounge. He enjoyed conversing in Italian, which he spoke fluently, and from the very beginning he and I became friends. We shared a common love of opera, and more important still we were both golf fanatics, and played together two or three times a week in the mornings before the start of our labours. Indeed, so keen were we both about the game that occasionally our work suffered as a consequence. In 1953 the great golfing legend Ben Hogan came to compete in the Open at Carnoustie, so at the crack of dawn one morning Willie Dickie and I took off in a car to watch our hero in action. Motor cars were much more liable to breakdowns then than they are now, and a puncture plus a minor mechanical failure lengthened the return journey so as to make the two of us very late for our respective duties. In my case this did not matter much; I had a well-trained staff who could cope for a few hours without me; but Willie Dickie's unexpected absence at the opening curtain brought down on his head the wrath of the stage manager, who had been forced to make some very inartistic changes to the continuity of his Revue.

Roman Sauschek, an ex-Polish army officer and a refugee from his country, now occupied by the Russians, was also a daily visitor to the Café. At the end of the war, Glasgow and the west of Scotland played host to thousands of Polish refugees. These expatriates were readily identifiable by their garb and by their behaviour. They all seemed to be dressed in long light col-oured raincoats, invariably carried flat briefcases under one arm and always seemed to be in a perpetual hurry. These idiosyncrasies were seized upon by stage comedians of the day, and in every variety show the appearance of a raincoated briefcase-carrying individual who spoke fractured English was always good for a laugh. Roman Sauschek spent hour after hour in the Silver Lounge, drinking interminable cups of coffee and smoking innumer-able cigarettes fixed ostentatiously in a long ivory holder. Each cup of coffee was laced liberally with vodka from a large flask, which he carried in a hip pocket; a veritable horn of plenty, for it always seemed able to produce as much alcohol as he required in the course of the day. He was a graduate in Science and Engineering from Warsaw University, spoke several languages, and could speak with authority on many subjects. He was, too, an inventor of sorts, and could spend long hours doing nothing but drink, smoke and talk, thanks to the income generated by a gadget he had patented and which had been taken up and produced by a local Cowcaddens engineering firm, Howden's. This consisted of a hydraulically controlled expanding cylinder which could be accurately calibrated to serve as a time-controlled opening and closing mechanism. He was employed by that firm to supervise production of his invention, and since this needed only about an hour's work each day he was free to do as he pleased for the rest of the time. The Silver Lounge was close by his place of employment, and he made his headquarters there, holding court for hours on end, discussing and discoursing on the events of the day and on life in general with whomever of interest happened to be on hand. I did not mind his occupying a table for long periods, indeed I wel-comed it. The characters drawn to his table by his presence were colourful and verbose, and what was very important too, they consumed gallons and gallons of coffee in the course of their animated conversations, all of which went to help swell profits.

He was very knowledgeable in matters of art and music, and it was on this last subject that he and Willie Dickie used to converse at length. Roman had an amazing ear for music: once, for a bet, he had listened to the BBC Home Service, which at that time used to broadcast only classical music in the mornings, and had correctly identified the composer of every piece played, much to the amazement of all present. In the field of art, Roman would boast of the second prize he had once received for a modernistic painting he had submitted to an exhibition of modern art in Warsaw in the mid-1930s. Then a student at Warsaw University, he had presented an interesting composition for evaluation. With the help of a shovel and pail he collected a sizeable quantity of fresh horse dung from the city streets. This he flung haphazardly on to a canvas suitably treated with glue to hold the manure, then when the mess had set, proceeded to spray the pattern with a variety of coloured paints. The composition was imposingly framed and hung, without a title, in the exhibition gallery. The painting was studied carefully by the panel of judges and considered to be worthy of second prize. On presentation of his award he was asked to name the painting. The next day a small plaque appeared on the wall next to his brainchild.

'Scheiss Am Wand' (Shite on the Wall) read the caption!

Roman, however had never heard Willie Dickie sing in the flesh. Several of his recordings had been listened to and appreciated, but Roman had never taken the few steps across to the Theatre Royal to hear his friend perform on the stage, despite continuing invitations to do so, with the excuse that he did not want to listen to the pot-boilers performed in the revue.

One day Willie appeared in the Café and declared that during the current week he would include the prologue from *I Pagliacci* in his performance. That particular aria is popular enough to be enjoyed by a musically unsophisticated audience, yet, reasoned Willie, serious enough to entice Roman into the theatre to hear him sing. Roman listened gravely to this information and agreed to be present at the performance. The two met in the café after the theatre had emptied, and Willie, still with traces of greasepaint on his face, awaited Roman's comments. The Pole looked at him gravely and slowly lit a cigarette.

'Villie my friend, I must tell you. I have listened to Opera in Warsaw, I have listened to Opera in Rome, I have listened to Opera in London, but never, never, never, have I heard anything so atrocious! Villie my friend, I am making better noises with my backside than you are making with your voice tonight on the stage!'

And he took him note by note through his performance, pointing out mistakes and inadequacies in Willie's rendition of the aria.

A chastened, but nevertheless good natured, Willie had to agree.

'Right enough, Joe, I wasn't at my best tonight,' he said, and joined in the general merriment at Roman's remarks.

Entertainment trends change, and after a few more years the Royal became an STV studio, and 'The Half Past Eight Show' was a thing of the past, as were William Dickie's visits to Glasgow. He continued as a singer until well into his sixties, then set up a school of music in London much sought after by aspiring young singers. I am told that any criticism of their efforts always included the remark that his flatulence made a better sound than their singing did!

A few yards along from the Silver Lounge in Renfrew Street stood the entrance to a rather dingy covered arcade which connected Cowcaddens Sreet to Sauchiehall Street via Stow Street. This walkway went by the name of the Queen's Arcade. It opened into Renfrew Street where the Thistle Hotel stands now, and continued across and through what is now Marks and Spencers into Sauchiehall Street. It boasted of a fine variety of shops of all types. At the Stow Street end stood Crockett's, the ironmonger, where one could buy anything from a pin to an anvil. Next to it was a small off-license premises, then came Da Prato's, the Italian delicatessen, then a couple of pubs, one of which, the Arcade Bar, had the unsavoury reputation of being the roughest drinking den in the Cowcaddens. Freddie Noble's butcher and fishmonger shop had a prominent frontage in the Arcade. It sold fish, bacon and eggs and various meats, all labelled as 'seconds', whatever that might have meant, but since the prices were almost half of those charged elsewhere, the place did a roaring trade. In those days of food rationing, not much attention was paid to such niceties as food hygiene and consumer protection, and the idea of a regulation making it necessary to label food products with a sell-by date was still to be born. Occasionally Noble's would advertise a batch of haddock or whiting 'seconds' at knockdown prices, and I would snap these up immediately to sell to my inebriated night-time clientele in the Savoy. Steeped for a while in a mixture of salt water and vinegar, the 'seconds' would lose the characteristic phosphorescent sheen of decomposing fish, and when fried in hot dripping, the temperature of which would effectively kill off any latent noxious organisms, the end product would look no different from a fresher and more wholesome piece of fish. The taste, akin to a pungently flavoured piece of dried cardboard, was another matter, but since The Savoy's late night customers were hardly possessed of a discerning palate, such a consideration was of small importance. Incidentally, Freddie Noble had been born and christened as Federico Nobile, but for obvious political reasons had changed his name by deed poll before the outbreak of war. This manoeuvre did him no good, however, for his shop was vandalised on the night of 10 June 10 1940, and although released after only a few weeks incarceration, he himself was arrested that night as an enemy alien.

The best known establishment in the Arcade was the West End Misfits, a new and second-hand gents outfitters and dress hire shop. The name of the shop was itself a misfit, since it wasn't in the West End, and since it boasted of being able to clothe anyone of any size, 'Misfits' didn't seem quite apt either. The proprietors were three Cockney brothers, Frank, Maurice and Benny Goodman, who had brought the name of their London shop with them at the time of their diaspora to Glasgow in the immediate post-war years. The move from London had been made necessary by the fact that a salvo of German V1 and V2 missiles had obliterated their premises together with several surrounding streets in the last months of the war, and so the brothers had come to Glasgow to re-establish their business. Trade was booming in Glasgow. Everyone had money in their pockets, but with everything rationed, there was nothing to spend it on apart from pubs, cinemas and dance halls. Clothing was especially severely rationed. The few clothing coupons issued to each person for a year could barely buy a couple of shirts, and so the West End Misfits, with its vast stocks of second-hand clothing of all sizes could barely cope with the volume of trade. Frank and Maurice were the smooth-tongued and persuasive salesmen of the business, whilst Benny, exuding trust, confidence and charisma, was the buyer of stock. Part of the purchasing strategy was a diligent perusal of the death notices in the Glasgow *Times* and *Citizen* newspapers. Benny would then see to it that the area in which the bereavement had taken place was circulated with pamphlets offering to buy male clothes of all kinds in good condition, and then a few days later, a fistful of pound notes in hand, the houses in the district, including of course the bereaved household, were visited. The yield from the bereaved households was always very good, and consisted often of the best quality pre-war suits, purchased from a disconsolate widow by a suitably sympathetic Benny at rock-bottom prices.

The Silver Lounge was Benny's favourite haunt. There he would spend hours chatting, exchanging jokes and betting on the horses with one or other of the bookies always to be found there. One day, he was approached by Peter McNulty, a local taxi driver, who offered to sell him an overcoat. The coat was a large and beautifully tailored article made from the best Crombie cloth with plush satin linings and a velvet collar, obviously worth not only a lot of money but also a couple of years' supply of clothing coupons. Benny snapped it up without asking too much about its origins. A reassurance from the seller that it was not stolen sufficed. Peter was known to be a bit of a head case, but his honesty had never been called into question. The magnificent coat was placed on prominent display in the shop window with a prohibitively high price tag, for Frank and Maurice were not in a hurry to sell it. It gave a touch of class to the window display. Had Benny enquired further as to the origin of the coat the following tale would have emerged.

In those days theatre and cinema attendance was probably at its peak. Apart from the wireless there was no other form of entertainment and distraction from the drabness of immediate post war life. It was certainly the era of the big touring dance bands. The American orchestras of the middle thirties, Ellington, Armstrong, Calloway and the like had been supplanted by smoother home grown dance bands. Ambrose and his orchestra, Geraldo and his orchestra, Lou Praeger and his band, Ted Heath and his band, Henry Hall and the BBC dance orchestra, Nat Gonella and his band, Ray Noble and his orchestra, all these were household names whose regular visits to the City Centre theatres and dance halls were eagerly awaited and booked out months in advance by an avid public. Many of the musicians in these bands stayed in the Garnethill lodging houses and sipped coffee in the Silver Lounge to listen to our large selection of records.

Prominent in these orchestras was the Lew Stone Band, a top class London outfit with a variety of gifted musicians and singers, amongst them the nationally famous drummer Max Bacon, a giant of a man with a pleasantly rasping singing voice whose solo act featured prominently in the band's repertoire. The orchestra had just finished a two week's appearance at the Empire and had been celebrating the beginning of a week's rest period, and to celebrate the occasion Max had given a party at his usual digs in Garnethill. As the time of his departure on the night sleeper to London approached, the jovial drummer was well advanced into a state of alcoholic fuzziness, so a taxi was called to take him to the Central Station, where he was duly poured on to the night sleeper by a helpful Peter McNulty, who was on his last job of the night. Next morning Peter was agreeably surprised to find a magnificent overcoat on the floor of his cab, and Max Bacon arrived in London minus his velvet-collared crombie, without the slightest idea as to where he might have left it. A phone call to his lodgings in Glasgow produced no results. Max resigned himself to the loss of his coat, knowing that the value of it was covered by insurance, even though the coat could not be replaced because of the lack of clothing coupons.

A month or so passed and the Lew Stone Band returned for a fortnight's visit to Glasgow. The crombie coat in the window of the West End Misfits, as yet unsold, still formed the centerpiece of the display. On Wednesdays and Saturdays, matinee days, Max Bacon made a point of having a meal of fish and chips at the Savoy, where, since his visits were always in the late afternoon, there was no possibility of eating anything but the best quality fish. On one of these visits Benny happened to be sitting in the premises, regaling his company with jokes and stories. He was a marvellous raconteur, using his slight Cockney accent to advantage, and Max joined in the general enjoyment of Benny's tales. From obviously similar backgrounds, pleasantries were exchanged and common haunts and backgrounds in London established. Max Bacon's identity and profession needed no introduction, he was a nationally known figure, but when Benny introduced himself as being in the clothing business, the musician's thoughts turned to the lost overcoat, as yet unreplaced. He mentioned that he might be in the market for an overcoat.

'I've got just the very thing for you,' enthused Benny. 'A beautiful piece of cloth. You won't find any better in Savile Row. Just your size too, I imagine. Second hand, but better than new. No coupons, and for you we'll make a special price. Come and see it tomorrow.'

The next day Max Bacon took one startled look at the coat on display in the shop window, said not a word, but turned on his heel to return ten minutes with a policeman in tow and confronted the mystified Goodman brothers with a demand for the immediate return of his coat, with muttered threats and accusations of theft and reset. The musician told the story of his loss to the policeman, and, his ownership finally established, retreated triumphant, proudly wearing the lost coat and still muttering threats and accusations. The brothers managed to convince the police of their basic innocence in the matter. They had bought the coat in good faith, they claimed. The fact that they had exhibited it in plain view in their window should be proof enough of their innocence, they continued. Had they anything to hide, the coat could have been disposed of long ago privately. Where had they got the coat? They made a great show of going through invoices and records. It must have been part of a job lot from some of their many sources, they concluded, and in view of the delicacy of the situation the police let the matter drop. They knew full well the unwritten law that prevailed in such a neighbourhood. If you don't want the roof to fall in on you, thou shalt not shop thy neighbour, especially if he is as well liked as Peter McNulty was. It took the naturally resilient Benny at least a day to recover from the shock of the loss of the five pounds he had paid Peter McNulty for the coat.

As we became more affluent, I found that I had more and more time to spend on leisure activities, and I had been accepted into the membership of Haggs Castle golf club, a club which already had a half dozen or so Scots-Italians as members. I had by now become inured to being blackballed on application for membership to sports clubs. Discrimination was usually on two grounds, religious affiliation and nationality. Religious discrimination was the order of the day in Glasgow in those years. Many firms would not employ Catholics, and since all job applications had to include educational qualifications, the name of the school attended would immediately have shown a person's religious affiliation. I could understand discrimination on ethnic grounds. The country had just emerged from a destructive war, and a lack of desire on the part of private clubs to admit persons of Italian extraction as members was perfectly understandable, but discrimination on religious grounds I could not comprehend. Whether Catholic or Protestant, all were citizens, both denominations had spilt their share of blood in the defence of their country in the war, all supposedly had equal rights, and why a person's religious beliefs should bar him or her from certain jobs or positions I could not understand.

Just recently an osteopath friend, Ian Baird, who had a clinic in Somerset Place, had proposed me for membership of the Arlington, a club which had been advertising for members in the local press for some time. I filled in the necessary application forms, and on the line with the question Religion? I marked in RC. Some days later a shame-faced Ian had to inform me that he had been asked to withdraw my application. The Arlington Baths did not accept Catholics as members. So I sought membership elsewhere. The Western Baths in Cresswell Street were approached, and this time, despite my double disadvantage of Italian name and Catholic religion, I was accepted as a member. I was to discover that the Western Baths membership was and always had been cosmopolitan and rich in variety, and had encompassed bookies, shopkeepers, actors, TV announcers, personalities from the nearby BBC studios, members of the professions, Catholic priests and Protestant ministers. Ethnic and religious background had never been a factor in the selection of membership. All that was required of prospective members was that they should measure up to a certain standard of behaviour and decorum and that they should be able to meet the relatively modest fees entailed by membership. The Baths was to go through many vicissitudes in its long history, and came near to ruin thirty years or so ago, when dilapidation and lack of funds drove it to the verge of bankruptcy. That it survived and prospered to become one of the best equipped establishments of its kind in the country is due entirely to the efforts and vision of the present chairman, Mr Willie Mann, who steered it through the difficulties of that period and saved it from extinction. In retrospect, after some fifty years of happy and rewarding membership of the Western Baths, I have to thank those members of the Arlington who denied me entry to their club all those years ago.

As a member of the Western, I was to find myself in a circle of new acquaintances, some of whom were in the course of time to become close friends. The members of the Baths tended to form themselves into little like-minded groups. The one I was drawn to was presided over by Eddie Collier, a little Jewish doctor, a bachelor and regular attendant at the Baths. His was the table frequented by a variety of interesting and colourful characters, and a more cosmopolitan group would have been very hard to find. Regularly stationed at Eddie's table were the likes of Roddy McMillan, the actor, James McLean, a well known Glasgow bookie, Bob Whitelaw, a doctor from Kilbirnie, the Reverend Leslie Hope, minister of the Renfield Street Church of Scotland, Alistair Gillies, the singer, Father Sidney McEwan, the internationally known singing priest, and Hugh Doherty, a publican. Hugh was the owner of two pubs, one of which went by the imposing name of the Symposium, a title hardly suitable for its location in a tough part of the Garscube Road. It was a fair bet that few if any of his customers knew what the word 'symposium' stood for. Eddie Collier and I became good friends. He took a great interest in our children, followed with interest their scholastic progress at university and proudly presented my son Lorenzo with his first stethoscope on his acceptance for the faculty of medicine at St Andrews University. To finish my mention of Eddie Collier I shall have to go forward in time.

One day in the early eighties, on our return from a fairly lengthy stay in Majorca I found a message from the Procurator's Office in Glasgow waiting for me. I was asked to get in touch as soon as possible. I was duly informed that my little friend Eddie had been found dead in his flat, and that a holograph will, naming me as executor, had been found by the body. The funeral was to take place the next morning in the synagogue at Lambhill cemetery. The funeral service in the little synagogue was sparsely attended, with two Rabbis, the undertakers and a handful of friends from the Western Baths the only one ones present. That afternoon, saddened by my friend's death, and touched by the trust he had placed in me, I sat in the Fiscal's office and read Eddie's holograph will. It was dated October 1974 and contained a request that I be appointed executor of the will. A few small bequests were made, after which the remainder of the estate was to go to the Royal Lifeboat Society in Troon. The last line of the will read 'I desire that on my death my body be cremated.' I looked at the Fiscal.

'Who made the funeral arrangements?' I asked

The fiscal didn't know. I turned over some of the documents in the box in which the will had been found. I looked at one of them and then at another, did some metal arithmetic and took a deep breath. I was over one hundred thousand pounds already. I phoned my lawyer friend Bob Martin, and in his office the following day, the documents were closely examined, to reveal that Eddie's estate amounted to more than £400, 000.

I read once more the line 'I wish that my body be cremated.'

Eddie had entrusted me with the implementation of his will, and I was deeply touched at his trust in me. Why had a burial and not a cremation taken place at the cemetery? Who had given instructions for the burial? I consulted the police, and was told that in view of the lack of relatives the body had been turned over to the local synagogue. Did the Rabbi know of the contents of the will? Surely someone must have known that Eddie wished to be cremated and not buried?

So I phoned the Rabbi who had officiated at the burial and explained my dilemma to him. I was met with an angry flow of words. Cremation was not in conformity with Jewish law, said the priest angrily. No Jew would want to be cremated, and although he did not practise his religion Eddie would always be a Jew, and he must have been out of his mind to have written such a request. I persisted. Did the Rabbi know of Eddie's request?

'It doesn't matter whether I knew or not,' was the answer. 'I would never allow a Jew to be cremated.'

I fumed for a while at the Rabbi's brusqueness and then explained my concern to Bob Martin. I felt that I would not be doing my duty towards Eddie unless his wishes were fully carried out. His body must be exhumed and then cremated, I insisted. Bob had never been faced with such a problem before and an advocate was consulted. The advocate read the will, listened carefully to my request and after due deliberation expressed his opinion. Let Eddie rest where he is, was his judgement. I could not blame myself, for the burial had taken place before I had known of Eddie's wishes. The Rabbi may well have acted in good faith and perhaps had not known of Eddie's request, and even if they had seen the will and chosen to disregard his wish, no law had been broken. The body was now buried in the Jewish equivalent of consecrated ground and the synagogue would fight tooth and nail any action to have the body exhumed and then cremated. An action might in the end be successful, continued the advocate, but the procedure, touching as it would on deeply held religious beliefs, would certainly be very acrimonious. In view of the intense opposition any such action would encounter the costs would be very high and might very well consume all of Eddie's estate, assuming of course that no one else was willing to foot the bill. The advice was repeated, let Eddie rest where he is.

The Jewish section of the Lambhill cemetery is a small space enclosed by a wall at the southern end of the Catholic burial ground. The headstones on all of the Jewish graves there were all of modest size and quality, and as I stood over my old friend's burial place I decided that his unwanted burial place should somehow be specially designated. I arranged for a magnificent and very expensive polished granite slab to be laid over the site. It stood out like a Taj Mahal in the unpretentious surroundings, as if to make the point that Eddie's grave was out of place there. There is no Jewish writing on the slab, as is the case in all the other graves in the cemetery. The inscription is in large golden English lettering. I pay an occasional visit to the grave; my own parents lie buried not so very far away in the Catholic section of the cemetery, and I sometimes make a short detour to pay my respects to Eddie. I still feel a slight sense of guilt in not having carried out his wishes. With the passing of the years I have noted that many of the surrounding headstones have been replaced by markers equal if not greater that Eddie's in their splendour.

Prominently set in one of the walls of the Royal Lifeboat station at Troon, a neat brass plaque acknowledges Eddie's bequest.

I joined the Western Baths in the late 1950s, and my membership has lasted to this day. My visits however, have become fewer and fewer. I have to drive to the Baths, and at my age I find it quite a strain to cope with the ever-increasing flood of traffic on the roads and parking spaces in the area are becoming more and more difficult to find. Moreover, most of my companions at Eddie's table have all passed on; in fact only one, Bob Whitelaw, remains, and his visits were becoming fewer and fewer too. In view of all this, not without a great deal of regret since it meant terminating a long and happy relationship, some months ago I handed in my resignation, which resulted in the following communication from Willie Mann, saviour of the Baths all those years ago:

Dear Mr Pieri,

I thank you for your letter of the 4th October and for your kind words expressing thanks to me. I also acknowledge receipt of your resignation from the Club, but I have to tell you that having spoken to some other Committee members we have decided not to accept your resignation, but rather to offer you honorary membership. According to our records you have been a member since 1957, almost 50 years, and we do not feel that we should let you go!

I do hope that you will accept this offer of honorary membership and that although you now find it difficult to come from Lenzie to the Baths you will call in from time to time and therefore make use of your membership. I and your many friends at the Baths would certainly be delighted to see you.

Kind Regards
Bill
WM Mann
Secretary

❧ 7 ❧
Expansion

After the opening of the Silver Lounge Ralph and I were perfectly content with the way business was progressing. The two shops were busy, the Savoy exceptionally so, and our income was more than enough to keep ourselves and our families in the good things of life. We also enjoyed the ample free time we could give one another away from business. As long as either one of us was there to look after things, we could take all the holidays and play all the golf our hearts could desire. The poverty and deprivation of the early pre-war years was now a distant memory, and our ambition stretched no further than what we had achieved. But often in life opportunities arise which cannot be ignored. Such an opportunity was presented to us by the conversion of the Theatre Royal at the top of Hope Street to the Scottish Television headquarters, which took place in the middle fifties just as a shop in Hope Street, just a few yards from the theatre stage door entrance, was put up for sale. This was an opportunity we simply could not overlook. We put a down payment on the premises, borrowed the rest, and so The Cappuccino, a coffee bar cum snack bar was born. It was an instant success, both with the general public and with the artistes and staff of the new Scottish TV studios. A favourite programme of those times was 'The One O'Clock Gang Show', a programme televised daily five days a week at 1pm. The names of the One o'Clock Gang soon became household names in Scotland. There was the Tommy Maxwell Trio, Charlie Sim, Dorothy Paul and Roddy McMillan; there was Peggy O'Keefe, the popular pianist and singer, and Larry Marshall, the comedian. Each day after the show they congregated in the Cappuccino to draw up plans for the next day's performance, consuming cup after cup of coffee in the process.

Then, literally by chance, a fourth shop was added to our possessions. My father was friendly with a Mr Biagoni, a man of about his own age, who owned a fish and chip shop in the Anderston district. He had one daughter, Anna, who had recently married, and the shop was now being run by his son-in-law. In 1948 the two went off on a motoring trip to Italy, and on the road back were involved in a dreadful crash at Abington on the Carlisle Road, a notorious accident spot which claimed the lives of several motorists each year. Mr Biagoni was devastated by the loss of his family, and being elderly and in somewhat poor health he decided to sell the business and return to his native Italy. Given the gruesome circumstances of the accident and his own poor health it is remarkable that he survived the trauma of having to identify his daughter. Anna's head was all that was left to identify. She had been decapitated by the impact and her head thrown several yards away from the wreck. The rest of her body was burned to a cinder in the ensuing blaze.

There was a major problem in disposing of his shop. In the 1950s several districts in Glasgow had been designated as redevelopment areas, and the first of these was the Anderson district, in which the Biagoni shop was situated. A date for the compulsory purchase of his shop had not been set, and the property had no attraction whatsoever for anyone looking to purchase a business. Who in his right senses would put money into a place which at some time in the very near future would be taken over by the local authority? Compensation would of course be paid to any dispossessed owner, but since the redevelopment of Glasgow had not started no one had as yet any idea how such compensation would be calculated, or how much or how little it would be. So Mr Biagoni was stymied. He could not get rid of his shop, even though he had been doing excellent business. By observing his purchases at the fish market and from the reports we had heard about the number of sacks of potatoes he went through in a week, we had a rough idea of what his takings were, and they were not to be sneezed at.

We discussed the matter with our solicitor, and our suggestion to Biagoni was that we take over his business, with no money changing hands, that we pay him an agreed amount each year as rental for what the market value of the goodwill would have been under normal circumstances, and that these payments would cease when the Glasgow corporation acquired the ownership of the property or when the agreed market value had been reached by our payments, whichever was the sooner. Any compensation from the local authority for the property would go to Mr Biagoni. Compensation for the goodwill would go to us. We stood to benefit by the acquisition of a busy shop which would literally pay for itself, which would put trading profits in our pocket plus a lump sum of money in our hands when the shop was taken over. For Mr Biagoni the attraction was that he was immediately rid of a business he could not sell, but he was gambling on the time factor as to when the property would be taken over by the local authority. The longer the shop traded the better it was for him, and the better the chances of the full goodwill figure being reached. We gambled nothing. We would get something out of the deal no matter how the future went. All we were putting into it was our labour.

Bob Martin put our idea into legalese, submitted it to Mr Biagioni's solicitor, the offer was accepted, and we took over the running of his shop. The business proved to be as profitable as we had thought, and although we had difficulty insofar as staffing and supervision were concerned, due mainly to our lack of expertise in such matters, we were more than satisfied with our acquisition.

But then disaster struck us once again. The Cowcaddens was declared a redevelopment area, and our main earner, the Savoy, together with the Silver Lounge Café and the Cappuccino, were now threatened with compulsory purchase by the local authority. So although we had four good earners in our newly formed company, we had nothing, it seemed. We were on the verge of losing our livelihood at the stroke of a pen of a local authority bent on the modernisation of the peripheral districts of Glasgow. Nobody could give us an indication as to how matters might develop. The axe could fall upon us at any time, and so, threatened by the certainty of the loss of our livelihood at some time in the near future, we panicked somewhat and overrreacted. The wise thing to have done would have been to take our time in looking for other sites, continue to work the existing shops in order to accumulate enough capital to relocate without borrowing, and to wait for the eventual monetary compensation for the loss of our businesses. But instead we began somewhat wildly to seek immediate alternative accommodation for our shops. We could see no further than that area of the Cowcaddens which made the Savoy and Silver Lounge such cornucopias, and we began to borrow in order to purchase nearby premises for relocation, not having realised that once redevelopment started the business potential of the area would change completely. We opened two shops in quick succession, each one a stone's throw from the Savoy.

The Cappuccino in Hope Street, next to the Theatre Royal in Hope Street, was meant eventually to be a substitute for the Silver Lounge, and round the corner from that we opened the Rio, a restaurant specifically designed to be turned into a replica of the Savoy once that establishment would no longer exist. However, there is a world of difference in the running of one shop, where everything is under one's personal control, and the running of five. We had no formal business experience in the running of what had now become a chain of shops. Our acquired expertise lay in the ability to work hard and in the control of everything within touch and sight. The running of five shops with a total of about 120 employees was another matter. Managers had to be installed in each, cash and stock control had to be introduced, an office organisation had to be set up, and proper book-keeping would have to be resorted to, rather than the somewhat ad hoc system heretofore used by us. Suddenly, with five shops on our hands, we were earning less than we had been with only two, and our headaches had multiplied. No longer could we take all the holidays we wanted to and arrange for ample free time to devote to our families. Although we no longer dirtied our own hands cooking and serving fish and chips, constant supervision of our expanded little empire took up all our time. The carefree days of the Silver Lounge and the fraternisation with our colourful customers had gone. And yet, like a drug addict who does not realise that his habit is growing, we expanded still further.

The Malvern Restaurant, at the corner of Hope Street and Sauchiehall Street was owned by a Greek, Charlie Pattison. He wanted rid of the property so as to devote his energy to the opening of a gambling casino. He was in the fortunate position of not needing any capital for his project, and we could not raise any more money to purchase the Malvern from him, so a deal was struck. We would take the property off his hands and pay him an agreed monthly sum over a period of five years. At the end of those five years we were bound to pay him the agreed value of the property. The proposed deal bore more than a passing resemblance to the one we had agree with Mr Biagioni some years before, and again, without a penny passing hands, we took over a business. There was a big difference, however. While the Anderson restaurant was a going concern and making money, the Malvern was operating at a loss, so something had to be done to keep us from sliding further into an economic mire. We converted the pavement level premises to a fish and chip shop and named it the Savoy Grill. On the first floor we modernised the already existing lounge bar, and on the top floor we opened a plush restaurant, the Rialto. Business there went so badly that we toyed with the idea of renaming it the Morgue, and it ate up all the profits earned by the pavement level Savoy Grill. After a deeply worrying time, however, the tide began to turn our way. The Anderson shop was finally taken over by the local authority and compensation was paid to us for the goodwill and to Mr Biagioni for the property. The sums paid were more than generous, and when these were translated into what we might receive when the Savoy, The Silver Lounge and the Cappuccino finally went under the bulldozers, we could see financial brightness at the end of what had been a long and dark tunnel of worsening debt. Never mind that the plush Rialto was losing money hand over fist and that it had to be subsidised by the profits of the downstairs Savoy Grill, all we had to do if the burden became too great was to close the place down or let it out to someone better qualified than we were to make it profitable, a course which we actually did take after the passing of a few more months.

It was at this juncture that the benefits of having two brothers such as Ralph and I were, working hand in hand with complete trust in one another were made manifest. One night without any warning I collapsed, and was taken to hospital, where I was diagnosed as having suffered a perforated duodenal ulcer, probably brought on by the stress and tension of the preceding months. For two months or so, until I was able to take up my duties again, the entire burden of the business lay on Ralph's shoulders. Years later I was able to reciprocate in kind when Ralph in his turn collapsed, in his case with a blocked prostate, which laid him *hors de combat* for a period, and I was also on hand when Theresa, his wife, was stricken with Legionnaire's Disease and he had to devote much of his time to her. The nature of our business and the manner in which we had developed it required a personal hands-on approach which no stranger could have supplied. For fifty years Ralph and I worked together and depended completely on one another. It is a measure of the bond which tied us together as brothers that it lasted unbroken for the whole period of our working lives despite the occasional differences, some serious, which arose between us in the course of those years.

Then, after my return to health, another opportunity presented itself, this one a rock-solid certainty for making money. One day I noticed that Bailey's Wine Shop, a famous off-sales situated at what was arguably the best trading site in Glasgow, at the corner of Renfield Street and West Regent Street, diagonally opposite the Odeon Cinema, was closed and that a To Let sign lay in the window, in preparation for affixing to the outside wall. Ralph and I were as one in our evaluation of the site, and immediately asked the ever-dependable Bob Martin to investigate. He came up with the information that the owner was a Mr Stone, of the British Bank of Commerce and of the Kirkcaldy Linoleum Market shops, with whom we had already had some satisfactory dealings in the past. Mr Stone informed us that he already had a positive enquiry from a serious source, but that, in view of our happy dealings in recent years he would rather let it to F. Pieri & Sons Ltd. The snag lay in the time factor. To obtain planning permission for what we had in mind, another fish and chip shop, a lengthy procedure would have to be started. Permission would have to be sought from the neighbours for the erection of a ventilation flue on the rear of the building, and plans would have to be approved by the planning authority for the whole project. All of this could well have taken months, and Mr Stone was disposed to wait for only a few weeks for an offer from us.

It was here that Oscar Catani came into the picture. Oscar was a shopfitter, a first-class one at that, and had fitted out the Rialto block, as we called it, for us. To put it as euphemistically as is possible, he was also the biggest pirate in the business. If there was a corner to be cut, Oscar would know of it, if there was a specification in a job that could be avoided to his profit, he would find it, if there was someone in the planning department who could be approached to facilitate matters, Oscar would know of him. He was a pirate, but he was a likeable one. Moreover, all his work was first class and he produced results where no one else could. So we approached Oscar and explained our problem. First things first, he said, let's see if there is an internal flue in the building we could use for an internal ventilation shaft, thus doing away with the necessity for an outside flue with all the planning complications and permissions from neighbours such a structure would give rise to. He gave instructions to one of his men to take a chimney sweep's iron ball to the top of the building and drop it down our shop's flue. It came clattering down the chimney and stopped at a satisfied Oscar's feet.

'You're in business,' he said. 'I can get a flexible tube down that flue and you can use it for an exhaust for cooking fumes. No approval from neighbours necessary.'

There remained, however, the small problem of obtaining in a few days a planning approval that would normally take many weeks. He pondered for a moment and instructed us to write him two letters, one predated by two months and the second with the current date.

The first letter, to be dated two months previously, was to instruct him to prepare plans for submission to the planning dept in respect of the shop at 63 Renfield Street and submit them to the planning authority for approval. The second, dated currently and written in the strongest possible terms, was to enquire as to the position regarding the application for planning permission, warning him that if we were to lose the lease of the shop because of his failure to submit plans in good time we would hold him responsible for any financial loss sustained by us. Armed with these two letters he tearfully approached his friend in the planning department. He had been ill and had been unable to submit the plans referred to in our first letter, said Oscar to the official. He railed against the two Pieri brothers, who were threatening to bankrupt him because of his failure. They were hard, heartless men who didn't care one jot about his health. Could his friend help him in any way? Four days later the triumphant Oscar produced a set of fully approved plans at a meeting in Mr Stone's office, who couldn't quite understand how we had managed to produce in two weeks what would normally have taken two months to achieve.

Oscar went to work with his usual skill and energy, and a few months later another Savoy was opened at 63 Renfield Street. In view of his expertise in navigating through the murky seas of planning procedures, we did not question the grossly inflated bill presented to us by Oscar for his services. The matter did not finish there, however. On our opening day the irate tenants of the upstairs offices came storming in with a complaint. They were being assailed by noxious fish and chip fumes and smells, and insisted that I go with them to see for myself. I could barely see inside the offices through the blue haze of cooking fumes which permeated every room, and my nose twitched at the sharp smell of fried fish. I could not deny that there was, as I put it, 'Just a wee bit smell' and promised to look into it. I called on the Iona Ventilation Company, a firm who occasionally did work for us, to investigate. Back came the report. There was no flexible metal tubing inside the chimney, and the cooking fumes were leaking through the brickwork into the offices. I complained bitterly to Oscar, who came immediately to examine the cause of the complaint, claiming that the necessary tubing had been properly installed. He saw for himself that there was only bare brickwork in the chimney and after some deep thought came up with a magnificent explanation for the lack of metal tubing.

'Some bugger must have stolen it during the night!'

I could not help but laugh at the humour of such a colossal blatantly impossible excuse. Obviously no metal tube had ever been installed, but I could not remain angry with him for any length of time. Without his expertise in cutting corners we would never have got our hands on the shop, so we ruefully paid Iona Ventilation for a metal tube to be put where Oscar had failed to put his. Shortly after, Oscar retired to the beautiful little estate he had bought on the Balmaha Road by the side of Loch Lomond. It had a Gaelic name which I cannot remember, and brother Ralph is no longer around to be asked. We remained good friends and saw a lot of one another until his death some years ago, but he always did complain that he should have been allowed to replace the stolen metal tube at 63 Renfield Street!

The Renfield Street Savoy was the most profitable shop we ever had, and we traded there for some twelve years before our retirement in 1982.

✤ 8 ✤
New Friends

My internment experience had changed me in one respect. After my return home I was unable to be completely at ease and express myself unreservedly when in the company of my old pre-war Scottish friends. Although there was nothing in their manner which was in any way different from what it had been before the war, I suppose that subconsciously there was imprinted at the back of my mind the fact that for three years I had been locked away as an enemy of the people I was living amongst and called friends, and this, to a certain extent, inhibited my freedom of expression. I had become wary of saying the wrong thing, of expressing any opinion that might be at variance with those of the person or group I happened to be with at that time. To be completely at ease I had to seek out the company of those who had shared my experiences of the war years, and because of this my circle of Italian friends became much larger than it had ever been in the years prior to the outbreak of war. I sought the companionship of the likes of Joe Guidi, Peter Nesti, Angelo LaMarra, Dante Toti, Peter Buonaccorsi, all of whom had been with me in Canada, and all of whom shared my newly acquired diffidence in their relationship with the locals.

I kept in touch with my London-Italian friends from the camp, and spent many a weekend in London with John Tontini of the tunnel escapade, and especially with Romeo Capitanio, from whom I had learned so much during my three years confinement. From London occasionally I would carry on to Hythe, near Southhampton, where George Martinez, he of the escape attempt to be mentioned in a later chapter, lived. My first attempt to find his home was not a propitious one. I arrived in Hythe by train, close to midnight, without the foggiest notion of how to get to Dibden Manor, the place in the country where George lived with his family. Hythe Station was just a small village stop, and at that time of night no taxis were available. Although George was expecting my arrival I had no wish to disturb him at such a late hour, so I walked into a Police Station next to the railway, explained my predicament to the sergeant in charge and asked if there was anywhere in the village I could spend the night. No, there wasn't, came the reply, but if I was stuck for a place to sleep I was welcome to spend the night in one of the cells. There would even be a cup of tea for me in the morning, I was told. I accepted gratefully, and slept soundly on a mattress placed on the floor of the cell, the door of which had been left wide open during the night. Next morning I was awakened by the sergeant, who hailed me with a cheerful good morning and a mug of tea. I thanked him, washed and shaved in the confines of the cell, and as I was about to leave I suddenly remembered something. In those days, under the Aliens Act, which was passed in 1920 and not revoked until the 1960s, I had to carry an Aliens registration book with me everywhere I went. I had to have it stamped by my local police office if I left Glasgow for any reason, had to declare my intended destination, and at my destination I had to have it stamped at a police station there, a procedure to be repeated on my return to Glasgow. As a curiosity I still have this passbook, now old and frayed at the edges. Each page is copiously stamped with my movements, and one bears the inscription: 'Reports marriage to Mary Cameron, British Subject'. The stamp is dated 27/4/50. I did toy with the idea of not producing it; I should have done so on my arrival the previous night, but then if I did not have it stamped here I might have questions to answer on my return to Glasgow, so I pulled the book from my pocket, presented it to the police sergeant and explained. He examined it, looked at me severely and remarked that I should have presented the book at the time of my arrival the night before. I apologised, and remarked that tiredness and the lateness of my arrival had pushed it from my mind. I wondered if the cell would have been forthcoming had I done so. The sudden change in the policeman's demeanour made me doubt it.

To return to the subject of my friends in Glasgow. My closest friend of pre-war days, Johnny Clapperton, had been killed during the war, and I had grown out of my relationship with the McMeighans, whom I now saw very infrequently. Francy Traynor still came around, and although our friendship was still as firm as ever, I seldom went into detail with him about my time in Canada. In view of his own experiences in the Merchant Navy, with 11 ships sunk under him, Warth Mills and the few slaps I had received at our arrival in Montreal suddenly seemed of no consequence. However, I began to form new relationships, this time with locals who had fought in Italy during the war, and who sought me out to tell me stories of the contacts they had made with Italians in the course of the campaigns there, of how they had been welcomed as liberators, of the hospitality they had received from Italian families, and of the shelter and food offered by people who could ill afford to part with it. They spoke too of the friendliness of the population in general, and of how many individuals had risked their lives in helping escaped British POWs. In later years I was to see for myself a letter from General Alexander, Commander in Chief of the Allied forces in Italy, framed and hanging on the wall of a little wayside café in Barga, in which the General expresses his thanks and gratitude to the owner, Enrico Clerici, for his efforts in sheltering British soldiers from the occupying Germans.

As had been the case before the war, the Savoy once again had become the meeting place of policemen who served out of the northern Police station in Maitland Street, drawn there by the police box which stood at the Hope Street door of the Savoy. This police box, in the days before hand-held phones and radio communication, was the only contact the men on the beat had with their headquarters. If their presence was required somewhere, the blue light on the roof of the box would flash, alerting the constable on the beat to get into contact with his headquarters, which he did by means of a telephone inside the box. The box could be clearly seen from the back shop of the Savoy, and here, especially on cold and rainy days, the men on the beat, having of course first patrolled their round to ensure that all was well, would sit and wait to be summoned by the flashing blue light, sipping tea or coffee and nibbling at a plate of chips, glad to be out of the cold and wind and rain. In the forty years of running the Savoy, I probably got to know every policeman who served out of the Northern police office in Maitland Street, and with two of them in the post-war years I formed friendships that were to last a lifetime. Joe Beattie, who was to rise to the rank of chief detective inspector, first appeared on the scene in 1946 after a wartime career as a much decorated pilot in the RAF, during which he flew Lancaster bombers and Mosquitos, the fast target-finder planes which flew ahead of the bombing squadrons to drop flares over the target area. He was a great companion and marvellous raconteur, who in the last years of his life was to provide me with much material for a book *The Big Men*, a series of stories about the Glasgow police which I was to write during my own retirement in years to come. The second of my policemen friends from those days is Alex Adair, still massive and strong at the age of eighty-four and who in his day was probably the most able man ever to walk a beat in the Glasgow streets. An ex-Royal Marine commando, Alex was a huge man, about six feet four inches in height, and when you add to that the seven or so inches of helmet worn by policemen until the late 1950s, the intimidating appearance he presented to malefactors can well be imagined. His stories too contributed in no small measure to the success of *The Big Men*, and like Joe Beattie, he first appeared on the Savoy beat in 1946, after his return from the Army. They had both served in the Italian theatre of war for some time, and both had nothing but praise for the Italians they had met. To men like these, who for the past five years or so had been risking their lives on an almost a daily basis in fighting Nazis, the problem of dealing with the toughs and hooligans of the Cowcaddens district was merely, to use the words of Joe Beattie, 'a piece of cake'. The type of man Alex Adair was and still is, can be seen from this narration from *The Big Men*:

I joined the Navy straight from my job as a fisherman sailing out of Wick,
where I was born, and when the war came I wanted to see some adventure

so I joined up. I was 18 at the time. I helped a bit to evacuate the soldiers at Dunkirk from a destroyer, and then I volunteered for Special Forces. We were trained in underwater stuff, you know the kind of thing, checking boats for limpet mines in the Med., underwater demolition and stuff like that. The Italians were using two-man subs to stick mines onto our ships in Gibraltar, they sunk one or two that way and when we got wise to how they were doing it we kept an underwater watch and knocked a few of them off before they could get to their target. We couldn't stop them with grenades or depth charges when they were near our ships. That might have set off their mines and sunk us.

Then we went to underwater demolition, to demolish barriers just off beaches, you know the kind of thing, steel rails and barbed wire and all sorts of junk like that sunk in the water to rip the bottom off landing craft and snag up the soldiers coming off and trying to wade on to shore. We saw a bit of action at Pantelleria and Sicily and at the Anzio landings, then we got posted back to Portsmouth. A couple of days before the invasion, we got our orders and we came off a sub just off the beach in Normandy, fifteen of us. We were loaded up with limpet mines. We had some strapped round us and some we were pushing ahead of us on inflated belts loaded with them and we had to stick them on to the barricades under the surface. These mines were timed, nobody knew when they were set to go off apart from the boys in London. The reason why they were timed was that when they went off the Germans would know that something was on and they would get ready. After the mines were set, and that wasn't an easy job either, under the water with the barbed wire and iron rails and things, we couldn't go back to the sub. We had just shorts on and flippers and we had to swim ashore.

When we got there the French resistance people were waiting for us. We had special wristbands for identification, just like a wristwatch but with a copper medal in place of the watch. The medal had the head of a French soldier on it and some writing in French, and that way they knew who we were. Come to think of it those wristbands must be something special now, there must be only fifteen of them in the world. We went with the Maquis and they fitted us out with clothes and guns and grenades for another job we had to do. The night before the invasion started the Maquis got a signal from London. We had to kill as many German officers as we could that night, not soldiers, just officers, so as to break the chain of command for the invasion starting. The Maquis knew where they all hung out, bars and restaurants and brothels and places like that, and during that night we burst in on them and killed a lot. It was a lousy dirty way to kill a man, when he's sleeping and not expecting it. It's different when you're in a battle, *you're facing somebody who can fight back, but lousy or not we had our orders and it had to be done. It didn't bother the Maquis, though, they hated the Jerries in a way that we didn't, the Jerries had taken their land and their women and they took a great delight in killing them that way. When the invasion started we helped the Maquis to sabotage things, blowing up railway lines and mining roads and stuff like that. It was a bit hairy, because we didn't know what was happening on the beaches and we didn't know how we would end up or whether we would see our own lads again. We weren't half relieved when our boys finally did break through and we could join up with them.*

My dossier from my years in Camp 43, listing my knowledge of languages and the fact that I had been camp interpreter for two years, had evidently been passed on to the local police, for one day in the early sixties I was asked if I were willing to be put on their list of interpreters for service in the Glasgow courts. I agreed, and from time to time I was called on to interpret in the courts, mainly in Italian and French. I enjoyed those experiences, although I have to admit that I was not always entirely impartial in the translation of individual testimonies. Before the proceedings, I always asked to speak to the person I was to translate for, usually the accused or a witness, so as to determine the accent or dialect I would be called upon to translate into English, and in these interviews on occasion I would form personal sympathies. These would sometimes result in me translating testimony in the manner I thought it should have been said, rather than in the sometimes incoherent way in which it was given by the person I was translating for. I occasionally had the impression, conveyed to me in the form of quizzical looks on the part of the sheriff or judge I was translating in front of, that my minute but effective alterations were being understood and noted. Lots of people, especially those in the legal profession, can after all, understand Italian and French, but never once were my translations brought into question. Any alterations I might have made were not ones of substance, but rather of emphasis and of presentation, but, I must confess, only to help those witnesses I was sympathetically disposed towards. However, on the several occasions I was to act as interpreter in cases involving Beltrami, the famous criminal lawyer, I had to be very careful, no matter where my personal sympathies lay, that my translations showed no bias in any direction. He was as good as, if not better, in Italian and French than I was, and would have noticed any discrepancy on my part.

One case I was involved in comes to mind. I was called one day to interpret in French for an Algerian sailor who was up on a charge of causing grievous bodily harm to three Glasgow civilians. The assault in question had taken place outside a Gallowgate pub, and had resulted in the three victims being taken for treatment to the Royal Infirmary and in the arrest of the Algerian. I arrived early for the trial to exchange a few words with the accused so as to acquaint myself with his manner of speaking, and was pleasantly surprised to hear him talk in a clear and distinct French. He was a very big and powerfully built man of about forty or so, and looked perfectly capable of putting three lesser men in hospital in the course of a fight. The trial was scheduled for 10.30am, but the morning dragged on and on; the first trial of the morning was obviously taking longer than had been anticipated, and lunch time arrived with our case still to be called. The court went into recess, and in the company of one of the fiscals I was acquainted with, I went for a snack in a cafeteria just round from the Sheriff court. There, already seated was the Algerian, accompanied by a police constable. We sat ourselves at an adjacent table, and I began to exchange pleasantries with the accused. He then told me his tale of woe.

He had gone into the pub for a quiet drink and had been accosted there by a prostitute, he said. He had rebuffed her advances, whereupon she had started yelling and swearing at him. He had thought it best to leave, finished his drink and went out into the street. Three men followed him out, and as best as he could understand, for his minute command of English was not up to deciphering the Glasgow accent of his confronters, they were demanding money from him to give to the maiden in the pub in compensation for the injured feelings she had suffered at his rebuff. He of course refused, whereupon the three set about him with fists and feet. The result was that with the aid of a blackjack he always carried in his pocket, for you never knew who you were going to meet when in a port, he had laid the three of them out stiff on the pavement. Next thing he knew two policemen had arrested him and there he was. The lunch break over, back we went into the court, where I was immediately summoned into the procurator fiscal's office. It had come to his attention, he said, that I had been talking with the prisoner. Did I not know that it was forbidden for any officer of the court, for that was what I was when acting as interpreter, to have conversation with a prisoner? No, I didn't, and steeled myself for what was to come. What did you speak about? he asked. I repeated the conversation to him. Did you believe him? asked the fiscal. Yes, was my answer, and went on to say that the Algerian seemed a decent enough type, adding that we all knew what Gallowgate pubs were like. The fiscal looked at me, then at his watch. 'I'm going to dismiss the case,' he said. 'We're running late enough as it is, and I don't want things to get carried on till tomorrow.' The Algerian was released. I bet he wondered why the charges against him had been dropped, for I never saw him again to explain.

Despite the many friendships I was to make amongst the Scots in the post-war years, the fact remained, and remains to this day, that the only persons with whom I could be utterly and unreservedly at ease were those Scots-Italians of my own generation who had shared in my war-time experiences. The one exception was an ex-soldier and then medical student Vernon Nurse, who came to my attention as a daily visitor to the Silver Lounge, where he sat for hours drinking interminable cups of coffee as he pored over the medical textbooks he always carried with him in a large knapsack. Vernon was a mature student who had taken up the study of medicine after having seen active service in North Africa and in the Italian campaigns. There he had acquired a working knowledge of the language and had grown to love the country and its people. We shared a love of art and of music, and enjoyed the cut and thrust of debate on a variety of subjects, on many of which we shared diametrically opposed views. In the same way that I did, Vernon felt himself not to be completely at home in the society in which he lived, despite the fact of a distinguished war record. His feeling of estrangement was because of the fact that he was of mixed racial parentage. His father was a Nigerian and his mother a Scot, and in an era when ethnic background could and did lead to discrimination, he felt as being in some way apart from the society into which he had been born, and he could well understand my own feelings in such matters. Sadly, his health had been badly undermined by his wartime experiences, and he died before reaching his fiftieth birthday. His death deprived me of a good friend and confidant, the first ever to have taken the place of Johnny Clapperton in my esteem. Vernon's wife, Mary, is still with us, and although they had no children of their own, she keeps in constant touch with my own three girls.

Having said all that, the great irony is that the person I fell in love with and with whom I chose to spend the rest of my life with in marriage, was a Scots girl who had never been out of Scotland in her life, and whose background was as different from mine as it could possibly be. I first met Mary Cameron, the girl I was to marry, in the summer of 1947. The first time as an adult, that is, for Mary, who was eight years my junior, lived in Maitland Street, just a few yards from the Savoy, and, as I was to learn, before the war as a young girl barely in her teens was a frequent customer at the carry-out section of the Savoy, where I must have served her on numerous occasions. During the war she had been evacuated for safety with other Glasgow children to a small village near Perth, and had just returned home to Maitland Street at the end of 1945.

I had met up with Dorothy Dickinson, my pre-war hearthrob, again on a couple of occasions in 1946 when the summer shows and Christmas Pantos at the Pavilion and Empire Theatres had restarted. During the war she had served with ENSA and had rejoined the Bluebell Girls dance troupe immediately after the war. Her visits to Glasgow had started once more, and although we were pleased to see one another after all those eventful years, the spark between us had gone, and although we saw one another fairly frequently and went to the pictures together on many occasions, by mutual consent there was no further mention of a closer union.

It was by pure chance that I took up with Mary Cameron. One day, as I was standing chatting with Alistair Archibald, the owner of the dairy next door, we saw two stunning looking girls approach from the top end of Hope Street. Alistair and I were whiling the time away and discussing the possibility of going off for a couple of weeks golf together. I was still driving the Jaguar used in my black-market runs and we were thinking of doing a tour of the Ayrshire golf links with it. As the girls passed by we chatted them up. They introduced themselves as Carol Hart and Mary Cameron, and the result of the ensuing banter was that our golf outing was forgotten, and some hours later the four of us found ourselves in Prestwick, enjoying a fish tea in Johnny Moscardini's Lake Café and later took a dip in the open-air pool. For no reason that I can think of now, I was paired off with Mary Cameron. She was pleasant to be with, was a quiet, unassuming person despite her good looks and I found myself drawn to her, completely at ease in her company. So much so that the proposed golfing holiday with Alistair was never thought of again, and I found myself driving to the Clyde coast resorts and going to the pictures with Mary several times in the course of my holiday. We were perfectly relaxed and at ease in one another's company, and we began seeing one another on a regular basis after my holiday had finished. Mary was now working as a salesgirl in Allan's shoe shop in Sauchiehall Street, and passed the Savoy door every day to and from her work, and would pop in just to say hello. The attraction we had for one another was growing into something much more serious as far as I was concerned, and I could sense that Mary too was beginning to regard our relationship as something much deeper than just a friendship.

I took stock and weighed up the pros and cons. Was I sure that I wanted to carry on the relationship with Mary? That road would inexorably lead on to marriage, and I could imagine the reaction of my family if I was to announce my intention of marrying a Scots girl. It was the general expectation amongst Italian families that an Italian should marry one of his or her own kind, and it was taken for granted by my own family that eventually I would do just that. There was of course no doubt as to my parents' reaction, especially mother's, had I announced my intention of taking 'una Scozzese' as a bride.

There was a further complication. As already mentioned, my brother Ralph had married an Italian girl, Theresa Nicoletti, just before the outbreak of war. Theresa had a sister, Rena, of about my age, whom I used to meet at their house on Sundays, and in view of the occasional jocular remark with serious undertones made at these gatherings, I had the distinct impression that it was expected that I might be drawn to Ralph's sister-in-law Rena, thus completing a cosy Nicoletti-Pieri family circle. But there was absolutely no attraction between myself and Rena; she was an attractive girl and we mixed well in company, but she was no more interested in me than I was in her.

So, to clarify things in my own mind, and to put my relationship with Mary to the test, I took off on a long holiday. I had some money in my pocket, I had no commitments, apart from my relationship with Mary, and so, having arranged with Ralph for a leave of absence from the shop, I set out on an extended holiday. My first stop was London, where many of my Camp 43 colleagues hailed from. There I stayed with Romeo Capitanio, a quiet and studious Venetian employed in the foreign trade department of a French bank, the Credit Lyonaise. We had formed a close friendship during our years in Canada, and from his home in Stockwell as a base, I visited the many London-Italians who had spent the years with us behind the wire on Ste Helene's Island. Romeo had come to Britain at the same time as I had. His father had arrived here also in 1919 with a wife and two children in tow, but with one great difference. His father was not an immigrant devoid of skills and with only the strength of his back to rely on for work. Romeo senior was a skilled stonemason, a monumental sculptor, and his skills were much in demand in the building boom which London was under-going in the post-First World War period. His work is still to be seen in the London of the present day on buildings which survived the German bombings of the Hitler war. There are numerous financial institutions in Lombard Street, the financial centre of London, still housed in traditional buildings whose portals are supported by giant stone figures of mythology. These monumental statues are all the work of Capitanio senior, executed in a workshop set up by him on his arrival in London. He had seen to it that his family should receive the best education he could afford and had had the satisfaction of seeing his son gradu-ate from university with a BSc two years before the outbreak of war. Then, for no apparent reason, without the slightest hint of any prior illness or depression, without a note to his family to explain his action, Romeo senior hanged himself from the rafters of his workshop. Romeo spoke to me of his father's life and death on many occasions. The manner of his parent's death had left a scar on his soul. However, Romeo also had no family commitments, and it was not difficult to persuade him to seek leave of absence from his bank and to accompany me on a tour of Italy, a tour which was to last several months.

The only advisable means of travel in Europe in 1947 was by train. We did consider the use of a car, but quickly came to the conclusion that, given the unreliability of the cars available in the immediate post-war era and the unknown condition of roads and services in a Europe devastated by war, the train was the best available option. However, even on the railway, travel was erratic and slow, and timetables very seldom adhered to. Almost the entire rail network of France and Italy had been destroyed during the war and was in the process of being restored. Travel through France was not too difficult, for the bulk of the fighting had taken place in the northern and central part of the country, with the routes to the south and to Italy via Switzerland relatively untouched, but in Italy chaos still ruled. There the main railway lines running north and south the length of the peninsula had been literally bombed out of existence. There was nothing left to repair. A whole new railway network was in the process of be-ing built, with track being laid along the side of the old bombed-out network, with new stations appearing by the side of the rubble which marked the sites where the old ones had stood. The awesome power and destructive capacity of the Allied bombing was to be seen as the train crawled through what had been the city of Bolsano, just south of the Brenner Pass. There was not a building left standing there, just shapeless heaps of debris to mark the spot where a handsome city had once stood.

We eventually reached our destination: Rome. There was no bomb dam-age to the city there. Only the railway marshalling yards had been destroyed, and a brand new structure of stainless steel, marble and glass had arisen on the bombed-out ruins of the old Stazione Termini. We stayed in Rome for a full month and saw the city in the best conditions possible. There was virtually no motor traffic. There were no tourists. There were just the citizens of Rome go-ing about their daily business, and we had all the time in the world to saunter through what must be the most enthralling city in the world. Layer upon layer of history lies there. The Roman Forum, the Palatine Hill, the Coliseum, the Arch of Constantine, the Arch of Titus, the Temple of Vesta, the Basilica of Maxentius, the Baths of Caracalla, the Appian Way, the Tiber, where Horatius defended the bridge against the Etruscans, the Catacombs, where Christians lay in hiding during the reign of Nero. Then on to see the great monuments of Christianity, St Peter's Cathedral with its massive dome by Michelangelo, and the same artist's Sistine Chapel frescoes. We stood in wonder to admire his in-credible Pieta, the Descent from the Cross, executed by the artist when still in his early twenties. We visited the protestant cemetery where Keats and Shelley lie buried in the shadow of the Caius Cestius Pyramid, and later we stood for a long time marvelling at what must be the most beautifully proportioned church in Christendom, St Paul's outside the walls. We sat on a pew in the church of Quo Vadis on the Appian Way, where legend has it that Jesus appeared to St Peter as the apostle was fleeing from Rome, and only a few yards away visited the emotionally charged Ardeatine Caves in the newly built mausoleum, where the bodies of the 335 hostages shot by the Nazis lay buried. We stood and marvelled inside the Pantheon and strolled in the spray of the fountains of the Villa D'Este and walked for miles alongside the ruins flanking the old Appian Way.

I steeped myself in the atmosphere of the Rome I had heard so much about during my stay in the 'Little Italy' of camp 43, and fell in love with the diversity of this city on the Tiber, which two thousand years ago ruled almost the whole of the then known world and whose laws and language and religion was to shape the continent of Europe.

Romeo and I then did a grand tour of all of the major cities north of Rome. We spent weeks in Florence, where we admired Benvenuto Cellini's *Perseus* and gaped in awe at Michelangelo's *David*. In the Florence Cathedral we saw Michelangelo's last work, *A Pieta*, sculpted by the artist just a few months before his death at the age of ninety-two. We stood on the Ponte Vecchio, the only bridge left untouched over the river Arno by the retreating Germans. The story is that Kesselring, the German general in command in Italy, was an art lover, and while he blew up every other bridge over the Arno, left the Ponte Vecchio untouched because of its historic and artistic value. However, so as to block the Allies' advance, all the buildings on the north and south of the bridge were dynamited, effectively sealing off the bridge at both ends. We left Florence to spend some time in Venice, where Romeo's uncle Gino, a glass blower who worked on the island of Murano, took charge of us in exploring the canals and backwaters of La Serenissima and the majestic rooms and paintings of the Doge's Palace. We spent a day with him at his glassworks in Murano where he had worked all his life, and where the rumbling roar of the white-hot furnaces somehow reminded me of the Dixon's Blazes in the Surrey Street of my childhood. We watched as he plunged a steel pipe into the white-hot embers and waited until the metal itself glowed white with an intense heat. Then, with a quick and graceful movement, he plunged the pipe into a nearby vat of molten glass, turning it over and over until a desired vase-shaped lump of molten glass adhered to it. He let it cool slightly, then with his other hand he dipped a series of white-hot steel pipes into vats of molten glass of various colours, all to be added to his original shape in a series of swirling patterns and designs, creating a work of grace and colourful beauty.

Romeo and I then went north to Merano, a German speaking town in the extreme north of Italy in the shadow of the Dolomites. That particular area had not suffered during the war, and to walk through the prosperous and well-kept streets of the town with its elegant shops and coffee houses was in stark contrast to the destruction we had seen in the rest of the peninsula. From Merano we went on to Trafoi, on the road to the Stelvio pass, which was still blocked by snow, even though we were well into a warm month of May. The roads there were still patrolled by Allied troops on the lookout for nazi and fascist collaborators who had taken to the mountains to evade capture. Then on to Milan, Turin and the Lakes, and a glorious week on Gardone Riviera, where we walked for hours in and around Gabriele D'Annunzio's villa Il Vittoriale degli Italiani, the home and showpiece of one of the most flamboyant figures of the early years of the Italian nation. D'Annunzio was a soldier, an aviator and a poet with three major claims to fame. He was the first pilot to bomb an enemy city, not with high explosives, but with pamphlets which he unloaded over Vienna in the early days of the First World War. His second exploit was the hoisting of the Italian flag over the town of Pola in protest at what he called the betrayal of Italy by the 1919 Treaty of Versailles. This he did by sailing a destroyer into the port of Pola and by capturing the Town Hall and declaring the Pola peninsula to be part of Italy. His third claim to fame was the notorious love affair he had with a belle of the day, the actress Eleonora Duse. He proceeded to write an erotic poem about the affair, which so shamed the woman that she retired to spend the rest of her days in seclusion. Which just goes to show how values have changed over the years. Such an event nowadays would open to her the gates of world-wide fame and acclaim through television and the media. On the coming to power of Mussolini, the Pola incident became the stuff of fascist legend, and D'Annunzio was given his showpiece home in Gardone as a gift from a grateful nation. The destroyer used in the Pola exploit was dismantled and rebuilt in the gardens of the *Vittoriale*, the name given to D'Annunzio's new home, where it stands to this day as a tourist attraction.

However, even during this holiday, with so many new places to see and things to do, there was a nagging void within me. I missed the company of Mary Cameron more than I would have thought possible, and so, when my money finally ran out and I had to return to my work place behind the counter at the Savoy, I did so with a firm purpose.

❧ 9 ❧
Marriage

On my return I wasted no time in knocking at Mary's door and I heaved a sigh of relief when she told me that she had missed me as much as I had missed her. Over an ice-cream at the local café, the Luxor in Cambridge Street, I proposed that we marry and then prepared for the storms to come from family quarters. I was not disappointed. First there was a frigid silence, then a torrent of objections. Why did I not marry a good Italian girl? Nothing good could come from marrying a Scozzese, etc. etc., and mother, God bless her, started to say the rosary frantically to save me from perdition, but father, who had kept a frowning silence through it all, later in private slapped me on the back and told me to marry whomever I pleased.

Despite all objections, Mary was my choice, and marry we did, two years later in April 1950. I was after all more than thirty years of age, and my family must have realised that, apart from stating their opinion, they could no longer influence me in such decisions. We married in St Aloysius church in Garnethill, and our best man was Francy Traynor, my good friend from our days in Butter-biggins Road. Mary Kane, my wife's cousin, was best maid. The wedding was a quiet one, with no Italian guests, a fact which speaks for itself. Mary Kane, who in a few years time was to become Mrs James McLernon, has remained a lifelong friend.

Our honeymoon was a repeat of the journey I had made in Italy two years before with Romeo Capitanio. After a three day train journey we arrived in Rome, and to a girl who had never been south of Prestwick the experience was entrancing. However, our honeymoon visit to Rome started off with a somewhat disconcerting event, and although I shall always remember it as something of an adventure, it did not have the happy connotations of the rest of our stay there. We were married on 27 April 1950, and although we had left Glasgow imme-diately after the ceremony, we did not arrive in Rome until the evening of the 29th, for a trip of that nature fifty-five years ago required four changes of train, not to mention a Channel crossing by ferry. On the taxi ride from the Termini station to our hotel, the Anglo-Americano in Via Quattro Fontane, opposite what was then the Scots College building, I had noticed that many of the side streets were barricaded off. On enquiring of our driver we were informed that the annual May Day parade was to take place in Rome on the first of May, and that many of the streets had been closed to all traffic so as to make the job of the police in controlling the procession easier. It has to be remembered that in those immediate post-war days in Italy, the country was on the verge of being taken over by the communists. With the smashing of the fascists and the end of the Mussolini dictatorship, the simmering socialism that had lain for decades under the surface of the political scene in Italy had come to the boil. Togliatti, the leader of the Communists, had returned from his twenty year exile in Moscow, and his Communists were now by far the largest single political party in Italy. What the consequences would have been for the rest of Europe if Italy had fallen under the control of a Communist dictatorship, God only knows, for all of Europe was in a state of ruin and political turmoil after the war, and in those Stalinist days, at the beginning of the cold war, America and Britain might have been faced with a Communist threat from the continent, to replace the Fascist one which had just been defeated. So all the right wing forces in Italy had joined together to meet the new threat. Elections were about to be held. The Church had created special groups of priests skilled in debate whose mission it was to go round the country to engage the local communist leaders in open political debate, and to put more pressure on voters; excommunication was threatened to those who voted communist; all political gatherings and processions were banned and riot police in military uniform patrolled the streets in strength, ready to put down any disturbance which might occur because of these draconian measures. The police, all mounted on military vehicles, heavily armed and in combat uniform complete with steel helmets, were led by the famous, or infamous, depending on which side of the political fence one sat, Colonel Scelba, who during the war had led the notorious Ariete division, and who, under Mussolini's orders, had been ruthless in Sicily in the extirpation of the Mafia.

One procession which the Government had thought it wise not to ban, for such an order would certainly have been followed by riots and by an immediate uprising of all the workers in the country, was the traditional May Day parade in Rome, when workers from all over Italy, including tens of thousands of peasants from the surrounding countryside, converged on the city to take part in the march and to listen to Togliatti in the Piazza del Popolo. Their enthusiasm was all the greater since all such parades had been banned during the years of the fascist regime, and the workers were determined to make full use of their new found freedom.

So early on that beautiful sunny morning of the first of May, Mary and I stepped out of our hotel and proceeded to walk along the pavements of Via Nazionale. The procession had started, and tens of thousands of workers, all waving red flags emblazoned with the hammer and sickle motif, were marching in the middle of the street, shouting communist slogans and singing snatches of *L'Internazionale*, the communist hymn. The pavements were lined with riot police wearing body armour, all armed to the teeth and wielding heavy batons, with which they pushed back any marchers who tried to break ranks and walk on the pavement. Some did so, however, and two stalwart looking peasant girls ran up to Mary and me shouting *'Camerati, venite con Noi'* (comrades, come with us) and placed red flower garlands round our necks. They were roughly manhandled and pushed back into the body of the procession by police, who began to throw us dark and suspicious looks. We hurriedly tore the garlands off and threw them away, only to have the same process repeated by girls breaking out of a different section of the marchers. This time the police did not just look, they themselves removed the garlands from our necks and asked with menace *'Siete Comunisti Voi?'* (Are you two communists?) We disclaimed all connection with the party. We were two honeymooners just arrived in Rome and had nothing to do with politics, and Mary offered her passport as proof.

'Then what are you doing wearing the colour of communism?' asked one, and pointed to the red bordered T-shirts we were both wearing.

'Don't you know that only a communist would wear that colour today? Better take them off if you don't want any trouble.'

Suddenly apprehensive, we took refuge in a nearby café, where the offending garments were taken off and thrown into a dustbin. Minus the T-shirts, our attire must have looked a bit unconventional, but at least no more garlands were thrown our way and we were no longer running the risk of having our heads cracked open by a police baton. With the exception of that somewhat disconcerting beginning, the rest of our stay in Rome was as perfect as we had imagined it would be.

We did all the things that tourists are expected to do in Rome; more or less the same things I had done with Romeo some two years earlier. Only two things had changed since then. There was more traffic in the streets and a handful of foreign tourists, mainly from the USA, were beginning to make an appearance. We browsed through the Vatican museum, with its corridors lined with statues of antiquity, Greek and Roman, and stopped to read the inscription under the massive head of the emperor Hadrian, parts of whose wall still stand at the border of Scotland and England. The words are attributed to Hadrian as he lay on his deathbed:

> *Ephemeral soul of mine, guest and friend of this body,*
> *say whither now wilt thou fare, pallid and rigid and bare,*
> *with the game now at an end?*

Which seem strange words to have been uttered by a pagan who ought to have known nothing about the Christian concept of 'soul'.

We threw coins into the Trevi fountain to ensure our return to Rome, and fearfully put our hand into the gaping mouth of *Bocca della Verita*, 'The Mouth of Truth' effigy close by the Temple of Venus, where, so the story goes, the truth of a person's declaration could be tested. He or she would be made to put an arm into the effigy's mouth. If the arm came out with the hand cut off at the wrist, then that was proof that the person had lied. If the arm came out untouched, then that was proof of that person's veracity. Even in the twentieth century, when you knew full well that no gladius-wielding soldier was stationed behind the effigy, ready on order to cut off your hand at the wrist, it was with a tinge of apprehension that one plunged one's arm into the dark recess of the statue's mouth.

We prowled the dark passages of the Castel Sant'Angelo with its centuries of memories and I thought of Benvenuto Cellini, charged with the defence of the fortress against the Spanish by Pope Clement, who, as payment for the artist-warrior's services, offered him absolution for all his sins, past and present, and any he might commit in the future! We visited the church of Trinita'dei Monti, in whose grounds and gardens Galileo had been confined by the Pope until he recanted his heretical astronomical theories, and where he had been visited by Milton, who later was to write the words:

> *Where Galileo, less assured, observes*
> *imagined lands and regions in the moon*

We stood awe-struck at the size and majesty of St Peter's. How could the hands of man, with the comparatively simple tools at their disposal, have built such an edifice? We lay on our backs in the Sistine chapel (unimaginable now, given the crowds who nowadays crush into the little space) to marvel at Michelangelo's ceiling. We gazed incredulously at the magnificence of the Villa Borghese and its priceless works of art. We walked the streets of Rome marvelling at the diversity of its fountains, and sat for hours on the Pincio hill seeking out the landmarks of the city below. We rested and ate deliciously prepared fettuccine in unpretentious trattorie far from the tourist centres, and washed them down with sips of a cool and refreshing *Vino Deli Castelli*. At night we sat at the cafés on the Via Veneto, where the price of a coffee or a drink could have bought two full meals and all the wine you could consume at the above mentioned trattorie, a price, however, which allowed you to sit at a table as long as you wanted to watch the world go by. I have another memory of Rome. One night before taking a seat at a pavement table of a Via Veneto café, Doney's, if I remember the name correctly, I bought a copy of *Time* magazine from a street kiosk, and sat leafing through the pages as we awaited the arrival of our order. I looked at the front page, which each week carried the photograph of some noted personage. I looked at it again, then nudged Mary, who in turn glanced at the cover, then lifted her glance to follow my discreetly pointing finger. She gave a squeak of recognition, for two tables away there sat the person depicted on the cover of *Time* magazine. We tried not to look, but the object of our attention had become aware of our interest. He stood up, came over and said in a thickly accented Italian-American accent.

'You recognise my picture? Where are you folks from?'

I explained, and he laughed with a childish pleasure at having been recognised. He called the waiter over.

'*Una bottiglia di ciampagna per gli sposi*' (A bottle of champagne for the honeymooners), and Lucky Luciano, the subject of that week's *Time* cover story, toasted us with a glass of champagne and left. The article featured the story of the New York gangster's services to the American government from his cell in Sing-Sing prison where he was serving a life sentence for murder. In exchange for his freedom he supplied the Americans with a list of all his Mafia connections in Sicily, all of whom had been arrested by Mussolini and exiled to the Lipari islands in his attempt to crush the Mafia. Most of those arrested had spent some time in America, all were anti-Fascist, all spoke English, and on the invasion of Sicily by the Allies they were freed and put into political positions of importance throughout the island. Thus was the Sicilian Mafia returned to their seats of power, stronger and more deeply entrenched than ever. Lucky Luciano's freedom had not been without conditions, however. One of these was that he be deported to his native Italy, where the Italian government refused to allow him to return to his home in Sicily, and confined him to the Rome-Naples area. In 1962 he was to die of a heart attack in a street in Naples.

An added attraction had been added to the many already on offer to the tourists who were beginning to appear in small numbers as the railway system, bombed out of existence during the war, was getting back to normal. In what perhaps is the most impressive site in all Rome, in the ruins of the old Roman Forum and the Palatine, historic sites which give some small idea of the majesty of ancient Rome, we were spectators at an unforgettable spectacle. A 'Son et Lumiere' was being staged every night there, with the commentary on alternate nights in English and delivered by Orson Welles. Bench seats which could seat many hundreds of spectators had been unobtrusively placed on the Palatine Hill overlooking the Forum, and from there we were treated to one of the most enthralling sights and sounds I have ever experienced. To the accompaniment of appropriate music and sound effects, searchlights of varying colours played over the ruins of the ancient city as Orson Welles intoned the history and legend of each selected backdrop. From the site where Romulus and Remus were suckled by the she-wolf to the steps of the Senate where Mark Anthony had delivered his oration over the dead body of Julius Caesar, spotlights illuminated the majestic ruins, and dramatic music and sound filled the warm Roman night air as Welles, in his magnificent baritone voice, recited the apposite words:

> *Lars Porsena of Clusium, by the nine Gods he swore, that the proud*
> *house of Tarquin would suffer wrong no more—*

To be followed by the sounds of clashing swords, the noise of battle, and the shouts of soldiers as Horatius defended the bridge over the Tiber. Then the words of Mark Anthony over the dead body of Julius Caesar as magnificently imagined by Shakespeare:

> *Friends, Romans, countrymen, lend me your ears,*
> *I come to bury Caesar, not to praise him.*

The 'Son et Lumiere' presentation with the voice of Orson Welles in the heart of the Roman Forum was an experience which will forever stay with me, as it did with Mary during her lifetime. After the spectacle, which lasted until well after midnight, in the warm velvet air of a Roman night, we walked through the ghostly remains of the great buildings, arches and temples of the Forum and Palatine, sat in the midst of the towering ruins of the Baths of Caracalla and watched the same stars that had shone down on the great figures of Roman antiquity.

On our twernty-fifth wedding anniversary in 1975 we decided to repeat our honeymoon trip. In Rome we stayed at the same hotel as we had in 1950, and were greeted by the same familiar sights. The 'Son et Lumiere' was no longer being staged, but after a late dinner we decided once again to take a midnight stroll through the ruins of the Forum. We walked towards the Arch of Constantine from Piazza Venezia, and as we went to cross the road into the entrance to the Palatine we were stopped by a cruising police motor patrol. We were asked politely what our intentions were at that time of night. We explained, to be met with the reply:

'Non e' da consigliare. Di notte c'e' troppa malavita in giro per le rovine. E'meglio ritornare in albergo.' (That's not advisable. Too many criminals loose in those ruins at night. It's better that you go back to your hotel.)

How Rome had changed in the course of twenty five years! In 1950, still suffering from the deprivations of a destructive war, Rome, despite the relative poverty of its inhabitants, was a city where one could walk the streets at night in safety. In 1975, despite the affluence visible on all sides, but probably because of that same affluence, the streets of the city were no longer safe.

From Rome we travelled north to Venice, where we arrived at the railway station early one foggy morning. Venice is a beautiful city when seen in the proper light of day. Seen for the first time on a foggy, dank and gloomy morning it bears every resemblance to the setting for a horror movie, and Mary clung on to me apprehensively as we awaited the arrival of a vaporetto to take us down the Grand Canal and across the Lagoon to the Lido. It was cold as well as being foggy, and since the first vaporetto was not due to leave for another hour or so, I hailed a workmans' barge which was about to set off down the Grand Canal.

'*Buon giorno, Siamo in luna di miele.*'

We were on our honeymoon, I said to no one in particular amongst the swarthy boatmen and workmen.

'*Andate per caso al Lido?*' Were they by any chance going to the Lido?

They were, was the answer. Could they give us a lift? My new bride was cold and hungry and we wanted to get to our hotel as quickly as possible.

'*Ma certo, venite, venite*', and we set off down the Grand Canal with the grey ghostly shadows of Palazzi on either side barely visible through the morning fog and with the Rialto bridge seemingly suspended in the mist over the grey waters as we passed under it. The atmosphere was rendered all the more sinister by the pirate-like appearance of the barge's swarthy passengers, some of whom sported rings dangling from pierced earlobes. Their dialect was incomprehensible as they chattered and joked amongst themselves, chewing on their breakfast of bread and cheese, washed down with an occasional swig from the wine bottle each one carried hooked to the back of their belts and which was offered to us, and politely refused, each time it was uncorked. At last we arrived at the Lido, with Mary very subdued and wondering as to what watery slum I was bringing her. I produced a half-bottle of whisky for the boatmen as a token of our thanks for the ride and carried on into our hotel, followed by a few ribald jokes and friendly hoots of encouragement from our fellow passengers. As the day wore on the sun dispersed the mist, and the full magnificence of Venice was revealed for Mary to admire. Piazza San Marco, the Doges Palace, the Bridge of Sighs, the Rialto, Santa Maria della Salute, all were explored and their beauty marvelled at. Tearful on her arrival because of the strangeness and bleakness of the scene, Mary was tearful at our departure, but for a different reason. She cried because of leaving so much beauty behind her.

Our next stop was a visit to my birthplace, Bacchionero, and there Mary was subjected to a culture shock, the same culture shock in reverse that Italian immigrants to Glasgow must have endured on their arrival there. Bacchionero was deserted. No-one lived there now. Some of my male cousins had been killed during the war, all of my female ones had married and now lived in Lucca, so we stayed with my Aunt Rosa in the mill-house Carletti, where the family still eked out an existence and were making plans to emigrate to France. Mary had never seen the likes of these crofts set high in the Tuscan hills, devoid of any of the amenities that a Glasgow dweller, even in the poverty-stricken pre-war days, would have regarded as essential for living. No running water, no toilets, just an outside barn with a wooden plank with a hole in it and a manure pit underneath, always buzzing with an assortment of bees and insects and redolent of a ripe unaired cowshed. To wash in we had an enamel basin with a water jug which we filled with ice-cold water from a nearby spring. We were given the best room in the house, with a huge bed and straw mattress. Under the bed was the mandatory chamber pot to be used during the night in an emergency. In the years before the war my parents used to make up parcels of old clothes and such-like luxuries to send back home, and these parcels would be made up with a unique wrapping. In our Savoy we used a special flour, 'King's Own' to make the batter for fish frying. The flour came in linen sacks, which mother washed thoroughly and then used as packaging for the gifts to be sent back to her relations. In Bacchionero the women of the house kept the sacks, bleached out the 'King's Own' lettering and made bedsheets from the material. It was in between such sheets that Mary and I slept during our fortnight's stay in Carletti, and it must, in all truth, be said that no hotel bed was ever more comfortable than the one we were offered in my aunt's house. The mill house now boasted of an amenity unheard of in those remote hills: electricity. This was generated from the dynamo of a German jeep ambushed by partisans in the late years of the war, which had been fixed to the mill wheel and turned by the water of the stream flowing under the house, thus generating enough electricity to illuminate a few low wattage light bulbs. But the warmth of our welcome more than compensated for the lack of amenities. We were greeted with open arms, and my aunt and cousins clapped their hands and cooed with delight at the sight of my new bride from the far and distant land of Scotland who had managed the arduous trek up from Barga and who could speak and understand Italian, for Mary during our two year courtship had taken Italian lessons at evening classes for mature students held at one of the Glasgow colleges. I could not but wonder at the difference of outlooks between the Italians who had emigrated to places such as Glasgow and their relations who had stayed behind. Here in Carletti, all my relations were genuinely delighted that their cousin Giuseppe had married *'una signorina Scozzese'*, whereas back in Glasgow my immediate family and friends all had their reservations if not downright hostility about the union. However, with the passing of time Mary was to be accepted into the family unreservedly by my parents. She was a loveable and friendly girl who did her best to fit into the culture of her marriage, and after a time both my parents found her *'molto simpatica'* and were to become genuinely fond of her.

On our return to Glasgow we set up home in a tiny so-called 'utility' house at the top end of Kessington Road in Bearsden. These houses were so named because work on them had been started before 1940 and had their construction interrupted by the outbreak of war. Work was resumed in 1946, but because of the lack of building materials the finished article had to be of a certain 'Utility' standard. This meant that our little semi-detached bungalow had dormer windows and a floored loft with the same area as that of the ground floor accommodation, but no stairs leading up to it. This, and any rooms required upstairs, had to be put in by the buyer. The price of the house, a three room semi-detached bungalow with kitchen, was £1200 pounds. To give an idea of my finances at the time, to obtain a deposit on a building society loan I had to sell my car of the moment, a ten year old Austin eight, on which I realised the princely sum of £200, enough for the deposit on a loan from the building society with a few pounds left over for furnishings and curtains. In the months to come I was to put the finishing touches to our new home, but given the impossibility of obtaining wood and other materials, I had to resort to some rather unorthodox solutions in the building of the upstairs rooms The upstairs partition walls were built with the wooden boards on which cakes and bread were delivered to our Savoy, the return of which to our supplier I frequently overlooked. The stairs leading up to the floored loft were built by a proper joiner from heavy floorboards we had ripped up from tenement house floors during one of our many expansions of the Savoy into adjacent houses. The joiner was a man called Duncan (I forget his second name) who had a little joinery business in Cathedral Street, and who did all our odd jobs in the shop. In those pre-town planning days you could alter the interior of any property owned by you and use it for any purpose you desired, without bothering to consult the local authority. I also used some of those heavy floorboards in the construction of a garage in anticipation of the day when I could once more afford to buy a car.

The floorboards left over from the erection of the staircase, however, had a rather strange and unique embellishment. Fused into the wood were the fossilised skeletons of the hundreds of rats which over the years had used the space between the wooden flooring of the ground floor tenement flats and the earth beneath as a dying ground. Duncan tried to chip away the fused bones, which formed a rather pretty herring-bone pattern on the wood, but that was a slow and time-consuming process, so, having cleaned up enough of these boards to build the stairs we came to a somewhat unorthodox solution as far as the building of the garage was concerned. The garage was built with the herring-bone pattern facing outwards and then painted over, to give a rather pretty and unusual appearance to the outside walls of the structure. Visitors and neighbours would ask as to how I had managed to create the attractive plastic paint herring-bone pattern on the outside walls of the garage! I kid you not. At the back of our old house in Kessington Road there is still a little public park which I occasionally visit when taken by nostalgia. I pause sometimes at the railings at the back of our old garden to admire the sturdy garage at the side of the house. The colour of the paint has changed since my day, fifty-five years ago now, but a distinct and rather attractive herring-bone pattern still enhances the appearance of the structure. I am sure that the feature adds somewhat to the value of the house.

With the increased responsibilities that come with fatherhood I thought it wise to begin thinking about taking out some life insurance. In the early years of the family I had no assets worth mentioning that would have been of value to Mary and the children, so I attempted to take out a fairly large insurance policy on my life, £5000 or so, which is nothing in today's terms, but quite large by the values of the 1950s. I completed the necessary forms, and was asked to produce proof of my age, which at that time was about thirty-three. The obvious document would have been a birth certificate, but I did not have one, and the insurance company concerned would accept nothing else. My Aliens registration book and Italian passport were the only official documents I had on which my date of birth, 6/1/19, was registered, but these were not acceptable to the insurance company as proof of age. Only a birth certificate would satisfy them.

Given the chaos which still reigned in the various regions of Italy just a few years after the destruction of the war, and given the high standard of inefficiency and apathy of the Italian civil services in general, and of the consular services in particular, the consul in Glasgow could or would do nothing for me. So I wrote to Aldo Nardini of Lucca, a great friend of my father, who was in charge of a department in the Lucca town council, the *Ufficio di Protocollo*, a department which dealt with the issuing of pensions. During the war Nardini had served on the Yugoslav front and also for some weeks in Russia, and bore a deep scar on his back as the souvenir of a grenade attack by a Russian guerrilla. On the collapse of the Axis armies there and on the fall of Mussolini he had made his way back to Lucca on foot, a journey which had taken him the best part of four months, given that he and his companion, also from Lucca, could travel only by night for fear of being arrested as deserters and shot. Aldo was a kindly man and had achieved great popularity in the Lucca area amongst the elderly residents there because of the help he had given them in the procurement of documents to substantiate their pension claims. In a land which had been devastated by a war, such documents in many cases had been destroyed, and Aldo Nardini would simply issue new ones based on the claimant's own affidavits. He was very elastic in his evaluation of a person's claims, and it was said that no applicant had ever been turned away or come out the poorer from a visit to Aldo's office.

I explained my problem and asked for his help. All this was done by letter since it was next to impossible to get a telephone connection to Italy then. Some weeks later I received his answer. I had been born in the district of Barga, which in itself came under the jurisdiction of Lucca. Unfortunately the county buildings in Lucca had been bombed out of existence during the war and all birth certificates relating to that area had been destroyed. He had gone to the little church in Bacchionero in the hope of tracing a certificate of baptism, but had found nothing there, the place was abandoned and going to ruin. Effectively, there were no documents of any kind in existence anywhere relating to my birth. However, that was his job, the issuing of new documents of such a nature. What age would I like to have put on a new birth certificate, he asked me. He could arrange for any age to be put on any document, so now was my chance to pick any age I wanted to be! Plus or minus five or ten years? I had just to say the word and I could have had any date of birth I wanted! Although I thought about it for a while, I could see no material advantage in asking for any other age than that which I actually was, or, given the lack of an official document, the day I had always been told was my birthday, 6 January 1919, and in due time a birth certificate with that date on it was produced to the satisfaction of the Insurance company. Perhaps in retrospect I could have saved on a few insurance premiums by making myself younger than I actually was, or gained my old age pension before the time by declaring myself older, but such thoughts did not occur to me at the time, nor, I suppose, would I have acted any differently if they had.

Another problem kept ticking over in the back of my mind. Here was I, an Italian subject who until not so very long ago had been classified as an enemy alien and had been imprisoned because of my nationality, now married to a Scottish girl and on the verge of raising a family. The world was still a very un-settled place. The Cold war between the West and Soviet Russia was a fact of life, and Italy was teetering on the verge of electing a communist government. The Korean War was raging between north and south Korea, with America and China heavily involved. What if a real war were to break out between East and West? In the event of such a war what would Italy's position be? Would I once more see myself labelled 'enemy alien' and again forced to look at the world from behind barbed wire? What would happen to Mary and any possible future family? These thoughts troubled me, and I turned to a new-found friend for advice. Tom Mullins was a local authority worker in the field of pensions, and he and his sister Del, a school inspector, had become regular customers in our new Silver Lounge. We had become quite friendly, to the extent that in a few years time they would become Godparents to our as yet to be born son, Lorenzo, and since Tom had many political connections in the local Labour party, I thought he might be of help in my problem. He listened and introduced me to a friend, Alice Cullen, Labour MP for the Gorbals district, who was already beginning to make the headlines as a castigator of the Conservative party and as a highly vocal campaigner for social equality and justice in the community.

I explained my problem: born in Italy, lived in Glasgow all my life; had taken no interest in politics, but had been arrested on the night of Mussolini's declara-tion of war and had spent three years in a Canadian POW camp as an internee. I produced my Aliens passbook which had to be stamped by the local police each time I changed employment or status or travelled outwith the district, and voiced my fears about the future to her. With the war so recently over and with the memories of it still fresh in everyone's mind did she think the time propitious for me to apply for British Nationality? I must confess that before approaching Tom Mullins I had thought very long and very hard about such a move. Most persons are introspective, I think, to a greater or lesser degree. I know that I am, and I believe that I know my weaknesses and faults. They are many, but I do not think that hypocrisy is one of them. If my circumstances and responsibilities had not changed I don't think I would have given a second thought to the question of naturalisation. Such a move would have entailed making all sorts of declarations, loyalty and allegiance to the King, for example, and Royalty was an institution I cared about not one jot. I lived here, I earned my living here, but that living was earned through my own efforts. I had been born to an Italian father and mother in Italy and the language learned at her knee was Italian. In my childhood and youth I had been subjected to insults and slights because of my background, and also because of my Italian heritage I had spent three years behind barbed wire. Now to ask for the privilege of waving a flag because of expediency was indeed hypocritical, but I had to think of my duties to Mary and any possible future family. I did not voice these reservations to Alice Cullen, of course. I simply asked her if she could investigate the possible naturalisation of a former enemy alien so soon after the war.

Some weeks later I sat in front of her desk in the local constituency office. She had a few notes before her. Was it true, she asked, that I had helped organise a mutiny in the camp? Was it true that I had attempted to help two other prisoners in an escape attempt? Was it true that I was somewhat of a thorn in the side of the camp authorities by my constant quoting of the Geneva Convention to them?

I sheepishly had to answer in the affirmative to all her questions. But it's not as bad as it sounds, I said to her. The mutiny, which had lasted all of three days, had consisted of all the prisoners refusing to do any kind of work until their grievances were addressed. The first complaint was that in winter we were being made to stand at attention in the compound for long periods to be counted at roll call, sometimes as long as half an hour in temperatures of as low as minus ten or minus fifteen degrees. The second complaint was that we were not allowed access to outside news, which was contrary to one of the articles of the Geneva Convention. The third complaint was that the letters arriving at the camp from our families were so heavily censored that they were not worth reading, and the fourth complaint was that all the expert chefs we had in the camp, arrested at their place of work in some of the finest hotels and restaurants in London, were working in the officer's mess, and that since they were prisoners like the rest of us they should be allowed to cook for us and not just for the Canadian officers. By chance, the so-called mutiny coincided with the visit of a group of International Red Cross officials to the camp, who listened to our grievances and took them up in our favour with the Camp authorities. The escape thing was maybe a bit more difficult to gloss over, although there is nothing in the Geneva Convention which states that prisoners should not attempt to escape from their captivity.

During the summer a small workshop had been erected at the far end of the compound for the purpose of packing Red Cross bandages into large wooden crates for shipment to Halifax. These crates were made by the prisoners in an outside workshop. The bandages were delivered by van to the workshop each week and once a week, always in the afternoon, four or five filled crates were taken from the camp by van to the railway station, there to be loaded on to a freight train for Halifax. With this as a background, George Martinez, one of my closest friends in the camp, had drawn up a plan of escape, together with a ship's mate by the name of Festa. The plan was that on the day of the shipment of the crates, two of them would be emptied of bandages during the midday break when the workshop closed for one hour. Martinez and Festa were to take the place of the bandages, then would be loaded on to the lorry and driven out of the camp. Once on the train, the two would break out of the crates and make their way to the USA. Since the crates were handled by prisoners as far as the train, the extra weight would be ignored and the escape should go undetected until evening roll-call. The opening and unpacking of the crates, the disposal of the surplus bandages and the sealing of the crates with the men inside was to be carried out by a sailor named Lardaro, a tall, taciturn Sardinian who served as Festa's batman. But one man as helper was not enough, given the time element. Someone was needed to help Lardaro. George looked at me hopefully. I thought for a moment. Life was boring, dull and repetitive. What the hell! Why not? Anything to break the monotony. The plan was worked upon, every detail gone over and when one morning the workshop was alerted to prepare five crates for dispatch that day, the plan swung into action. That morning, under the supervision of the French-Canadian sergeant in charge of the workshop, the crates were neatly packed and labelled and on the stroke of midday the whistle blew for the noon break. The prisoners filed out and the sergeant locked the door behind him as he left. Five minutes later I opened the side door of the workshop with a duplicate set of keys and gave entry to my three companions.

Quickly the lids of two of the crates were prised open and the contents of each emptied on the floor. Martinez and Festa squatted down, one to each case and were packed in tightly with piles of bandages. A cardboard tube was placed in the vicinity of their mouths, taped to the side of the crate, and holes punched in the wood to allow for ventilation. Finally their heads were covered over with bandages and the crates lightly sealed, making it possible for them to be opened easily from inside. Apart from their weight the crates were indistinguishable from the three others awaiting the arrival of the van.

A heavy snow fall had taken place during the night before, with deep drifts piling up in the narrow space between the hut and the fortress walls, so Lardaro and I gathered up the excess bundles of bandages, with the intention of throwing them out of a rear window for burial in the snowdrift. With difficulty, we prised open the window and the bandages were shoved through the gap, which we then tried to close. But the intense cold must somehow have affected the window sashes, for strain as we might, a two-inch slit remained open and we were forced to leave the window as it was, and just managed to slip out through the side door a few seconds before the entry of the sergeant.

One by one the prisoners drifted back to their place of work and the crates moved to a position near the door ready for loading into the waiting van. The window gap had gone unnoticed by the sergeant as he busied himself issuing orders to his prisoners, nor had he seen that two of the crates required a great deal of effort on the part of the handlers. It was only when the main door had closed behind the loaded lorry that he became aware of a cold draught behind him. He looked a bit puzzled as he noticed the open window, and his curiosity increased when he saw that the snow on the sill had been disturbed. He forced the window open fully and caught sight of the piles of bandages blending into the whiteness of the snow outside. An officer was called, the prisoners were ordered to shift the crates back into the workshop, and the lids were prised open. One by one, the heads of Martinez and Festa, red and sweating from the heat in the packing cases, popped out like jack-in-the-boxes and the two were marched off under armed guard to the detention cells. The obvious question arose: who had put the men in the boxes? Despite intensive questioning the two men refused to give an answer. Our Camp Leader was summoned to the colonel's office. Unless the culprit or culprits gave themselves up, he was told, all privileges in the camp would be cancelled, the canteen would be closed and the weekly cinema show indefinitely withdrawn. This news was conveyed to the prisoners. I conferred briefly with Lardaro. There was no point in both of us going to the cells and besides, a confession from me would satisfy the military as to the manner of entry to the hut and knowledge of timetables. So the two men in the cells were joined by a third, and there we spent the next 30 days in the expiation of our sins.

Alice Cullen listened to my explanations sympathetically. However, she said, in view of all the circumstances it might be best if I waited a few more years before making an application for citizenship. Best to wait a while until attitudes changed, as change they would, rather than risk a refusal now, she advised. In the event, the years passed; I never did get round to making an application for British citizenship and I remain as I was born. My Italian nationality has never been a hindrance to me in anything I have ever undertaken, nor, as far as I know, has it ever in any way been of detriment to my family, although it might have been had any of them sought employment in any type of civil service job. I refer to the experience of Albert Risi, a long-time Scots-Italian friend. Anxious to break away from the drudgery of café work, in the early fifties he took a course at Skerry's, a further education college in Glasgow, so as to apply for a civil service job when the necessary qualifications had been obtained. His diploma acquired, on applying for a post he was informed that even though he himself was born in Britain, all government jobs, even that of a postman, were barred to him because his parents had been of Italian birth. He now gives heartfelt thanks, for he then was forced to embark on what was to be a very lucrative business career.

After a couple of years of marriage our first child, Luisa, was born and two years after that Linda appeared on the scene. The utility house in Kessington Road suddenly began to seem somewhat small, despite the utilisation of the upper floor, and since finances were much healthier, with the shops working well, we decided to look around for larger and more substantial accommodation. We found a substantial semi-detached villa in Campbell Drive in the heart of Bearsden and lived there very happily for close on ten years with our children, who by now were four in number, with the addition of a son, Lorenzo, and another daughter, Laura. Some years after our move to Campbell Drive we learned that at the time of our purchase one of our neighbours had attempted to draw up a petition amongst the residents there to prevent the property being sold to an Italian. Apart from his own, I was told, not a single signature did he get for his petition.

With the passing of the years and the growth of the family our Campbell Drive house too began to feel a little cramped, and Mary spent her days looking for bigger and better accommodation. One evening she tracked me down at one of the shops and said excitedly over the phone that she had found a dream house and that I should meet her there straight away, so that I could view the place and be introduced to the owner. The house, The Firs, was in Milngavie, at 23 Craigmillar Avenue, to be exact, in a beautiful secluded spot overlooking Tannoch Loch. As I write this, the selfsame house is up for sale, some 28 years since we last lived there. I quote from the present sales brochure:

> *The Firs is one of the most coveted properties in Milngavie. It has belonged to just a handful of families in its century long existence. Standing in extensive grounds of about an acre that include a tennis court, this house is the epitome of high Victorian prosperity. With 12 rooms, it covers 4000 square feet and is magnificently proportioned.*

I found the address, and as I drove through the wrought iron gates and up a winding drive I began to think that perhaps I had taken a wrong turning into a park, but no, as I slowly approached a large beautifully-proportioned building, there was Mary standing at the door engaged in conversation with a tiny old white-haired lady. She was introduced to me as Mrs Allan, the owner, and was invited in to view the house. We first went into the kitchen, itself bigger than any room in our present house, and there seated were our four children tucking happily into biscuits and lemonade. The rest of the house was nothing short of magnificent, but as soon as I had stepped over the threshold I had decided that such a huge mansion was not for me. Apart from the purchase price, which as yet had not been revealed to me, I was mentally calculating the running costs of such a place, the heating of it, the running repairs, although everything seemed to be in perfect condition, and the maintenance of the huge garden. Out of politeness I followed the little lady as she pointed out the various features of her home, but although I listened politely I was more interested in her paintings and collection of bronzes, some of which alone were worth more than our house in Campbell Drive. I commented on them and Mrs Allan seemed to be interested in the fact that I could identify the artist behind some of the pieces. We paused before a beautifully executed bronze head of a child. Mrs Allan commented that this was her favourite piece, that it had been in the family for many years, but that she did not know the sculptor. I had recognised it immediately as a bronze head of a child by Rodin, one of his earlier and more romantic works, and could also tell her that it was one of a batch of twenty-five made from the original mould, after which, as was the norm in casting such a work, the mould had been destroyed. Mrs Allan was impressed, and thanked me as we took our leave.

Back at our own comparatively meek and modest dwelling Mary pleaded with me: you must try and get that house, Joe. It's a dream house. It's perfect for our family. We could be very happy there. Please Joe. She went on and on and on. To please Mary, and if truth be told, to keep her quiet, I decided at least to go through the motions. There was no way I wanted to buy that house. It simply was not a practical proposition. It was completely out of my league. It was too big, it was too grand. The running costs would be too great. Mrs Allan's deceased husband had owned tea plantations in Ceylon. I was co-owner of a few fish and chip shops in Glasgow. There was no way I wanted that house. But I had to keep Mary happy, I had at least to go through the motions, so we went to consult Bob Martin, who had been well coached by me beforehand. I had not bothered to have the house surveyed, and Bob's instructions were to offer the basic asking price, £29,000, and not go one penny over. The offer went in, a week or so passed, I was beginning to forget about 'The Firs' when a phone call from Bob plunged me into the deepest gloom. Our offer had been accepted! Mary's joy was at the other end of the spectrum of my gloom as we visited our new acquisition and were greeted by Mrs Allan.

'You know, Mr Pieri, I had several offers for The Firs,' she said to me, 'all of them larger than yours, some considerably so. But money is not a consideration with me. I'm going to be living just a few yards away in The Firs Cottage across the road, and I would rather have your family for neighbours than any of the others who came to view. And I was impressed with the way you could identify my husband's pieces, especially the Rodin.' and she presented me with a little plaster replica of the *Head of a Child*.

'I've had this made for you, if you promise to keep it in exactly the same place as I kept the original.'

I thanked her, of course, but thought that a present of the original would have gone a long way to healing the scar the unwanted ownership of The Firs had left on my psyche.

However, despite all, we lived for nine glorious years in The Firs. My lifestyle had to change, however. Such a huge garden, over an acre, required a lot of attention, and for those nine years I played no golf and resigned from the Hilton Park course; the garden had taken over my spare time. In winter, in my free time from the shops, I pottered around the place. We had a garage, originally stables, which could house four cars with room to spare, and in my time away from the shops I could spend hours there messing about with cars and tools and things. I would stop my pottering occasionally to take a swig from a never far distant Chianti bottle, and would muse over the strangeness of the ways of Fate. From Surrey Street in the Gorbals, through Renfrew Street in the Cowcaddens by way of a utility house in Kessington to a tea planter's mansion in Milngavie, with Lord Fraser of Allander as a neighbour three houses up. Not that we ever fraternised!

I had not been far wrong as to the upkeep of the place. The heating bills in winter were astronomical. To spread warmth evenly throughout the house, an extra gas boiler was installed beside the oil-fired installation, and these had to be augmented in the coldest of the weather by the use of electrically heated radiators in all the rooms. The maintenance and repairs too were as expected, but here I was able to make use of our shops' handyman, Sigmund Antosik, a Polish ex-soldier whom we employed to do any repair jobs required in our premises. There was never a week passed but what the willing Sigmund would be employed in replacing roof tiles, in pointing windows and in doing all sorts of maintenance jobs. The place required as much attention as the Forth Railway Bridge, and the good Sigmund served us well in that regard. After my initial despair I never regretted the purchase of The Firs, but after nine years we were literally driven to sell and move on.

One morning, as I was driving down to the gates, I had to stop in the driveway to allow the entrance of a police car. One of the constables held a silver jug in his hand which they had found in the avenue by the side of our hedge. Mary identified it as a silver coffee jug normally kept in the main lounge. We investigated and found that the room in question had been ransacked during the night. Despite an elaborate alarm system burglars had broken in and had cleared the room of all valuables. The alarm had been circumvented by the cutting of a large panel through a window without disturbing the metal alarm strip (this was before the introduction of space alarms), and by the placing of wooden slats over the alarm mats in front of each entrance point. The burglars must have dropped the silver jug as they were making good their escape. The CID came to investigate, and we were informed that a sophisticated gang of burglars were active in that district and that their *modus operandi* was the one used in our robbery. The officers inspected the house, and were of the opinion that in view of the valuables in the rest of the rooms, the thieves probably would be back. They asked for permission to have two policemen sleep in the Firs for a few nights in case they did return, but their surveillance was fruitless. The effect that all this had on Mary can well be imagined. There were just three of us left at home; Lorenzo was at university in St Andrews, and Luisa and Linda were married and in houses of their own. Our young-est daughter Laura was the only one left. I was at the shops until midnight or so, and Mary would await my arrival fearfully, afraid even to put on the lights in case someone was watching from the bushes outside. Then ten days after the first burglary and three days after the police had withdrawn, the thieves struck again in the middle of the night. They used the same method of entry, but to a different room this time, and this time the alarm went off. As the thieves were ransacking drawers in the dining room, the loose lid of a silver coffee pot fell off and rolled on to one of the alarm mats, setting off the siren. I was jarred awake by its scream and without thinking I leapt from bed, dashed downstairs to the electric cupboard and switched the alarm off. Noting from the alarm panel that the siren had been set off by pressure on a mat in the dining room I pulled open the door to that room, and was just in time to see a pair of legs disappearing through the window. Again the police were called and again we had the same routine with the CID, who were chagrined at the fact that if their surveillance had lasted a few more days the thieves would have been caught redhanded.

Mary and I had had enough of living under siege. Four weeks later we were sleeping in a newly acquired flat in Kelvin Court in the west end of Glasgow, and The Firs, my unwanted purchase of nine years ago, was up for sale. It was months before I lost the feeling of claustrophia that flat life created in me after the space I had become used to in Milngavie.

We sold the Firs to an up-and-coming young Italian entrepreneur, who in time was to become prominent in Scottish business circles, Mario Romano, for £105,000. He sold it two years later to a Glasgow lawyer for £175,000. The Firs is now up for sale at offers over £950,000! It is said that it will probably fetch about 1.3 million. If only! But this is a silly wish, for there was no way I could have afforded the upkeep of The Firs in my retirement.

It is interesting to note that all of the homes we lived in before my retirement and our move to a flat in Lenzie were all the subject of burglaries. Our first modest home in Kessington Road was broken into the day before we were to hand over the keys to the new owners. A back window was forced open at a time when the house was empty, and the house ransacked, but since there was nothing of any value left the burglars had to make off empty-handed. I can still see the look of dismay on the faces of the new owners when they were handed the keys of their new home in the presence of two policemen who were investigating a robbery which had just taken place there! About a year or so later our second home in Campbell Drive was very skilfully and clinically burgled by thieves who knew exactly what they were looking for and how to go about getting it. In a corner of the study I had installed a fairly large safe, about two feet six inches high, and had covered it with a decorated cloth topped with a large plant. In the safe I kept all the family's private and personal documents, and at weekends I would put into the safe the Saturday takings from two of our shops, prior to banking on the Monday morning. This money, not to exceed £1000 (a fair sum in those days) was insured as 'Cash in Transit', and the insurance company had approved the make and the installation of the safe.

Every Sunday, dressed in our Sunday best, the family were given to attending eleven o'clock Mass at the newly opened St Andrews church at Bearsden Cross. On returning home from the service one Sunday, I drove up the driveway as usual, and as I opened the front door of the house, became aware of a strong draught of wind. The back door was lying ajar, almost torn from its hinges. Nothing in the house itself seemed to have been touched, but when I checked in the study a large empty space where the safe should have been confronted me. Apart from the broken door no other damage had been done and nothing else in the house had been disturbed. The burglars knew exactly what they were after, had dragged the safe on its carpet base to the back door, and there presumably had loaded it onto a van or car and made off. The safe weighed well over a hundredweight, and would have required a fair amount of strength to manoeuvre. I immediately called the police, and the CID took down all particulars as to the contents of the safe.

I made a list of all the stolen items for them, with one glaring omission. The day before the robbery, for safekeeping I had placed a German Mauser machine pistol with two clips of armour-piercing ammunition into the safe. The pistol was in pristine condition and carried Japanese markings on the butt. How could I, an ex-enemy alien who had spent three years behind the wire during the war, explain the possession of such a weapon?

The explanation was that the day before I had loaned a certain captain Laurie Nurse, late of Ord Wingate's Chindit army, the sum of twenty-five pounds, and that he had insisted that I take the Mauser, a war souvenir taken from a Japanese officer in Burma, as a deposit for the loan. Moreover, since he was bent on a night's drinking binge, he wanted to leave the pistol in a safe place. Why should I do such a thing for Captain Nurse? For the simple reason that he was Vernon Nurse's brother, the same Vernon who was such a close friend, and I had been sworn to secrecy in the matter. So I did not report the loss of the Mauser to the investigating officers. The actual robbery and my own losses did not bother me too much. I was fully insured for cash in transit, and the stolen documents and damaged door could eventually be replaced. I informed Laurie of his loss, which at first he accepted philosophically, but he too wanted no mention made of it to the police; all such weapons should have been long ago surrendered up, and there would be only trouble in store for him if the loss were reported.

But the matter bothered me more than a little. The thought that such a lethal weapon with a considerable amount of ammunition was now in the hands of criminals disturbed me. As I have mentioned elsewhere I had become very friendly with a young up-and-coming policeman from the Northern Division, by the name of Joe Beattie. I trusted Joe implicitly, so I sought him out with the full story of the robbery and of the contents of the safe. Not to worry, he said, after hearing the full story. He would see to it very discreetly that the proper people got to know about the full facts of the contents of the safe. No names, no pack drill. The next morning I was paid a very friendly and understanding visit by the inspector in charge of the investigation. With regard to the non-object which had not been in the safe at the time of the robbery, he said, could I describe to the best of my recollection what the thing looked like, and he showed me a series of photographs of German pistols. I was immediately able to identify the type which Laurie had given me for safe keeping, and was able also to pick out the type of ammunition clips which had accompanied it.

I heard no more about the robbery, apart from the fact that the safe was found blown open and dumped empty in a field, but I was kept informed as to the progress the pistol was making. A post office in Wick was held up at gun point by two men, one of whom had menaced the staff with a heavy German-type pistol. A similar robbery was carried out days later in Oban, and finally, two days after that, two men were arrested in a caravan park near Aberdeen and found to be in possession of stolen money and of a German Mauser machine pistol, the very one which days later I was called upon to identify as having been stolen inside my safe some months previously.

Laurie's philosophical acceptance of his loss did not last long. He began to pester me for compensation for the loss of his war souvenir, and I had finally to tell him off in no uncertain terms, pointing out that I had been the only real loser, twenty-five quid's worth to be precise, which I had loaned to Laurie with the pistol as security, plus all the subsequent aggro with the Police. Despite it all we remained friends!

The two robberies at The Firs in Milngavie which made us decide to search for more secure accommodation I have already described above, but little did we know that our experiences in that regard were as yet not over and that housebreakers would follow us to what we thought was the most secure living accommodation one could possibly find, the apartments at the Kelvin Court complex at Anniesland. We were no sooner installed in our first floor apartment there than our last remaining daughter, Laura, decided to get married. Her chosen spouse was a dentist from Lenzie, Aldo Ceresa, and the two immediately bought a large house in Victoria Road. The house had once belonged to Kenneth McKellar, the singer, who, incidentally, was now our upstairs neighbour in Kelvin Court. The house in Lenzie had not been properly surveyed, however, and as the decorators moved in it was discovered that the place was riddled with dry rot. Every piece of wood had to be stripped out, the stonework treated, and the house practically rebuilt. Basically what the newlyweds had paid about £60,000 for were four stone walls with no roof. Everything else had to be stripped out and rebuilt. Their situation was not as grim as it might have been however. Mary and I by this time had acquired a flat in Majorca, so arrangements were made for them to move into our Kelvin Court flat and we prepared to spend six months or so in Majorca until such time as their Victoria Road home was made habitable. Finance was not a problem either. Aldo's earning capacity was great and I supplied a necessary loan, promptly repaid, so that the necessary repairs could be carried out.

During their first week at Kelvin Court, during the night, cat burglars squeezed their way through a tiny window into one of the first floor rooms and, as Aldo and Laura slept, proceeded to fill sacks with every article of value they could lay their hands on. They then tried to make their way out of the apartment through the front door with their swag. But we had instilled in our children the habit of locking the front door with a mortice lock during the night and removing the key, so the burglars could not get out with their loot, and they had to retreat back through the window they had entered by, minus everything they had hoped to steal! And our daughter and her husband had slept through it all, to become aware of what had happened only on awakening the next morning.

We were informed of the event, and our immediate reaction was to give a sigh of relief that we had not been at home to live through that trauma. On our return home months later, we had special burglar-proof window locks installed on all the windows, and our subsequent fifteen years in Kelvin Court went unmarred by any such incident. As a matter of record, that was the very first time that a robbery, or at least an attempted one, had taken place in Kelvin Court. Other apartments were to suffer robberies in the years to come, but Mary and I were never again disturbed by thieves during our stay there.

It was during this period that I made another new friend, one who, with his wife Chris, was to figure large in the story of our family. Walter McNair was a property factor to whom we had been introduced by Bob Martin, our lawyer, at the time of our acquisition of the Savoy and Silver Lounge properties. To acquire these two shops we had also to take on board the tenement block in which they stood. To manage all this, the services of a factor were needed. Walter was a pleasant, outgoing man about twelve years older than me, with a charming wife, Chris, and a young twelve-year-old daughter, Christine. Chris and Mary met and hit it off immediately, and although Chris was a good twenty-two years her senior, so young was she in appearance and outlook that the age gap made no difference. They had common interests and values and enjoyed one another's company. Despite our completely different backgrounds, with Walter born and bred in Glasgow into a staunchly Protestant family, and I from a croft in Tuscany and raised as a Catholic, and despite our cultural differences, we were comfortable in one another's company. In the course of my life I have met but a handful of persons whom I would have trusted implicitly in all things: one of those was Walter McNair. In 1960, the Olympic Games took place in Rome, and Walter and I consulted our respective wives and were given permission to attend them. We went by car, and I drove all the way, because Walter had never been out of the UK in his life; even during the war he had done his service as an RAF armourer in Belfast, and he did not relish the idea of driving on, as he put it, 'the wrong side of the road.' He was fascinated by the European cities we motored through and, as I thought he would have been, despite his Calvinistic tendencies, he was utterly amazed at the glory and diversity of Rome. There, we were lucky enough to gain entry to the finals of the boxing events, and although the name did not mean anything to us at the time, we saw a certain Cassius Clay, later to become the famous Mohammed Ali, gain his gold medal in the heavyweight division. Walter waxed enthusiastic about his trip, and soon after another was arranged, this time with Mary and Chris in tow.

The four of us did a six weeks' motoring tour of Italy, with all stops planned and all hotels booked. From Glasgow we motored to Stratford-on-Avon. From there on to Le Touquet and from there we motored leisurely to Paris for a three day stay. From Paris we took the car-sleeper to Munich, and from Munich we drove for a four days' stopover in Innsbruck. From Innsbruck we carried on to Venice, where Chris literally simpered with delight at her first trip on a gondola. We celebrated Walter and Chris' fiftieth wedding anniversary on a pinic area on the autostrada to Mestre, with a special cake baked by their daughter Christine for the occasion and hidden in the boot of the car until their special day arrived. After five golden days in Venice our next stop was Viareggio, where my father's house was our headquarters, and from which we visited all the tourist spots, Pisa, Florence and Lucca. Then a drive for a three-day stay in Barga at the foot of the Apuan Alps, with short drives to the surrounding villages, where Chris and Walter were able to observe a way of life which was rapidly disappearing, the way of life led by my parents some half a century before. And so to Rome. One week there for Walter and Chris to drink in the sights and sounds by now so familiar to Mary and myself, but overwhelming in their grandeur to any who had as yet not visited the eternal city. From Rome to an overnight stay in Siena, then a long drive to Nice, where we stayed for three days, then the car-sleeper to Calais, and car-sleeper from Dover to Glasgow. Six memorable weeks during which the best part of four thousand miles were clocked up with me doing all the driving, with never a puncture, never a scrape, despite negotiating some of the hairiest roads in Europe, with never a hiccup from our big six-seater Lancia.

Tired out by my efforts, the day after our return I decided to pay a visit to the Western Baths for a well-earned sauna. I found a parking place a few yards from the entrance, and as I was about to enter, I was brought to a halt by shouting and yelling and the sound of horse's hooves clattering on the tarmacadam. There were still a few horses and carts to be seen on the streets of Glasgow in the late 1960s. A horse pulling one of them had bolted in Cranworth Street, dragging an empty cart behind it. The horse came to a halt with its hooves halfway up the Lancia's rear window, which shattered until the impact of the flailing horseshoes. Four thousand miles without a scratch on the Continent, only to be landed with a bill for £250 for the damage done by a horse in the middle of the West End of Glasgow!

Christmas was a special time for the three Pieri families. All our shops closed on that day, and we gathered en masse in Borland Road at Nonno and Nonna's house, as father and mother were now known. Between us Ralph and I had presented them with seven grandchildren, and their little bungalow bulged at the seams as we gathered to celebrate the one day in the year when the families could gather and celebrate together. The Christmas dinner would have been prepared by Nonna, whose skills in the kitchen seemed to have grown with the passing of the years. She was now helped in the home by their companion, Clara. Clara Marandola had come to them at the age of seventeen from the town of Cassino, or what was left of it after the war, through the same agency that had brought our father to Scotland: the Church. She was, in fact, a post-war refugee. Her family had been forced to flee from Cassino at the beginning of the six month long battle for the town and for the hill-top monastery, and had watched from the neighbouring hills as their town and everything around it was being pulverised by Allied bombardments in an attempt to dislodge the Germans from their fortifications. For six months Clara and her family had scavenged for food on those hills, seeking shelter where they could, but her father and mother had sickened and died, and at the end of the battle Clara and her brother were taken into shelter by nuns from a nearby convent fortunate enough to have escaped the destruction of war.

At that same time Ralph and I had decided that because of their advanced years, our parents now needed help and companionship in their home and we approached the Xaverian fathers in their retreat in Nitshill to seek help and advice in the matter. They suggested that we bring over one of the many homeless children and adolescents being looked after by church agencies in war-ravaged Italy, and one month later Clara arrived in Glasgow, wide-eyed and fearful of the new and strange environment into which she had been plunged. A quiet and retiring girl, she fitted in well with Nonno and Nonna. Green and leafy and well-kept and peaceful, her new Bearsden environment could not have been more different from the war-devastated countryside in which she had lived for the last three years. She was glad to be in a comfortable and safe home, and our parents were delighted to have found a daughter in her. She stayed with them for almost twenty years before returning to her native Cassino, and now, almost seventy years of age, Clara lives in Cervaro, a little town in the shadow of the Monte Cassino monastery which had seen so much fighting during the war. Her street carries the name *Via Medaglia d'Oro* (Gold Medal Road). It is so named because a member of the Marandola family lives there, and two members of that family, one a brother of Clara, and the other a cousin, were each awarded a posthumous gold medal by the Italian government to honour them for their defiance of the Nazis in the last months of the war. In the last few weeks of the Italian campaign, as the Germans were systematically retreating north towards Germany, a German platoon was ambushed on the road leading up to Fiesole, a little town near Florence, and several German soldiers were killed. Clara's brother and cousin were in the group of local partisans who had carried out the attack, and had been captured. A German officer offered to spare their lives if they divulged the names of their companions, tied them to a tree and gave them one hour to decide. They refused the German's offer and were promptly executed. That spot, just under the Franciscan monastery at the top of the Fiesdole hill, is now marked by a bronze plaque with a bas-relief depicting two dead men. The plaque is engraved with the name Marandola and a brief account of the incident. The street where they were born in Cassino was later renamed.

Those Christmas days at Borland Road were days to be remembered. The Christmas tree was swamped by the masses of presents piled under it, and the children would squeal with delight as each parcel was opened and disclosed its secrets. The food was magnificent, with a flavour that no kitchen of a five star restaurant could ever reproduce. The ravioli were homemade, with the filling made by Nonna from a recipe handed down from her own grandmother, and each individual piece sealed by the hands of our girls the night before. The bolognaise sauce was also from an old family recipe and flavoured with finely chopped dried mushrooms gathered from the chestnut valleys of the Bacchionero forests. The meal would last for hours, with long periods for small talk between the courses and time to listen to the traditional Italian arias softly played on Nonna's old gramophone. Those were the early days of television, and on Christmas day a special film would be shown and so, replete with food and drink, the families would gather tightly around the smallish black and white screen to watch the new marvel. The day would pass only too quickly, but then we had Boxing Day to look forward to. That was the day when we went to the cinema with the McNairs, Walter and Chris and their daughter Christine. The cinemas now equipped with the new marvel, Cinemascope, always reserved a blockbuster film for the Christmas period, and I remember *Dr. Zhivago, How The West was Won* and *It's a Mad World* being viewed on three consecutive Christmases. The children especially loved New Year's Day, for that was the day that Ralph took them all to the Kelvin Hall Circus. He loved children, he loved to entertain them and our four had a great affection for him. Those days represented family life at its best, with the children in their formative years and each of our families a closely knit unit within themselves, untroubled as yet by outside influences.

Christmas was also a time to be reunited with Mary's relations. Mary Kane, now Mary McLernon, and her husband James. They had remained close to our family, and her father Hugh, who had recently been widowed, was a great favourite with our children, who looked forward eagerly to the occasional visit from their Uncle Hughie and to the festive lunch prepared by Mary a few days before Christmas for the Scottish side of our family.

Those days came to an end in 1965 with the death of our father Francesco. He was eighty-seven years of age and died of heart failure, nursed and cared for at home by our mother until his last breath. She lived on for a further seventeen years, active and with a crystal clear mind, until she herself passed on in 1982 at the age of ninety-seven. If any death can be described with the word beautiful, then surely the passing away of our mother can be so described. She died after a short stay in St Margaret's Hospice in Clydebank in the care of the nuns who ran it. She was surrounded by her entire family, Mary and I and our four children and Ralph and Theresa and their three. Our mother was a good woman in every sense of the word. She had lived and worked and sacrificed for her family, she had tried to instil in us the values which she herself held dear, she never spoke ill of anyone, had never done anyone a wrong and always tried to help those she considered to be less fortunate than herself. If the heaven she believed in exists, then she will surely be there.

❦ 10 ❦
Family Life

By the end of the 1950s our family was complete. The 'Four Ls' we called them; Luisa, Linda, Lorenzo and Laura. Mary devoted her life to her children. The girls were always immaculately turned out, this in an era when mothers still took a pride in the appearance of their children, before the advent of jeans, ragged trousers, wild hairdos and beads inserted in earlobes and nostrils, all of which make some of the youth of today resemble stone age throwbacks. Education took top place on our agenda for the children. Neither Mary nor I had been given the opportunity of aspiring to a higher education, and so we saw to it that the 'Four Ls' had every opportunity to develop their potential to the full. Ever mindful of the poverty of my own youth and my own lack of qualifications for any sort of professional career in life, I deemed it important that our children should have an education. Society was changing, the importance of education in a rapidly evolving world was becoming more and more evident and the idea that a son should follow in his father's footsteps in jobs or in trade had disappeared.

The girls passed the entrance exams for Notre Dame, the Montessori Girl's School in the west end of Glasgow, and Lorenzo, who had received his primary education in a local school, St Charles', was eventually given a place in St Aloysius, but not until a great deal of pressure had been exerted by Mary and myself on that institution. As was the case for entry to Notre Dame, applicants for admittance to St Aloysius had to sit an entrance exam. Mary and I were sure that Lorenzo would be selected, for we had some inside information as to his performance in that test. Lorenzo's godparents were Tom and Del Mullins, a brother and sister with whom we had become very friendly through their visits to our Silver Lounge café. Tom was a civil servant and Del was a school inspector for the Glasgow area. During a visit to St Aloysius she was able to see the exam results and could tell us that Lorenzo had come out near the top of the participants, which meant that his acceptance was assured, or so we thought, given that the intake that year would be of forty or more students. Imagine our consternation when a polite refusal arrived for our son through the post, with no reason given for the decision.

We reacted swiftly. I wrote a series of letters to the order of Jesuits who ran the school. What was the point, I asked, of subjecting young boys to the stress and worry of an entry exam if the results of that exam were to be ignored, making it plain that I knew the result of that exam as far as our son was concerned. If other criteria were of greater importance why bother with an exam at all? An applicant's academic qualifications could be ascertained by past school reports after which their own criteria could be applied. The setting of an exam which seemed to have no meaning smacked of casuistry, which should have no place in the type of school St Aloysius purported to be.

I made a nuisance of myself to the extent that Mary received a phone call from Father Dempsey, the Jesuit priest who had officiated at our wedding, suggesting that perhaps a moderation of my attitude might achieve results, in view of the fact that some of the places offered at St Aloysius had not been taken up and that perhaps Lorenzo might be allowed in by the side door, as it were. As a result of that conversation Mary asked to see Father Tracy, the headmaster at the time, with the result that finally Lorenzo was fitted out in a St Aloysius school uniform.

The children's school days were happy days for us. We took pride in their achievements and shared in their disappointments, of which there were relatively few, for all our children did very well in their studies. However, the one event which has remained vividly in my mind of the Notre Dame days was a singularly embarrassing occurrence which can now be laughed at for its humorous side but which was anything but funny at the time. The headmistress at Notre Dame in the 1960s was Sister Anne Consuela, a middle-aged nun who could well have stepped out of a Victorian novel. Prim and precise, she was a strict disciplinarian who demanded and got the highest standard of behaviour and decorum from her pupils. She always terminated the scholastic year for the sixth form students with a banquet at one of the best restaurants in the city centre. Unfortunately, the one chosen for that particular year, the posh Ca'D'oro at the corner of Renfield Street and Gordon Street, burned down just two weeks before the occasion was to take place, and Sister Anne was left without a venue for her celebration. She hurriedly got in touch with a half-dozen or so other hotels and restaurants, but there was nothing available anywhere for that particular Saturday night.

At that time we had opened a restaurant just a few doors down from the Savoy, the Rio, a very spacious eating place on two floors, with the upstairs section divided into two rooms, each room capable of seating 100 or so diners. The Rio was at the lower end of the restaurant spectrum, whose customers were perhaps a little higher on the social scale than those of the Savoy, but by no stretch of the imagination comparable in any way to the upper class frequenters of the Ca'D'Oro. The Rio catered mainly for office workers during the day and the usual rabble of late night customers out for a quick snack before a visit to the pictures or for something slightly more upmarket than a fish supper to alleviate their hunger after a visit to the local pub.

Sister Anne somehow or other had got to know that the Pieri family owned a restaurant which could easily accommodate her party of eighty girls, and one day as I went to collect the girls at school she waylaid me with her predicament. Could I possibly accommodate her party? She was desperate, she did not want to disappoint her girls; could I possibly fit them in on the Saturday night in question? I sought to dissuade her. I didn't think the Rio would be a suitable venue for her purposes, I explained. It was in no way comparable to the establishments she normally held her function, and besides, I did not know if it was available on the night in question. I spoke to the manager, Jack Sterlini. He confirmed that one of the upstairs rooms was available, but that the other had been booked out by a wedding party from the Springburn district. Yes, he supposed that at a pinch he could take another party of eighty, but at such short notice that would put a strain on the service. Jack would have squeezed customers in with a shoehorn if necessary, his bonus consisted of a percentage of turnover, and another eighty diners represented another few quid in his pocket.

I reported back to Sister Anne. Yes, a room was available, but again I did everything to dissuade her. The accommodation might not be suitable, I said. Morover,we were catering for a wedding party on that same night, which might be a bit more noisy and boisterous than she was used to. Would it not be better to cancel the occasion until a more suitable venue could be found? She would have none of it. She insisted, and against my better judgement I gave in and instructed Jack to prepare for her party. That Saturday night I did my usual rounds of our shops and stopped in for a look at Sister Anne's party. I took one look and did a hurried retreat. The two upstairs rooms, in one of which the Notre Dame party had been accommodated, were bedlam. The members of the wedding party were in varying stages of inebriation and their raucous singing could be heard from across the street. I could well imagine what it must have been like in the adjoining room. The toilets could be accessed only through the room reserved for Sister Anne's party and a steady stream of diners was passing through her tables on the way to disposing of the plentiful wine and beer consumed in the course of the evening. I saw one celebrant approach the sister, give her a friendly pat on the back, and say something to the effect that that was a braw bonny bunch of lassies she had there, and could he offer her a drink, even though he wasn't a Catholic. The icy look on her face could have frozen the Clyde. As said before, I beat a quick retreat. Two days later I received a letter with a Notre Dame heading, complaining bitterly about the venue and the company she and 'my lovely girls' had been forced to associate with.

I replied, saying that I was extremely sorry that her evening had not come up to her standards, but pointed out that I had warned her that the Rio might not be a suitable place for what she had in mind, and that she had insisted over all my attempts at dissuasion. I repeated my apologies and said that in view of the circumstances I would not be sending a bill for the night's catering. Sister Anne had her secretary contact the manager, Jack Sterlini, and insisted that a bill be presented. Her cheque was duly cashed, which ensured that Jack received a small percentage of it in his monthly bonus. I did not show any of my girls Sister Anne's letter. They would have been just too mortified at the unfortunate event and might never have wanted to show their face at Notre Dame again. Many years later I came across the letter and showed it to them, occasioning yells of laughter from the three girls.

The 'Four Ls' all did well at school, all went on to University, and all achieved degrees in their respective studies; Luisa earned an MA, Linda a BSc, Lorenzo an MbChb and Laura an MaLlb. These degrees at least gave them the keys to paths in life very different from my own. Have they been better or happier persons in their lives because of the acquisition of academic qualifications and the paths they have taken because of them? An old friend of mine from the Western Baths, Hugh Doherty, used to say that there was more money to be made in three feet of shop counter than in all the University degrees put together, which is probably true, but his saying does not take into consideration the satisfaction given by one's calling in life or the security offered by a professional career. One thing is certain, had our children not acquired their respective degrees, none of them would have met the persons they eventually were to marry. Only they are in a position to judge whether their choice in that regard was wise or not. Possibly it is the old Italian streak in me that says this, but as I look back, I can perhaps see some merit in the old custom of parents so manipulating and channelling events that their offspring would be steered to a partner deemed suitable for them, without going to the extremes of an arranged marriage. And yet I myself had baulked at parental wishes, and I had fifty-three years of happy life with my own choice of partner, far removed from what my parents, especially mother, would have wished for me, so I should not be the one to advocate such a procedure. All I can say is that Mary and I enjoyed our children and had some of the happiest moments in our lives in the raising of them. We were proud of them, we rejoiced in their achievements and we did what we thought was best for them in all things. One's children are to a very large extent hostages to fortune. We raise them, help them to reach their potential, teach them the difference between what is right and what is wrong and help them until they have chosen their own path in life. Our approval or disapproval as parents for their choices and for their actions is of value only to us.

In those years I occasionally thought of my own experiences as a child and as a schoolboy, of being called 'a dirty wee Tally', of being jeered at in the school playground and of being discriminated against in later life. I once asked my children if the fact that they bore an Italian name had ever been an embarrass-ment to them, or if they had ever been subjected to bullying and ridicule because of their Italian background. The question drew uncomprehending stares from them. They simply did not know what I was talking about. No such problems had arisen for them because of an Italian name. There is a world of difference, I suppose, in growing up in Bearsden in the 1960s rather than the Gorbals in the 1920s, and in being educated in the best schools in Glasgow rather than the academically excellent but somewhat rough and ready St Francis and St Mungo's of my own boyhood.

Each period in one's life has its own special appeal and its own special memo-ries. Special amongst these periods and memories are the years we devoted to the raising of our children and the time we spent together as a family, sharing in events, Sunday outings, theatre and cinema visits and holidays. During the summer months Ralph and I would take turn about on Sundays in taking our by now aged parents in car trips to the nearby Clyde resorts, with Largs, because of its plentiful cafes and other amenities, a great favourite. This was in the heyday of the Moorings, the famous café-restaurant-cum-dancehall on the corner at Largs pier, and we would always pay a visit there, either for an ice cream in the sumptuous café at street level or for a fish tea on the first floor restaurant. The three Castelvecchi brothers who had built the complex came from our home town of Barga, and one of them had seen action with my father on the Isonzo front during the First World War, and they would sit for a time exchanging stories of the hard times they had experienced together in wartime. On our 'free' Sundays we would roam much further afield. Turnberry was a great favouite. Mary and the three girls would be deposited in the hotel dining room to partake of a meal and Lorenzo and I would go down to the golf course snack bar for a pie and chips, to be followed by a round of golf on the magnificent Ailsa course. Play there was restricted to clients of the hotel, which in a very restricted sense we were, and a view of our hotel car park ticket was enough to persuade the amenable starter to accept our green fees and to allow us on to the hallowed fairways. There was hardly a town or resort of any size within an eighty-mile radius of Glasgow, ranging from Culzean Castle in Ayrshire to Inverness in the north that we did not visit regularly during those years. For a time St Andrews became a favourite at weekends. Lorenzo did the first part of his medical degree at the university there, and during his three years' stay we grew to love the picturesque Fife coast town.

Our summer holidays together as a family were occasions to be eagerly looked forward to. My parents now had a large house in Viareggio, and as soon as the children were old enough to travel Mary and I would spend a month or more of the summer there. This was a marvellous arrangement. The children could enjoy the marvellous beaches of the resort, always supervised by the grandparents who took a great delight in their grandchildren, and Mary and I, not being particularly enamoured of sea and sand, could drive at our leisure around Tuscany to take in the wealth of art in its towns and cities and enjoy driving around the lovely countryside. Within a fifty-mile arc inland from Viareggio there lies some of the most naturally beautiful and artistically embellished spots on Earth. Every little hilltop Tuscan town encountered in a trip along the valley of the river Serchio is a thing of beauty, and there is not one which does not contain a medieval or renaissance building, painting or statue of artistic worth. The countryside itself is breathtaking, and if one takes the road to Florence the views become doubly spectacular as one passes Montecatini and the gently sloping hills of Serravalle. And what can one say about Florence itself? I sometimes daydream about the traffic-free days when we could drive directly into Piazza della Signoria with our little Triumph Mayflower, park directly under Cellini's bronze *Perseus* at La Loggia dei Lanzi and eat an ice cream in the shadow of the Palazzo Vecchio, its portals guarded on the one side by a copy of Michelangelo's David and on the other by an equally huge marble Hercules.

Mary and I also made a point of going off on our own to Rome for a few days during these holidays, to visit and renew acquaintance with the by now familiar attractions of the city. One such visit remains clearly remembered. In the early days of our marriage, with just three children in tow since Laura was as yet to be born, we arrived in Viareggio after four days of driving through England and France. We raised the possibility of leaving the children with the grandparents and carrying on to Rome for a few days there. The weather was unseasonably cold and wet, and my father, possibly put off by the prospect of having to entertain indoors three young children ranging in ages from three to eight for a few days, announced his intention of coming with mother to Rome with us.

Father was a man who never took no for an answer in family matters. We all squeezed into the little two door Triumph Mayflower, which, although perfect for three small children and two adults, was cramped to say the least when two more adults squeezed themselves into the back seat. No autostrade in those days, just a rather badly maintained Via Aurelia down the coast to Rome, which, together with the interminable toilet stops for the kids, made for a full day's drive to reach our destination. Fortunately I knew Rome well, and could drive straight to a hotel strategically situated behind Bernini's colonnades at St Peter's. Early next morning we piled into the car and drove the few hundred yards to St Peter's Square and parked under one of the two Bernini fountains. Given the fact that now no vehicles are allowed into the square, and that traffic in the surrounding streets are jammed wheel to wheel, it may be difficult to believe that in those days when private cars were few and far between, one could park literally anywhere in Rome.

There was a bigger crowd than usual waiting in front of the basilica, and on enquiry we were informed that the Pope would be shortly giving a blessing in the Raphael room at the top of the staircase, which, as tradition has it, came from the temple of Jerusalem and is known as 'The Holy Stairs'. So the seven of us, four adults and the three children, took our place in the slow moving queue as it moved towards and then onto the stairway. It was an imposing sight to see, the broad staircase with a row of Swiss guards at attention every half dozen steps or so, and at the top the broad portals of the Raphael room. The two girls, Luisa and Linda, had no difficulty in climbing the steps, but Lorenzo, only three, had to be carried up by me, still seated in his little folding pram. We found a seat on one of the row of benches, and there, in the majesty of the Raphael room, with his paintings surrounding us on the walls, proceeded to await the arrival of the Pope. The minutes passed, they lengthened into half an hour, and father began to fidget, casting repeated glances at a timepiece which he produced from a waistcoat pocket. No ordinary timepiece this, but a massive Elgin gold pocket watch which he clicked open and then clicked loudly shut after having consulted the passage of time.

'*Ma quando viene questo Papa?*' (When is this Pope coming?)

Another half hour passed, and father stood up.

'*Andiamo ragazzi, ho aspettato abbastanza, e' ora da mangiare.*' (Let's go, I've waited enough, it's time to eat.)

And he began moving along the bench, squeezing past the seated congregation. He beckoned us to follow him, and we did as we were told, my face red with embarrassment as I hefted Lorenzo up in his pram and murmured and gesticulated excuses to our neighbours as I trod on their toes on the way out. We ran the gauntlet of Swiss guards back down the holy steps, and finally emerged into a hot and sunny and near-deserted St Peter's square. My father was a man you did not argue with and a man you did not keep waiting. So we made our way to my favourite trattoria, San Pietro, set in a corner behind Bernini's colonnade and there we forgot our disappointment at not seeing the Pope by consuming a plate of fettuccini and drinking a glass of Vino Dei Castelli. Mary and I had to wait another twenty five years or so before we were to have the chance of seeing a Pope close up, a story recounted in another chapter.

In later years, with the children approaching their teens, Viareggio took on an ever greater importance in our family life. Each year at school holidays the car would be loaded up and off we would set on the long drive to Italy. I remember one year, we tied a folding bicycle on to the roof of the car, a Rover the car was, and did it not come flying off as I negotiated a curve on Maryhill Road, about two miles from our point of departure! No damage was done, but I did have to put up with some caustic comments on the part of the family on my ability as a packer! The journey to Italy used to be always as enjoyable as the actual stay in Viareggio. There were no motor roads then; the journey to Dover or Folkestone took two days, it could have been done in one if you were willing to exhaust yourself, but the English countryside was there to be enjoyed, as were the stopovers in Stratford-on-Avon and in Dover. In Stratford we always stayed at the Falcon Hotel, a rather old-fashioned Tudor type place in the middle of the town, with creaking floorboards and slightly tilted floors, where the children swore they could hear the ghost of William Shakespeare creeping around in the middle of the night. Our overnight stay in Dover was invariably at the Dover Stage hotel, near the car embarkation point, and it was a great adventure to see the receding white cliffs of the English coast as the ferry set off across the channel. The journey through France also took two days and there we stopped wherever the fancy took us, in a variety of picturesque little towns and hotels of varying quality. One year, as happened frequently then, French farmers were on strike and had taken to barricading the main roads with farm tractors in protest at something or other, and well south of Paris we were forced to make a long detour through unknown countryside to bypass a farmer road block. We were lucky to find sleeping accommodation in a little village, I forget the name, where we were given two rooms numbered *douze et douze bis,* 12 and 12A, and I remember Linda's comment, uttered in a high pitched quavering falsetto twelve-year-old voice 'I don't like this place!' For years afterwards when she encountered something not to her taste she would utter *'Douze et douze bis!'* in a high falsetto voice. The remoteness of the village can be imagined when I tell you that I filled up with petrol at a pump powered not by electricity but by a hand lever! At least they called it petrol, but the belching smoke from the exhaust and the diminished power of the Humber seemed to say otherwise.

Then there was the great adventure of the crossing of the Alps, usually by the Mont Cenis Pass, and the descent into the plain of Lombardy on the other side. One more mountain pass had to be negotiated before Viareggio was reached; this the Bracco Pass in Liguria, which began at Santa Margherita Ligure and wound its way for about fifteen kilometres over wild mountain terrain. The road was then a very difficult one with bad cambers and heavy commercial traffic, and although I normally enjoyed driving I always heaved a sigh of relief when finally we were at sea level at Genoa, then on the coast road at Carrara for the last few kilometres into Viareggio.

The family house there was near the beach, and a bathing cabin with folding chairs and a sun umbrella would have been taken for the summer at the bathing station *'Reginetta'* at the northern end of the long Viareggio promenade. The same families were there every year and friendships were made which have lasted to the present day. Then every year Mary and I would take the road to Rome once more for a week or so to visit the places we loved so well. Our friend Aldo Nardini from Lucca, who himself had a passable baritone voice, each year organised bus parties for trips to the opera season held each year in the Roman amphitheatre in Verona, and if these coincided with our visits, Mary and I would be included in the party. To hear and see an opera in the Verona amphitheatre is quite an experience. The operas we saw there were the spectacular ones; *Carmen, Aida, Nabucco, Turandot,* with part of the floor of the arena serving as a stage. The changing of the scenery for the different acts of these operas involved a great deal of time and effort. In *Carmen,* for one of the acts a whole village had to be constructed over the entire floor of the stage, which entailed a break of half an hour and more. This meant that the performance of a complete opera could last the best part of five hours, a taxing procedure when one considers the complete lack of toilet facilities for the thousands of aficionados sitting on the concrete steps of the huge amphitheatre. I recall on a couple of occasions climbing to the top of these steps, and there, in the company of several other males, relieving myself down into the street fifty or more feet below. The resultant fine spray falling gently on to the heads of the tourists strolling along below was probably thought by them to be a fine drizzle of light rain mysteriously falling from a cloudless, starlit sky.

Mary with Pope John Paul II in 1981. Shortly afterwards the Pope was nearly killed in an assassination attempt

On the day of Joe's retirement in 1984, with a picture presented to him by his three daughters

The Firs, home of the Pieris

Thor, the Great Dane, with daughter Linda

The clubhouse at Son Vida golf course

The 9-30 Golfing Society
Ladies' Night 1985
La Vileta Restaurant

Invitation to Gala Ladies Night at Son
Vida golf club

At the prizegiving of the 9.30 Golfing Society. The members apart from the author included Count John de Prêt, Reidar Mathisen and Wing Commander Bob Simpson, DSO and bar

Mary and daughter Linda by the swimming pool in Majorca

Mary at Lake Moraine in Banff National Park, Canada, in the 1990s

Mary and Joe with son Lorenzo

The author with Jack MacLean, journalist and writer, 1997

Mary, Joe and friend Bernard

Joe and Mary with Chris and Walter McNair

Joe and Mary with grandchildren Maria-Luisa and Xisca on the verandah of the house in Son Vida

Mary with the Spanish family at the poolside, Son Vida

(Below) Joe with his grandson Alessandro on his first communion. On the author's left are daughter Linda and granddaughter Xisca, with Italian son-in-law Ennio on extreme left

Presentation of the Medal of St Christopher to author in recognition of services to Scots-Italian understanding. With the author are Archbishop Mario Conti and Umberto Sereni, Mayor of Barga

❦ 11 ❦
Majorcan Days

Linda, our second daughter, was the first to spread her wings and leave the family circle. By 1974 she had graduated from Glasgow University with a BSc in biological sciences and had gone on to teach at a Glasgow school, St Columba of Iona. With a desire to broaden her horizons, she began scanning the various professional journals which advertised openings for teachers, and wrote to a London address which offered teaching positions abroad for graduates of British universities. She was interviewed and was offered the post of science teacher at a school, King's College, a British-run school in Palma on the island of Majorca. She accepted and Mary and I went to Majorca with her to help find accommodation and were immediately struck by the beauty and diversity to be found on the island. The package holiday phenomenon had been well established by then, and the word Majorca conjured up for us visions of a cheap and cheerful Mediterranean resort frequented by a young set bent on cheap booze and willing sex. Although that was certainly true of one small aspect of the island, we were amazed at the overall picture, for much of the island was as yet unspoiled and offered facilities and amenities with a beauty and character not to be found in any of the more traditional and developed resorts of the Mediterranean.

King's College, where Linda would now be teaching, was a British-run private school which, although open to all nationalities, catered in the main for the needs of the families of the many British living on the island. There was also a large American presence in Majorca, since the oil fields in Libya, just a few hundred miles south across the Mediterranean, employed many American engineers and technicians. Libya was to them an alien environment devoid of familiar amenities and, with few exceptions, these Americans preferred to make homes for their families in Majorca and enrolled their children in Kings College to be educated.

For Linda, her new place of work could not have been more different from the school in the Garscube Road district of Glasgow where she had set out on her teaching career. Set in the middle of a beautiful countryside and surrounded by olive groves and orange trees it was as far removed from the grimy and depressing tenements of that part of Glasgow as could be imagined. Moreover, from a teacher's perspective it was attended by well-behaved children who wanted to study and learn and who did not require the presence of a policeman to make them behave, as was the often the case in St Columba. A year after starting work there she met a young Mallorquin, José Borras-Oliver, an architect and builder. Six months after that she became engaged and one year later she married and became Senora Linda Pieri de Borras. I like the Spanish custom of incorporating the bride's name into her new marital one, for it ensures the continuity of her own heritage into married life.

Linda's move to Majorca and subsequent marriage created a couple of problems for Mary and myself. At the time of her departure we were living at The Firs, the house described in the previous chapter, and there Linda kept two dogs, one a great Dane who answered to the name of Thor, and a golden retriever, Shane. The retriever was no problem to us and required a minimum of care. He was a free-roaming dog, who used The Firs purely as a place to eat and to sleep, and who spent his days wandering and sniffing around in the nearby fields and padding through the streets of Milngavie, where he was a well-known and popular pet. He was especially well known at the local butcher's, at whose door he would sit patiently until given a freshly scraped bone to run off with, contentedly wagging his tail. Thor, however, was another matter. Although friendly and in no way aggressive, he was a huge dog and could never have been allowed out of the boundaries of our home. He had to be exercised daily, and after Linda's departure he was taken round Tannoch Loch and the nearby Mugdock reservoirs on a leash, sometimes by me, sometimes by our youngest daughter Laura and on occasion by both of us together. Each of us had many times suffered the indignity of having been dragged to the ground when Thor decided to give a sudden lunge after a cat or another dog. The problem arose when we decided to give up The Firs and make the move to a flat in the Kelvin Court development at Anniesland Cross. Shane we decided to take with us, but Thor simply could not have been housed in a flat, no matter how spacious, and had somehow to be disposed of. He was a fine specimen, and a local vet was more than pleased to take him off our hands as a gift. But the free spirit of Shane could not take to life in a flat. Anniesland is a very busy area with fast-flowing traffic and there he could not have been allowed the unfettered freedom he had been accustomed to in Milngavie. Already quite old, about twelve or so, Shane began to deteriorate quite rapidly after our move, and reluctantly the decision was made to have him put down, so one morning I put him into the car and drove him to the vet. I swear that he knew the fate that lay in store for him. He sat motionless in the rear seat with sad and reproachful eyes staring at me, and as I left him in the vet's office he whimpered and stretched out an imploring paw as if to beg me not to consign him to such a fate. When I think about it, even now, thirty years and more after the event, I can still see the pleading eyes and the outstretched paw, and I still feel a stab of guilt, as though I had sentenced a faithful friend to death.

The second problem lay in Italy. After father's death, Ralph and I had inherited the family house in Viareggio and had found that the inheritance had created a certain conflict of interests for us during the school holiday periods, which were obviously the best time for the two families to make use of the house. The problem had been amicably resolved by the selling of my share of the house to Ralph, with the proceeds going to the purchase of an apartment nearby. Moreover, our focus now had shifted. The family were all grown up and quite rightly wanted to make their own holiday arrangements, and since Linda was about to be married in Majorca we decided to sell the newly acquired Viareggio apartment and to purchase one near Linda's new home. The Viareggio apartment sold quickly, but we were left with the problem of transferring the money received from the sale over to Spain. There were very tight currency controls in place in those days, as far as the transfer of money from one country to another was concerned. Indeed, as I remember it, an individual could take with him no more than £40 or the equivalent in foreign currency on travelling outwith the UK. This would have posed no problem as far as a transfer from the UK to Italy or vice-versa was concerned, for I was well acquainted with the various methods of bypassing such irksome laws, but a transfer of funds from Italy to Spain was another matter. I knew no-one in Italy with Spanish connections, and José, who, being a Mallorquin, was a past master in navigating through turgid Spanish legal waters, had no local connections who could help me in my problem.

The problem could have been solved simply by putting the cash from the apartment sale, about thirty million lire, £27,000 or so, into a suitcase and taking it over as part of our luggage, but that ran the risk of the cash being found by the customs and sequestrated, not to mention a hefty fine for attempting to evade the Italian currency laws. I sought another way, and finally, and not without a certain amount of trepidation, put my trust in the very untrustworthy Italian and Spanish postal systems. I put the cash, in large denomination lire notes, into a series of envelopes and posted them off from a dozen or so different places to my daughter's address in Palma. The Gods must have been smiling down at me, because contrary to the odds, all of the envelopes arrived at their destination, some after days, some after weeks, but arrive they all did, and I was able to put the money, now converted to Pesetas, to the purchase of an apartment in Illetas, a resort just a few kilometres along the coast from Palma. The apartment block was in the process of being built by my new son-in-law José, and I was given my choice of apartments, which resulted in Mary and I being the proud possessors of a spectacular flat suspended over the bay of Illetas with magnificent views over the sea to Palma. It was about this time that Ralph and I had been making plans for our retirement, and Mary and I were looking forward to spending some months each year in our new Majorcan home. Moreover, Linda's marriage seemed to have lit a fuse amongst our other children, for in fairly quick succession the remaining three had found themselves partners and had married; Luisa to Ennio Bilucaglia, an Italian schoolteacher she had first met during her years at University, and Lorenzo to an Army nurse met during his service in the Forces, where he had enlisted as a doctor immediately after having gained his degree. Laura followed soon after with her choice of spouse, Aldo Ceresa, a Glasgow Scots-Italian dentist. All of which left Mary and I completely free to do as we pleased in retirement.

Linda's move to Majorca and her subsequent marriage there had opened up new horizons for us, and had given our life new dimensions. Possibly because I have been bilingual since childhood, I find it easy to learn a language, and since Italian is not that far removed from Spanish it was not long before I could mix freely and fluently with José's relations and friends. Linda's father-in-law, Nicholas, had a background which did not differ much from that of my own parents, apart from the emigration part of it. He came from a family of campesinos, peasants, whose way of life was not all that different from the one my parents had known in the hills above Barga. If anything, life in Majorca was even harder, for, given the lack of water on the island and the scanty rainfall, there was not much arable land in Majorca and not many crops could be sown, and what could be grown did not fetch much in the markets of Palma. Tourism and the package holiday, the industry that eventually was to make the island very wealthy, lay far in the future. To be sure, Palma had three or four luxurious hotels on the Paseo Marittimo, the city's promenade by the sea, but these opened only in the winter for the convenience of the wealthy mainland Spaniards from the north of the country who came to enjoy the relatively mild Majorcan winter weather. Before the advent of air conditioning these hotels closed in summer, for the weather was simply too hot to be comfortable. At the age of eighteen, Nicholas was caught up in the Spanish civil war of 1936, when Majorca and the rest of Spain was torn apart by a conflict which set brother against brother and neighbour against neighbour. After a month or two of savage and intense fighting, the Franco forces on the island overcame the Loyalists and Mallorca was then used by the Italian and German airforces as a base in thanks for their aid to Franco. It was from their air base near Palma that the German Condor air division launched its infamous raid on the Basque town of Guernica, an event whose horror was later to be immortalised by Picasso's famous mural. Impoverished and exhausted by the war, Majorca had then to endure four years of what amounted to a blockade by the British Navy, German U-boats and by what little remained of the Italian navy after the disaster at Taranto in 1941, where the bulk of the Italian fleet was sunk at anchor by British torpedo bombers. Ships from the Spanish mainland would not dare the crossing to Palma, and the island, already on its knees from the internecine killings of the civil war, had to face up to further years of deprivation. The strong always survive, however, and Nicholas, who had fought on

Franco's side, together with his friend Don Juan Tortella, an ex-officer in Franco's army, took to smuggling cigarettes and coffee from the North African coast to earn themselves a peseta or two. Although the rewards were great, the risks were enormous. Their craft, a fast petrol-driven launch, had to run the gauntlet of the British navy and German submarines, after which they had to be on their guard against Arab gangs who would cheerfully have slit their throats as they picked up their cargo. Despite a lack of formal education, Nicholas was astute, invested his profits well, and so laid the foundations for future prosperity for himself and his only son José, now Linda's husband. Nicholas, who by the time I came to know him had become a very wealthy man by investing all his wartime profits in land and property, used to give advice to all and sundry in how best to invest money. 'Buy land,' he would say. 'You can bomb it, you can burn it, and an earthquake can shake it up, but it will always be there and it will eventually make earnings for you. Never entrust your money to others to invest; they don't care what happens as long as they have had their commission from it.'

I mixed in well with Linda's new relations. Their psychology was not all that different from that of the sharecroppers of Bacchionero, and I could cheerfully spend hours with them quaffing Rioja and indulging in the small talk of the day. I suppose I have always possessed a chameleon-like quality of being able to change my personality to suit the company I happened to be in at any particular time. In Italy I could be as Italian as the next one, with gesticulations to suit; in Glasgow I could discuss the relative merits of Celtic and Rangers with all the necessary expletives, and now in Spain I could sip Rioja, discuss the affairs of the day with all the required gestures and be accepted as one of them.

As a teenager in 1936 I had taken an intense interest in the civil war then raging in Spain. My political conscience was beginning to awaken in those years. The Sacco and Vanzetti case in America was only a few years in the past and was still the subject of controversy. Sacco and Vanzetti were union organisers at a time when the big American industrialists were trying to keep unions out of their sweatshop factories, and the two were accused of murdering a factory guard. The evidence against them had obviously been trumped up, but after a farce of a trial they were found guilty and sentenced to death in the electric chair. Worldwide attention had been focussed on the case and the verdict had brought universal condemnation on the American legal system and on the way the courts could be manipulated by vested interests. Unprecedently, the Pope himself intervened on their behalf, but to no avail. They were finally executed after seven years of legal wrangling. That event, and my reading of the various books by Upton Sinclair, the American socialist novelist and his English counterparts, AJ Cronin and JB Priestley, all of whom had strong left-wing opinions, had made me sympathetic to the Republican side of the war and I read all the material about the conflict I could lay my hands on. Moreover, during our post–war visits to Barga we would make a point of visiting Bruno Sereni, who had worked for a time in the Savoy and who was now producing the widely read monthly newspaper *Giornale di Barga*. During the Spanish civil war he had fought with the International Brigade against Franco, and over interminable lunches at the local trattoria he would regale us with stories of battles fought at Guadalajara and Teruel against the Fascists.

At the time of the civil war I was the proud possessor of a short–wave wireless receiver, and with this I could pick up broadcasts from both the Franco controlled part of Spain and from Madrid and Barcelona, both of which cities remained in Republican hands until almost the end of the war. The broadcasts from Madrid were often in English and the news bulletins were read by an American war correspondent whose name I remember to this day: Lester Ziffren. He had a very distinctive American accent, and that in itself was fascinating, since we were only just becoming familiar with such glamorous accents though the medium of the newly arrived marvel, talking pictures. Madrid was eventually occupied by the Franco army, and Lester Ziffren's broadcasts ceased abruptly. I often wonder what happened to him.

The civil war in Spain was a savage affair, and in no place was it more intense than it was for the six weeks or so that it lasted in Majorca, when it finished with the island being controlled by Franco sympathisers. Those six weeks of fighting resulted in the deaths of thousands of peasants and workers who had risen up against their wealthy landowners and bosses, and the execution of anyone ac- cused of communist leanings. The ruling classes of the island were lucky in that the Guardia Civil, the Spanish military police, had a training base there and the local and disorganised government supporters were quickly put down. I became aware that there were hardly any males of my own age in Majorca with left–wing ideas, and the reason was simple, they had all been executed at the time of the war and the reprisals which followed. When I was finally able to break down the suspicion with which any left–wing survivor regarded me, I was regaled with stories of atrocities and executions carried out by the Falangists, as the Franco supporters were named, and many spoke of mass graves of many hundreds of murdered civilians hidden in the wild interior of the island On the other side of the coin the Franco supporters told gruesome tales of communist atrocities, of priests and nuns violated and executed and their churches desecrated and looted. They spoke also of the summary execution of anyone who had shown any sign of wealth or who was suspected or denounced as being sympathetic to the Franco cause.

The excesses carried out by both sides in the civil war can perhaps be ex- plained by a streak of cruelty which seems to lie at the heart of the Spanish psyche. A manifestation of this, I believe, can be seen in the traditional Corrida, the bullfight, so beloved by all social classes in Spain. It is reported that every year 24,000 bulls are killed in Corridas in front of an audience of 30 million people. The circular arenas where this killing takes place all follow the same pattern of construction. There are six or more entrances to the seating places, and when you buy your ticket you can opt for a seat in the shade or for one in the sun. The shade seats are the more expensive, and are padded, as opposed to the cheaper ones, which are of concrete. To soften them, for one Euro, a cushion can be rented. The show starts with a parade of the toreadores, the bullfighters, after which the bull is let into the arena. For about fifteen minutes or so the animal is tormented by the banderilleros, the name given to the toreadores who run in front of the bull and stick short tasselled spears into its neck until the bull is literally bathed in blood. The closer the banderilleros dare get to the bull the greater is the applause of the audience. When the bull has been tormented enough, into the arena, mounted on horses, come the picadors, who proceed to cut the bull's neck muscles with long spears, thus preventing the bull from raising its head. This to ensure that a clear target will be presented to the matador's sword when it is time for the kill. Then the matador enters the ring for the final phase of the spectacle. He taunts the bloodied bull with a red cape, and the closer the bull comes to him in its lunges, the greater the applause and the shouts of 'Ole!' from the spectators. Then finally, after about six or so such pirouettes the matador finishes off the bull with a sword, slightly curved at the tip, with which he attempts to stab straight into the animal's heart. The blade is so shaped to ensure that a slightly misdirected blade will bounce off the bull's spine and into the target. The animal then sinks to its knees, keels over onto its side and dies, its lifeblood pouring in great gushes from mouth and nostrils. Occasionally, if the animal takes too long to expire, a toreador cuts its throat as it lies on the ground. If the kill has been carried out to the satisfaction of the audience the bull's ears are cut off and presented to the matador by the president of the Corrida, or by any famous local or national personage in the audience. The dead bull is then dragged away by a team of horses, trailing blood behind it. This is very quickly sanded over to prepare the arena for the next kill. Usually three bulls are disposed of in the course of one Corrida. Very occasionally justice is done and the bull gores one of its tormentors, sometimes fatally.

In this gory spectacle the horses must suffer extreme fear, for they are charged time and again by the infuriated bull, and although they are protected to some extent by heavy padding, they sometimes can sustain severe injuries. It has not been unknown for a horse to be disembowelled by the horns of an enraged bull, its entrails spilling out on to the sand. So as not to offend the tender susceptibilities of the many tourists who now attend these spectacles, the horses' vocal cords have been cut so that their screams of terror cannot be heard. I attended one such Corrida in my early years of visiting Spain, and that was more than enough.

Another national sport which the Society for the Prevention of Cruelty to Animals might not approve of is that of live pigeon shooting. In this sport, if one can call it that, the specially reared pigeon is taken from a crate, its tail feathers are pulled out and then the bird is stuffed into a compressed air mortar, similar in shape to the ones used on battlefields. A signal is given, the bird is propelled out, and since the tail feathers serve as a kind of stabiliser to the bird in flight, without them it flies erratically, thus presenting a more difficult target to the marksman. One afternoon's sport at such a shoot can result in as many as five hundred birds being killed. Multiply that by whatever number of such events take place across the whole of Spain.

As far as Majorca is concerned, and this is probably true of the rest of Spain, a new generation has now arisen with no memory of the excesses of the civil war and with only one commendable aim in mind, to become rich in the exploitation and development of modern technology and of the tourist industry. The pigeon shoots and the Corridas, however, are still as popular as ever

As much as we enjoyed the company of our new Spanish friends and in-laws, a further dimension to our life in Majorca now lay in wait for Mary and myself.

Twenty years or so before, in 1950, five years after the end of the last war, Majorca was only just beginning to develop from a backward and impoverished Mediterranean island into the wealthy tourist paradise that it has become. Although possessed of magnificent beaches, bays and seascapes, it was completely undeveloped and until then could well have been part of some third world country. Palma itself was a nondescript and dusty Mediterranean town whose only claim to fame was an imposing cathedral dating from the twelvth century, a magnificent location on a broad bay, and the fact that Chopin and George Sands had landed there before going for their winter sojourn in the picturesque Carthusian monastery of Valdemosa, a small hill village about fifteen miles inland from Palma.

After the end of the war with Germany and Japan, the great fear in the USA was the possible spread of communism in Europe, and so the Americans approached Franco for permission to build military bases on Spanish soil. El Caudillo, who had ruthlessly extirpated communism in his own land, was only too pleased to grant permits for American bases on Spanish soil, with all the money and investments that such bases would bring. American military advisers arrived in due time, and a small military contingent, commanded by Captain Steve Cusak of the US Air Force, arrived in Majorca in 1946. Cusak had been chosen for the post for two reasons: he was an able officer and he spoke fluent Spanish. Born in San Diego about thirty years earlier he had married into a well-off Californian Spanish family, and his training as an engineer before the war and his linguistic ability suited him admirably for the post of liaison officer with the Spanish in Majorca. He was struck by the natural untouched beauty of the island, and seeing the potential for development he decided to make an investment. Whilst still a soldier he was of course not permitted any business activities, but with his wife as a figurehead he began to buy up large tracts of land in the Son Vida valley set high in the hills just north of Palma.

This valley was an arid and seemingly worthless expanse of land surrounded by scrub-covered hills and surmounted by a huge abandoned castle, and before long Cusak was the owner of thousands of acres of land acquired for ridiculously small sums from owners who were only too glad to be rid of the parched and fallow Son Vida land, not fit even for the raising of goats. Such land, with its absence of water, was considered to be of no value, and the owners were only too glad to sell off to this crazy American who was seeking to buy land that nobody else wanted. But because of geological surveys carried out with his up to date equipment, Cusak knew something that the owners of the land in the Son Vida valley did not. The valley sat on top of an inexhaustible supply of water, flowing deep under the ground and accessible by means of artesian wells. Water in Majorca was, and still is, as precious as oil. There are no rivers on the island, rainfall is amongst the lowest in the Mediterranean, and the limited agriculture of the island had been made possible only by the water brought to the surface by primitive windmills, the ruins of which still dot the plains south-east of Palma. The availability of water was the yardstick by which the value of land in Majorca was assessed, and the value of a field could rocket a hundredfold upon the discovery of a source of irrigation.

Cusak had set up a development company with three others besides himself as shareholders, funds were raised, and the quid pro quo and the greasing of palms by which all business transactions were carried out in Majorca ensured the quick granting of any necessary permits. The latest in drilling machinery was obtained, and in no time the land in the valley of Son Vida was growing lush and green from the life-giving water which now spewed in seemingly limitless quantities from the parched earth. Steve Cusak was far-seeing. He raised more capital, restored the ruined castle and made it into a five star hotel, the Son Vida, which was soon to be filled to capacity by rich and free-spending holiday makers from northern Europe and Britain. After the war the implements of war had truly been beaten into ploughshares. The vast fleets of Allied bombers had been converted into passenger-carrying airplanes whose passengers invaded the hitherto quiet and unspoiled beaches of Spain and of the Balearics and happily poured money into the pockets of the local merchants.

The weather was as good as guaranteed, and things were dirt cheap in Spain then. A first class meal could be had for a couple of quid, a bottle of the local wine, rough though it may have been, was to be had for the equivalent of a shilling and spirits were literally cheaper than water, so people came in droves to visit the new holiday paradise. Inspired by the example of the golfing estates he had known in his native California, Cusak then embarked on the building of a golf course next to the hotel, and the area round the course was put up for sale in the form of plots of housebuilding land. Each plot was of two thousand square metres, strict building specifications were laid down and palatial houses soon sprung up, built there by oil-rich Arabs, English and German tax exiles and wealthy Spaniards. In the space of fifteen years, by 1965, one of the most select living areas in Europe had been created, and at its centre lay the Son Vida Club de Golf.

The new golf course acted as a magnet to the expatriate English who had begun to claim Majorca as their own. The development of the island had brought with it hundreds of retired English couples who had discovered that by living abroad life could be made easier: by electing to live away from the UK, no income tax would be paid there on their pensions and personal wealth, near perfect weather all year round was as good as guaranteed and the low cost of living on the island enabled them to partake of a lifestyle which only the very rich could enjoy back in Britain.

The new Son Vida golf course was very soon commandeered by those in the English colony who played golf. The game was practically unknown in Spain then. Ballesteros had as yet to arrive on the scene to make golf fashionable among the Spanish moneyed classes, so the English and a handful of Americans had the course almost to themselves. Almost, for soon undesirable elements, to the English and the Americans that is, in the form of German and Spanish golfers began to appear on the scene, and steps were immediately taken to consolidate the Anglo-American golfing dominance. The 9.30 Golfing Society was born, with Cusak, himself a keen golfer, as honorary president. The membership of the society was limited to thirty golfers, all membership by invitation of the com-mittee only, and since the committee consisted of Allen Martin Jenkins, retired Brigadier, Derek Lomax, ex-governor of the Sudan, Gibson McCabe, retired chairman of the American news magazine *Newsweek,* Count John De Prêt, an Anglo-Belgian Count, Wing Commander Bob Simpson, DSO and bar, late of the RAF, and George Turner, retired managing director of the Rootes car group, exclusivity was assured. The first tee was reserved for one hour for the Society from 9.30am on all days except Sunday, and a Majorcan golfing institution that was to last for twenty-five years was born.

By this time Ralph and I had retired from business and Mary and I had begun to spend more and more of our time in Majorca. Despite The Firs interlude, I had never lost my love for the game of golf and had become a member of Haggs Castle golf club, where I now played several times a week when in Glasgow. Each morning, as Mary and I drove from our apartment in Illetas up to Linda's home, built high on a hill overlooking the course, I looked with some envy at the sun-bathed fairways and decided to apply for membership. Since this was to be had simply on application, I paid a year's subscription, and I began daily visits to the course. Given that the 9.30 Society had the tee reserved for one hour in the mornings, it irked me a little to have to wait until 10.30 to seek a game, for that meant a late finish well into the afternoon, the speed of play on Son Vida being as slow as it was. It had never crossed my mind to approach the plummy-voiced group of Englishmen who assembled so possessively on the tee just after nine o'clock for a game, for to someone like myself, accustomed to the broad honest accent of Glasgow, there was something inherently alien and off-putting in the affectations of their upper-class English voices. A start very early in the morning was possible, but at that time suitable partners were hard to come by, and there was not much fun in playing golf alone. So I asked the starter, Eustacio, an obliging and golf-mad Mallorquin from the nearby town of Son Rapinya, whose new god was the newly emerged Severiano Ballesteros, to be put in touch with any single player who would like a partner to play with, and every morning at 8 o'clock I presented myself on the tee to see what my request might have produced.

There ensued a series of games with the most improbable variety of companions imaginable. Small, impeccably polite Japanese, hissing and bowing their way round the course, and Germans with their expensive clothes and ostentatious golf gear (mink club covers were to be seen in their golf-bags, no less).

By this time in the early 1980s, the 9.30 Society was showing signs of becoming somewhat thin in the ranks. Age and a surfeit of the cheap wine and gin readily available in Majorca had put paid to some, and as the cost of living began to keep pace with the island's growing prosperity, others had decided to return to their native England where the National Health Service could be relied upon to minister to the needs of their advancing years. The Society was now down to fifteen members, this even after the strict membership standards of its early days had been relaxed.

Then I had a stroke of good fortune. Joe Docherty and Jack McLean, bookie friends of mine from Glasgow, Joe from Wemyss Street round the corner from the Savoy, and Jack, a friend from the Western Baths, came to Illetas, where Mary and I had our apartment, for a month's holiday. They were both keen golfers, Joe with a five handicap, so I had them join me every morning for a game at Son Vida. We had the tee reserved for the slot immediately in front of the 9.30 Society tee-off. Our first contact with the English group was not a propitious one. As Joe Docherty was getting ready to drive his first ball on Son Vida to a background of suitable silence from the onlookers, Jacque Mahe's poodle appeared at the edge of the box led on a leash by a young caddy. Mahe was a French racing driver whose claim to fame was a win in the Targa Florio road race in Sicily in 1938 and a good record in the yearly Le Mans races. He was elderly now and had lived for some years on the island. The Society allowed his dog, a horrible-looking smelly poodle with bad teeth, to accompany him on the course. The poodle broke away from the caddy, ran over to Joe's golf bag and promptly cocked its leg, ready to pee. Joe poked at it with his driver.

'Get that effin' dug away!'

Although the Glasgow accent might have been incomprehensible, the motion of the club was not, and the caddy yanked the dog away, to the consternation of the Frenchman, who immediately leaned over to console his affronted pet while throwing a dark look at the stranger who had dared to chastise his poodle.

'Shoudnay huv a bluddy dug on the course anyway,' continued Joe, and rifled a long drive smack down the middle of the fairway. Joe and I followed suit. Although we were well into our sixtie,s the three of us played a fair game of golf and the quality of our play was not lost on John De Prêt, the captain of the Society, who followed us on the tee and who, given the slowness of the play, could observe our golf shots on almost every subsequent hole.

John de Prêt was a huge man of about fifty years of age, son of a Belgian Count and English mother, and a hard-drinking, hard-smoking, hard-wenching expatriate who had lived on the island for about fifteen years in semi-luxurious ease, thanks to a remittance cheque which arrived each month from his family in England. He was a fine golfer, especially when fuelled by several large draughts of whisky, and he could see in us three potential recruits for his beloved Society if our backgrounds did not deviate too much from the entrance requirements, and so he began to exchange pleasantries during the long wait on each tee. We three could moderate our Glasgow patter at will; soon names and identities were exchanged in a common language if not a common accent, and I, long experienced in these matters, noted the quiver of an eyebrow on the Count's forehead on hearing of my Italian and fish and chips business background.

As I was to learn later, we had been observed at play by some of the members, and at their next meeting the committee sat and discussed the question of extending us an invitation to join the 9.30 Society. John de Prêt was nothing if not pragmatic. The existing members, now somewhat depleted, could not take up the all the allocated time on the tee. If this depletion were to continue, that time would be shortened, and there might follow an encroachment of Germans and Spaniards into the morning's play, a fate which was to be avoided at all costs, he argued, even if it meant inviting two Glasgow bookies and a Glasgow-Italian fish and chip shop owner and their friends into their august circle. Besides, they were bloody good golfers, and knew the game better than most, which could only be to the advantage of their circle. Counter-arguments were put forward. The exclusiveness of the original group had been diluted far enough, some said. The Frenchman with his poodle was about as far down as one could go, and the idea of allowing a trio of rather uncouth Glaswegians to join, and one of them an Italian fish and chip man, no less, was simply not on. And who would the newcomers invite to play with them? More of the same ilk, no doubt. But they were good golfers, said others, a damn sight better than most of us, they certainly know all about etiquette on a golf course, and we do need new blood after all, they said. So a vote was taken, the motion that the three newcomers to Son Vida be invited to join the Society was passed, and the next morning the invitation to join was given to us by John De Prêt. We looked at one another. What did membership entail? A small subscription? No problem there. Weekly competitions amongst themselves and the occasional match with visiting groups from England? That sounded like fun. Monthly lunches for the members and one grand ladies' night each year? The women might like that, and so we decided to become members of the 9.30 Society, even though, as Joe said in an aside to me: 'This bloody snotty lot wouldnay even spit on us back hame!'

From then on I formed part of the group assembled on the first tee at Son Vida each morning, to be joined there by my bookie friends when they were on the island, our Glasgow accents now loud and prominent amongst the clipped and plummy reserved English tones of our new golfing companions.

It was a marvellous time for Mary and myself. New horizons had been opened up by Linda's marriage and by my membership at the Son Vida Golf club. Here we were, a thousand miles, a whole world and almost sixty years away from Surrey Street and Auchinleck, from the internment years of the war and from the hard work in the Savoy. Long gone and for the moment submerged in my river of memory were those places and the dingy rat-ridden tenements in which I had lived as a boy. Now here were Mary and I, on the threshold of our old age, about to savour the delights of a world and of a lifestyle undreamed of in our youth. We were introduced individually to the members by John De Prêt, the Society captain. I could see the look of disdain on some of the members' faces. But on the whole the 9.30 Society members were a pleasant and decent lot once you got used to the English mannerisms and accents, and I eagerly looked forward to my games with them. To promote familiarity amongst members and to bring variety into the morning pairings, all new members were allotted a different partner for each round by the captain. Some I enjoyed playing with, some I did not. My favourite partner was Reidar Mathisen, the son of a Norwegian father and Spanish mother who had lived on the island for a number of years. About sixty years of age and playing off a handicap of eight, he was a fine golfer and the perfect fairway companion. He concentrated on every stroke, was perfect in course etiquette, and yet could chat affably with his companions on the fairway in between shots. He was fluent in four languages and very popular amongst the members. We became good friends, and one year he and his charming wife Grete came to Scotland on holiday. It was 1986, the year Greg Norman won the Open at Turnberry, and they arrived two days after the last day's play to stay at the Turnberry Hotel. Mary and I travelled down from Glasgow to spend the day with them, Reidar and I to play a round on the course, with the ladies set to enjoy the amenities of the hotel. It was a beautiful day, with the course still set out for the championship, and with workmen just starting work on the dismantling of the spectator stands. We were both playing well that day, and at the final hole we drove two impeccable drives over the grassy mounds in front smack down the middle of the eighteenth fairway. We were of course playing from the forward tees, and so our drives landed well within iron range of the green. We then both hit two fine shots which finished no more than twenty feet or so from the pin. There were a score or so of workmen seated on the benches of the stand having their tea break, and as Reidar and I came striding down the fairway and on to the putting surface we were treated to a reception just as noisy and as enthusiastic as the one Greg Norman had received just two days before. We graciously responded by a doffing of caps and a wave of the hand.

Next on my list of favourite golf companions there was Bernard Metcalf, a retired printer from Birmingham, who despite his sixty-five or so years could still play a fair game of golf and was himself of a working-class background. Despite our class difference I also enjoyed playing with retired Brigadier Alan Martin Jenkins, late of the eigth Indian division of the British army, and with Bob Simpson, our club champion. Bob was a much decorated war pilot with a DSO and bar, who had been living on the island for more than twenty years and played off a handicap of two. During his visits to Majorca, Jack McLean the bookie always played with the Brigadier. Two more different characters it would be hard to imagine, one the polished and suave product of Sandhurst and the other the rough Glasgow street bookie with a rather thin veneer of education. They had one thing in common, however, as they had both fought for six months at the battle of Monte Cassino and had a world of shared experiences to talk about. In that connection Jack had a marvellous story to tell of an event which took place some weeks after the battle.

With true army logic, his sergeant, hearing that Jack was a bookie in civvy street and reasoning that a bookie should know all there was to know about horses, had elevated him to the rank of corporal and had put him in charge of the pack animals used to carry food and ammunition to the soldiers fighting on the Monte Cassino hill. The countryside behind the front line was foraged for horses and mules that could serve as pack animals, and these were put in Jack's charge. In the dark of night, for no movement was possible during daylight, the mules would be loaded with supplies and led up through the debris of battle in an attempt to reach the fighting troops. Even in darkness the losses were horrendous. Enemy flares would light the night, and any movement brought down heavy mortar and machine-gun fire, causing heavy casualties amongst Jack's animals and men. He emerged from all this unscathed, but when the monastery finally fell he was left shattered mentally by the weeks of battle he had endured on the murderous slopes of Mount Cassino. He was decorated for his bravery in the action, ordered to take care of the remaining horses and given some well-earned leave for rest and recuperation.

A few miles inland from Naples stood the shattered ruins of what was left of the town of Caserta. The Royal Palace close by had been untouched by bombing and the huge estate had been chosen as a rest area for Allied troops. There, relaxing after the stress of front line activity, were thousands of soldiers from a dozen nations. British Tommys and American GIs, white and black, rubbed shoulder with New Zealanders and Australians. The free French with their savage Goums from Algeria and Morocco, Poles, Czechs and Indians all mingled together, glad to have survived the intense battles of the last few months. They ate and drank the local wine and lazed in the sun and played interminable games of cards, betting with the wads of Occupation Lire issued by Army Command. The rate of exchange had been set at one hundred lire to the pound, and every man was flush with months of unspent back pay.

A few days of good food and wine and rest had been enough to restore Jack. His mules and horses had been put out to pasture in neighbouring fields, and he seized on an idea. These soldiers liked to gamble, so why not give them the opportunity to bet on horse races? With a few enthusiastic helpers, a rough and ready race track was flattened out in a neighbouring field, the horses and mules were graded roughly, races were organised and Jack proceeded to rake in thousands of lire in bets. His winnings were considerable, and when after a few weeks of racing activity he was ordered to report to his unit, he found himself in possession of a duffel bag crammed full of lire notes. What was he to do with all this money? In one of the few parts of Caserta which had not been destroyed by the fighting, he had noticed a bank, and there in the manager's office he sat with bundles of lire neatly stacked out on the astonished official's desk. The manager's protestations about the possible illegality of opening up an account for a foreign soldier were quickly dissipated by the gift of a couple of these bundles, and Jack left the premises with a bankbook containing a balance of some 200,000 lire, which as nearly as he could calculate represented about £2000, a princely sum indeed in those days.

The War lasted for one more year, and Jack, now raised to the rank of sergeant, took part in several other battles on the Italian peninsula, finding himself at war's end in Milan, far north of his Caserta bank. In the course of these engagements he had somehow managed to lose his bankbook, but he didn't worry much about that. He knew the neighbourhood in Caserta where the bank was. He had forgotten the exact name, banco di something, it was, but he remembered well the little manager, Signor Scopa, so on his first peacetime leave he made his way back to Caserta to take possession of his little fortune.

He was aghast at what he found there. The heaps of ruins had been cleared, new buildings were being built everywhere, street patterns had been altered and the place bore no resemblance to the ruined town in which he had lodged his money. Through an American interpreter who was helping with the reconstruction he told his story to an unsympathetic police captain who could offer no help. He knew of no Signor Scopa. He was probably a temporary official sent from some head bank or other in Naples, he said. The banco di what? How did the British Sergeant expect to find a bank if he didn't know the name? Besides, the whole town was being rebuilt, and if the bank in question had been in a damaged building it very probably would have been demolished to make way for a new structure, and a dispirited Jack was unceremoniously shown the door. He spent fruitless days making a tour of banks in the district, to be met everywhere with blank stares and shrugging shoulders. Did he not have a bank-book? Did he not have any document or receipt? Could he not remember the exact name of the bank? Was he sure that it was in Caserta? A defeated Jack was demobbed a few months later and was soon back in Glasgow to regale his friends with the tale of the misplaced fortune, and to pick up the reins of his interrupted career. His pitch became more prosperous than ever, and the memory of his lost lire grew less painful with the passing of the years and the growth of his business.

In the post-war years many a holiday did Jack spend in Italy, visiting the scenes of bygone battles, and telling all and sundry of how he had a lot of money invested in the Caserta area, if he could only remember where; a story he was to tell several times over to the rather sceptical members of the 9.30 Society.

The person I least enjoyed played with, a feeling shared by almost all the other members, was Major Tom Lyon, late of the Third Ghurka rifle battalion attached to Orde Wingate's Chindits. He certainly had an impressive war record, but as a golfing partner the retired Major was someone to be avoided. He was stone deaf and compensated for this by conversing with his golf partner of the day in a parade ground voice which carried across at least three fairways. His conversation, which was more of a monologue, since he could not hear any reply from his companion, was somewhat repetitive and consisted of stories of his exploits along the Irrawaddy river, which when heard once or twice were certainly interesting, but palled somewhat with constant repetition. Moreover, he was the slowest player imaginable, for he could not bear to lose a ball, a fixation which invariably caused long delays on a course where one could easily lose a ball on every hole if the fairway was missed. He would insist on spending all the time necessary to find his ball in the rough, and would not continue play until a ball, not necessarily his own, was found by his caddy. His old companions in the Society were well aware of this idiosyncrasy, and to keep play flowing supplied his caddy with half a dozen or so balls to be conveniently found when a reasonable time had elapsed in a fruitless search for the Major's wildly struck ball. John De Prêt introduced me to him:

170

'Perry, Perry,' repeated the Major. 'We had a Perry in our battalion. Copped his lot in Johore Baru. Any relation by chance?'

He paid no heed to my disclaimer, but went into a long description of the action where the unfortunate Perry had copped his lot. Somehow I survived my first game with the Major and made a mental note to avoid a repetition of the experience if at all possible. One morning soon after I had joined the society the Major decided to have a bit of practice on his own before his companions arrived and walked on to the fourteenth tee adjoining the clubhouse, meaning to play that hole and then the eighteenth, which led back to the first tee. Since there were as yet no golfers on the course and no caddies as yet available, he put a few clubs into a pencil bag, slung it over his shoulder and followed his drive down the fairway. The fourteenth safely negotiated, he walked on to he eighteenth tee and surveyed the hole. The eighteenth was probably the most difficult hole on the course. A dog-leg to the left of some 475 yards, the ball had to be hit along a sloping fairway which could gather up even a well struck ball and run it into a long lake which ran half the length of the hole.

The Major teed up his ball, aimed well to the right of the fairway in an attempt to eliminate the danger of the water hazard and hit a long hook which went well left of his intended line. The ball cleared the fairway and splashed into the water at the edge of the lake. He picked up his bag of clubs, walked down to the edge and saw his ball lying clearly in what seemed to be just a few feet of water. He knelt down, selected a suitable club from the bag, and leaned over to fish the ball out. His first attempt knocked the ball further away and as he leaned over further, he over-balanced and toppled into the still waters of the lake. The water there was deeper than it had appeared, coming nearly up to his neck as his feet touched the bottom. He waded over to the grass verge and attempted to pull himself out. To no avail. He kept slipping back down the steep moss-covered cement bank of the hazard, and try as he might could not get out and back onto the fairway. He paused for a moment and shouted for help at the top of his voice, but the sound failed to carry back to the first tee where some early morning golfers were preparing to tee off.

That same morning I too had decided to have a few early practice holes, and as I walked along by the lake on the eighteenth I heard a faint voice calling for help. I looked, and there was the Major, up to his neck in water, waving frantically at me. I managed to pull him back on to the fairway, soaked and covered in weeds, but none the worse for wear from his twenty minute or so immersion in the lake. Fuming with chagrin he walked back to the clubhouse, where he changed into dry clothes and began his belated round of golf to the accompaniment of unsympathetic comments from his friends, the consensus of their remarks being that he should have been left to drown where he was! It was not until he arrived at the third hole and went to pick a nine iron from his bag that he realised that the club had vanished into the lake, where it remained lost, together with the only ball he had ever failed to find in all his years of playing on Son Vida.

The culmination of the golfing year was the gala ladies' night, held in the La Vileta restaurant on the outskirts of Palma, a rambling hacienda-type place owned by Bob Edwards, a young Welshman who had lived most of his life in Majorca and who occasionally played as a guest with the 9.30 Society. The affair was planned each year by Bernard Metcalf, who designed striking invitations and menus for the event and by Bev Ives, a gin and tonic drinking Yorkshireman who had inherited a cricket ball factory in Pakistan from his father, which he promptly sold and dedicated his life to playing golf and to drinking as much gin as he could with the substantial proceeds of the sale. Our first gala night was due to be held just a few weeks after our joining; I attended with Mary, we had a marvellous time, and I could see that she was beginning to take to the Majorcan way of life. From time to time we played host to visiting English golfing groups to play a tournament for the Jim Large Trophy, a cup gifted to the Society by Jim Large, an English golf professional and one of the founder members. As well as being great golfing moments, these visits were most enjoyable social occasions, and for one of them, which coincided with one of our ladies' night dinner, I read out the following poem, *Ode to the 9.30 Society*, my first attempt at writing.

It was roundly cheered by the audience, who, given the wine-induced state of receptivity they were all in, would just as roundly have cheered a recitation of the twelve-times table.

Ode to the 9.30 Society

In fair far-off Majorca, every day at crack of dawn,
In the Kingdom of the Cusak, in the valley of Son Vida,
On the tee they stand together, Warriors great with drivers drawn.
From North and South and West and East they gather,
   Glorious in their pride and brawn.
They are there to hunt for eagles, but pars and birdies will fall too,
And for this they wield their mashies, wedge and cleek and niblick
   true.
There they wait for brave Sir Metcalf, Captain of this grand array,
Who, when all are there assembled, leads them forth into the fray.
A worthy captain is the grizzled Bernard, true ancient mariner of the
   course is he,
For of him the story's told that on a bleak cold winter's day,
He the tenth in two Homeric strokes did play, and thus an albatross to
   rest did lay.

Now on the tee the great Walloon De Prêt stands ready, driver in his
 powerful hand,
No finer hunter can be found than he, and foes in fear of him do stand.
With five-wood in his hand, from Portrush battleground in savage
 Ulsterland comes Hedley,
Best of all the Belfastmen is he, and by his side stands Norseman Reidar,
 fierce Viking from cold northern land.
With solemn mien there's fiery Pepper, fresh and eager for the fray,
And Bev and Norman and Lyon and Fishwick, stout English hearts of
 oak are they.
From deeds in far Cathay comes good George Turner, by him Stanley
 Wade does stand,
Whilst tall and brooding in the dawning, lurks Derek, noble Lomax of
 Sudan.
With DSO and bar from battles in the German sky comes Robert, of
 the Simpson clan is he,
And close by him there's Joe the Tuscan, Glasgow man from Italie.
Sir Roy, the Dean of Hazel, from far-off Turkestan has come,
 What eagles, pars and birdies will be in store for him?
And last but not the least there's Owen, a warrior from Scottish borderland
 is he,
And by his side tall Martin-Jenkins waits with soldier's courage on the
 tee.
Missing from this grand array is Yankee Gibson, in Winged Foot USA
 hunts he,
He seeks the eagle and the birde in the lands of Huron, Navajo and
 Sioux.
New warriors within the shadows wait, there's Ray and Alec and Ron
 from Heathergate,
And from Yorkshire Dale comes Ken the Hunter, who in days of yore
 from muck made brass,
And now with metal head and carbon shaft new fortunes seeks on fairway
 grass.
Tee up! Tee up! The clubs are out, the ball teed up, the first ball of the
 day is struck.
From deep within the valley comes the sound of battle's roar,
The drive is sliced, the bunker gapes, the pitch goes wild, no one es
 capes.
Breasts are rent and teeth are gnashed and hopes of fame are rudely
 dashed,
As putts that ought to sink go sliding past.

The last putt drops, the last flag flutters, and homewards go the weary
 warriors to reminisce,
On wedge shot shanked and putt that missed.
O ye ghosts of long dead golfers, Vardon, Jones and Hagen too,
Rest ye well in golf's Valhalla, for in far-off Spanish land, in the valley of
 Son Vida, in the Kingdom of the Kusak,
To carry on your great tradition, there dwells this small but gallant
 band.

JP, Ladies' Night, 1984

At this time Mary and I were spending much of the winter in Majorca, which was the best season of the year for golf, given the intense heat of summer on the island, and we would often play host to some of my Glasgow Haggs Castle golfing friends. Haggs Castle had a fair number of Scots-Italian members, about a dozen or so, and these were my preferred golfing companions there. Given that most of them had shared my own childhood and adolescent experiences as immigrants or sons of immigrants, we felt completely at ease and uninhibited in one another's company, and once a year we would form a team, the Haggs Italians, to play against a team chosen from the native Haggs Castle members. These were good-natured but intensely competitive matches, and I suggested that we Haggs-Italians should challenge the Son Vida 9.30 Society to a similar match. The match would be held at Son Vida in mid-winter, at a time when the course at Haggs Castle would be unplayable because of weather. John De Prêt was enthusiastic about the idea, and so a series of encounters between a team of fifteen or so Glasgow-Italian fish friers and café owners and the English clutch of leaders of industry, high officials of the civil service and high-ranking military officers who went to make up the 9.30 Society was arranged. The games were a great success and always played in a spirit of intense but sporting rivalry, with victory almost always going to he home team, not perhaps because they were better golfers, but because the Haggs Italians tended to be over-enthusiastic in their consumption of Rioja during their stay. The matches, played in a Ryder Cup format, were followed by a banquet held in the Son Vida restaurant. I re-member the beginning of a speech made by the winning captain, John De Prêt on the occasion of the prize giving:

'Two thousand or so years ago, the forefathers of the Haggs-Italians came to the shores of England, and their leader said the immortal words, "Veni, Vidi, Vici."

Two thousand years later the descendants of those Romans have come to this patch of England in the Mediterranean and are forced to depart with the words, "Veni, Vidi, and got soundly thrashed!"'

Because of its affiliation to the Son Vida Hotel, the course was visited often by VIPs and all sorts of celebrities. One day we were informed that Angel Miguel and José Maria Canizares, two outstanding Spanish golfers of that era, would be staying at the hotel for some days with their families, and that they probably would be playing a few rounds on the course. The two golfers were very friendly types and mixed in well with the Son Vida members at the nineteenth hole in the clubhouse. John De Prêt came up with an idea. Why not challenge the two professionals to a game, a fourball, better ball, with a suitable handicap of course, so as to make a game of it, the match to be followed afterwards by a party at the clubhouse. The match was suggested to Canizares and Miguel by the club starter, Eustacio, and promptly taken up by the two professionals as being a pleasant way to pass a morning. There was a condition, however. There should be a small wager on the outcome. The professionals suggested 100,000 pesetas a head, about £500. We baulked at this, but then, so anxious were our members to see such a match that they agreed to club together to raise the money for the wager. The problem as far as we were concerned was who would partner John De Prêt? Canizares and Miguel could speak practically no English, and since De Prêt could speak practically no Spanish, to make it a pleasant round for all concerned John preferred to be partnered by someone who spoke Spanish. Ability did not matter much, handicap would take care of that. It may be difficult to believe but there was no-one in the 9.30 Society apart from myself who could carry on a conversation in that language, despite the fact that many of them had lived on the island for many years.

They lived in a sizeable colony of English-speaking expatriates, all their business with the locals was done through English-speaking agencies, the waiters in the bars and restaurants had a working knowledge of that language, so why learn the local lingo? Not worth the bother, old boy, you'll always find someone who speaks English. I remember a match I once played with Roy Hazeldene, retired director of British Leyland Middle Eastern division, just retired to Majorca from his headquarters in Istanbul. We both had caddies, the euphemistic title given to the motley crowd of bag-carriers who could be hired at the course to carry your clubs for a couple of hundred pesetas. They were local lads from the village of Son Rapinya close by, of ages anything between fifteen and sixty-five years, and knew absolutely nothing about golf. They spoke no English, a deficiency which did not deter some of the players from shouting instructions at them in that language. At the first hole Roy was about to putt, and paused when he saw that his bag carrier, a boy by the name of Santiago, was casting his shadow on the line of his putt.

'Remove your shadow from my line, boy,' he yelled. Santiago looked at him blankly, with not a word understood. Roy repeated his words, in an even louder tone, and followed them with the question, 'what's the matter with you boy, don't you understand English?', which of course he didn't, but moved his shadow when I repeated Roy's request in Spanish.

Roy looked at me 'You speak Spanish? Quite amazing!'

Anyhow, since I was the only one in the society who could blether in Spanish, I was elected to partner John De Prêt, much to my delight. I was asked for my opinion on handicapping. Well, I said, the par on the Son Vida course was seventy two. The two professionals were capable of going round in a better ball score of sixty or even lower. For two golfers, one, myself, playing off sixteen, and John off six, to even dream about matching such a score, one stroke on the par four, two strokes on the par fives and possibly one stroke on the par threes would have to be given, since if John and I played at our very best we might achieve a better ball score of seventy eight or so. That meant that about twenty strokes or so should be given, making it possible for John and I to approach a better ball score of around sixty and thus make a game of it. After much argument Canizares came up with a suggestion. John and I would start on the first tee fourteen holes up with eighteen to play, he offered. He and Miguel would give us each a stroke a hole. John and I didn't even have to win a hole for victory. Four halved holes in the first fifteen would win us the match. As an added concession the game would be played from the middle tees, thus subtracting a good few hundred yards from the length of the course. We agreed and the match started, watched by a fair number of spectators. To cut a long story very short, John and I lost every hole and were able to half only one. Our fourteen up dwindled until we stood on the seventeenth tee with the professionals one up and two to play. The match finished on the seventeenth green, Miguel and Canizares the victors by two holes. They pocketed their substantial winnings and stood us all drinks at the bar.

Towards the beginning of our time in Majorca, a Spanish–American gambling consortium had drawn up plans for the opening of a number of casinos in mainland Spain and on Majorca itself. One had already been opened in Puerto Banus, near Malaga, and the one in Majorca, built next to the sea at a place called Cala Figuera about twenty kilometres from the capital Palma, was due to open in about six months time. The Casino Majorca, as it was to be known, was to be the last word in luxury and the consortium were hoping to attract big spenders from the Mediterranean gambling set, in particular the Arabs, who had money to burn and were building large luxurious mansions for themselves on the Son Vida estate. To make access easy for the Mediterranean millionaire yachting set, a series of jetties had been built in the tiny bay at the foot of the cliff where the Casino stood and these were to be connected to the casino by means of spectacular elevators, glass-fronted to give a magnificent view of the bay of Palma. There was to be no hotel attached to the casino, but a five star restaurant was to be part of the complex and the consortium were intending that it should be the gambling jewel in their crown. The setting was quite magnificent. One side of the gambling room consisted of a window the full width of the structure, and through it could be seen the wide bay of Palma, with the full spread of the city laid out in panorama. The décor reflected the brightness and colour of the Mediterranean setting. Gone were the heavy carpets, plush curtains and crystal chandeliers which usually formed part of the décor of the traditional casino. Here there were marble floors, tinted mirrors, subdued indirect lighting, and cascading fountains of water in the four corners of the gambling area, creating an ambience of grace and beauty.

But then, with everything in place and just a week before the date of the Gala opening, a bombshell fell. Someone discovered that the jetties and lifts provided for the arrival of luxury yachts could never be put to use. The harbour authorities had produced maps which showed that about five hundred metres out from the deep water of the bay there existed a rocky shelf which made the waters above it too shallow to allow of the passage of anything except the smallest of craft. You would have thought that with all the millions spent on planning, someone would have made sure that access from the sea for large craft was possible, but the mistake had been made and the dream of an invasion of a wealthy armada from the marinas of the Mediterranean evaporated. Such ineptitude in planning may seem difficult to believe, but it was to be followed by another of almost equal proportions. About twelve years ago work began on an an extensive motorway system to link the airport to the various holiday resorts. To arrive at Soller, a resort on the western side of the island, a five-kilometre tunnel had to be driven through a mountain. Work was started at both sides, the aim being for the two excavations to meet in the middle of the mountain, but the two tunnels failed to meet as planned. They missed one another by 105 metres, resulting in the bankruptcy of the building contractors and a delay of more than two years in the opening of the road network.

Casino Majorca opened as scheduled, but on a distinctly lower key than had been planned, with its customers made up of the local population and of holidaymakers from the local package holiday resorts, whose spending power was nowhere near that of the clientele originally expected. The Casino was certainly packed to overflowing, but instead of the stakes of millions of pesetas expected by the management, the roulette wheels were spinning to bets of a few thousand placed by giggling holidaymakers who seemed to regard the Casino as just another amusement arcade.

However, locals too began to frequent the place, and the restaurant, in its quite magnificent setting, became a favourite dining place with the Spanish from Palma. Mary and I used it occasionally as a place to reciprocate for hospitality received.

It was during this time in Majorca that the thought of writing a book came into my head. In the course of the interminable parties and social events that Mary and I took part in, the stories I had to tell of my early days as an immigrant in Glasgow and of my working life in the Savoy were much requested by the 9.30 Society members and their ladies. Possibly because I spoke of a way of life and of a background unknown to the likes of a Brigadier, such as Alan Martin Jenkins was, a Governor of the Sudan as Alan Lomax had been, and a captain of industry such as George Turner was, my stories were much in request at social occasions. Fuelled by a few glasses of Rioja I could wax garrulous about the many colourful characters who had been our customers in the Savoy and Silver Lounge and their exploits, and many were the times I had to recount the adventures of Johnny Myers with the knife stuck in his head, Benny Goodman of the West End Misfits and Max Bacon's coat, plus many others. I was often questioned at some length about my wartime experiences. I was quite naturally somewhat reticent about divulging these to the likes of Wing Commander Bob Simpson, DSO and bar, Major Eric Owen of the Highland Light Infantry and Count John De Prêt, all of whom had seen war in all its reality and by whose government I had been considered an enemy alien, but as familiarity grew I would intersperse my Glasgow stories with tales of my experiences in the POW camp in Montreal. They were well received and sometimes, after a few extra glasses of Rioja, I could become very expansive in the telling of them.

No-one listened to my tales with greater enthusiasm than did Bernard Melcalf, the printer from Birmingham, who kept saying that I should write a book around my stories. I toyed with the idea, but since my long-hand writing was indecipherable even to myself and my skills at a typewriter were limited to a tentative pecking with two fingers, which produced more mistakes than legible script, I went no further. But then one day Bernard showed me his latest electronic marvel, a word processor. I looked on with amazement as he demonstrated the powers of the machine. Mistakes could be easily put right. Whole chunks of words could be cut and transposed to another part of the sentence. Spelling mistakes were automatically corrected. To me the machine was a miracle which took the labour from writing. I immediately bought one, and a whole new dimension was opened up to me. I could now put down on paper the stories I enjoyed telling verbally, and slowly my first book took shape. *The Limbo Years*, I called it. It dealt with my internment and subsequent transportation to a POW camp in Montreal. I printed out several copies of it from my word processor, and posted them off hopefully to half a dozen or so publishers whose names I had found in the *Writers' and Artists' Yearbook*. The refusals came thick and fast, and after months of frustration I gave up sending off copies of *The Limbo Years*, and the pile of returned manuscripts gathered dust on the shelves of my study. They lay there for more than a year, until one day I happened on an article in the

Glasgow Herald by a journalist, Jack McLean, a regular writer in that newspaper. His article dealt with the Italians who had settled in the central Scottish belt, was very readable, had obviously been well researched and showed an insight into Scottish-Italian culture.

I wrote to him to say that, as one of those Italians he had written so penetratingly about, I had enjoyed his article very much, and that he in turn might be interested in my *Limbo Years*. I dusted off and enclosed a copy of the manuscript. I received no acknowledgement. Months passed and one day I received a phone call from a Glasgow publisher, Neil Wilson. It was to the effect that his friend Jack McLean had given him my manuscript, that he was interested in publishing it, with one or two changes, and that he would like to set up a meeting to discuss the matter. I accepted, of course, and immediately wrote a letter of thanks to Jack McLean. We have been friends ever since.

The changes I had to make to my manuscript taught me how to write and construct a book. I worked together with Liz Small, a lovely and charming young lady, who was Neil Wilson's editor at the time. I took note of her suggestions as to composition and layout, and had to admit that after her ministration, *The Limbo Years* read much better. The thing was, however, that it was no longer *The Limbo Years*. It had become *Isle of the Displaced*, a title which was not to my liking. I thought my own much, much better, but who was I to argue with the man who was going to publish my almost forgotten manuscript?

The book was published and sold quite well, especially amongst Scots-Italians, for it told of experiences which they themselves had undergone and problems which they too had encountered during the years Italy was at war with Britain. My appetite for writing had now grown, and a second book followed: *Tales of the Savoy,* a book of short stories about some of the colourful characters who frequented our shop. This was followed by a third, *The Big Men,* about the Glasgow police in the years preceding and immediately after the War. A fourth book entitled *The Wheel of Fortune* was to come next, but more about that in a subsequent chapter.

It was in Majorca that we met Hedley Best and his wife Joan. Hedley was a Belfast businessman who owned a holiday flat in Palma Nova, and one of a group of Ulstermen who came to the island as often as possible to escape the troubles in Northern Ireland, which were at their height then. In the group were Jim Hill and Wylie Geddes, the former an ex-Everton footballer who now owned a sports shop in Carrickfergus, and the latter a farmer whose father had been Mayor of Belfast some years before. They were all keen golfers and would come to play with the 9.30 Society at every available opportunity. Many were the enjoyable games John De Prêt and I played against Hedley Best and Jim Hill. These were played on a regular basis on their Santa Ponsa course, and were fiercely contested but thoroughly enjoyable occasions. After the round the losers would stand the beers at a local bar, the Rotunda, where the effect of a pint of cold beer after a round of golf in temperatures in the mid-eighties was startling to behold.

The best golfer in the Irish contingent was Tom Lennon, who, though originally from Belfast, now hailed from Hong Kong where he held the position of editor of the *South China Evening News*, the prestigious far eastern English language newspaper. Tom was a charming man and a great companion. He could talk with a great deal of authority on any subject, and could regale us with anecdotes about his career as a journalist. Despite all that, next to Tom Lyon, he was my least favourite golfing companion. He was too much of a perfectionist. He played off scratch, and did not suffer lesser golfers like myself gladly. I have always looked on golf as not only a game to be played as well as one can, but also as a pastime where the companionship of fellow players is there to be enjoyed. Competitiveness enters into it, of course, but a missed three-foot putt should not bring about a case of the sulks from one's partner. Tom Lennon was a veritable Jekyll and Hyde character, for away from the tensions of the course a more pleasant and affable companion than Tom could not be found. At the nineteenth hole the frowning concentration and bad temper shown on the greens and fairways were immediately shed, and a remarkable transformation into a laughing and amiable drinking companion took place.

Even when in Majorca, Mary and I would make our yearly pilgrimage to Rome. In 1981 Mary and I flew there from Palma for our mandatory yearly visit. We arrived late one Saturday night, and took a taxi to our hotel, the Visconti Palace, behind Bernini's colonnade just round the corner from St Peter's Square. Early next morning we walked the few steps through the colonnade and emerged into the huge space beyond. St Peter's Square was packed with people, all in groups of fifty or so, with each group carrying a banner on which was written the name of a town. We approached the nearest group, whose banner sported the name Crotone, and addressed a jolly little man who seemed to be in charge of the group. The Pope was to give a special audience in St Peter's to groups of pilgrims from a variety of towns south of Naples, he told us, and all these groups were assembled in the square ready to take their place in the Basilica. Entrance was to be given to groups only, and no casual visitor was to be allowed until the audience was over. Mary and I were crestfallen at the news, for it meant a long, long wait until we could make our customary pilgrimage inside the church. Where were we from, asked the jolly little man. I explained, thanked him for his information, and got ready to take our leave. Why didn't we come into his group, he asked. All we had to do was to stand beside him and walk with his group to a designated spot inside the Basilica, and a cry of assent came to us from his companions.

'*Si, si, venite pure con noi, E' peccato che siete venuti cosi' da lontano senza poter entrare.*' (Yes, yes, come on in with us. It's a shame that you've come so far and can't get in.)

We thanked the little man and his companions profusely and took our place under the Crotone banner. An hour or so passed, and as we waited the memory of the last time Mary and I had waited for an audience with the Pope in the Raphael room together with my father and mother and the three kids came back to me. I recounted the story to our hosts, to their great merriment. Finally we began to inch our way into the Basilica, where we were ushered by attendants to a spot labelled 'Crotone' behind the barriers erected around the sides of the church. We stood and waited and chatted as the church filled up, and then a hush descended as the Pope entered and began to make his way slowly round the barriers, stopping to bless each group and to shake as many outstretched hands as could reach his.

The little man from Crotone whispered to me.

'You and your lady stay close to me, I've got something arranged,' and as the Pope paused at our group, a photographer dashed out from behind the Swiss guards, stood at the side of the Pope and took as many photos as he could until the guards pulled him politely but firmly away. The little man took my name and address in Palma, with the promise of a photograph as soon as they were ready.

The audience over, the Pope disappeared behind the Baldacchino, and we began to file slowly towards the exit. We were about to exit into the brilliant sunshine of the square when yells and shrieks rang out.

'Hanno ammazzato il Papa! Hanno ammazzato il Papa!' (The Pope's been killed! The Pope's been killed!)

His Holiness had been shot and wounded no more than half an hour after he had greeted and blessed the Crotone group and had taken Mary's outstretched hand. Some ten days later we received this photograph with the best wishes of the little man who had arranged it all for us. He is the man in the photograph who is clutching the Pope's left hand just as Mary is about to receive a handshake from his right one. I wish I could remember his name.

One year during these visits from Palma to Italy we joined up there with Charlie Pacitti and his wife Gina, both of Glasgow, who were on one of their occasional visits to the village of their birth, Pietrafitta in the province of Frosinone. Together we motored north to Viareggio for a visit to my parents and relatives in that region. In order to differentiate them from the other many Pacittis in Scotland, in Glasgow they were known as 'The Russian Pacittis', for that is where Charlie's parents had lived for many years before coming to Scotland. Charlie's mother had been a seamstress in the service of the Tzarina, and his father was one of the many Italian workers imported into Russia to help in the decoration of the Kremlin. In 1917 the communist revolution erupted, the Royal family was executed, and the Pacitti family fled for sanctuary to Helsinki. From there they embarked on what they thought was a journey to America, as the unscrupulous person to whom they had given their money for the trip had told them, but instead of arriving in the promised land, they found themselves deposited on the docks at Portobello, the actual destination of the ship. Passports were as yet not necessary for travel in those days, so they remained in Scotland and were helped by a local priest to find work, and there in Portobello in the early twenties Charlie was born. Apart from an inborn business sense, which eventually was to make him very prosperous, Charlie was possessed of a unique facility. He was a fluent speaker of his native Neapolitan dialect, which, however, he delivered in a remarkable fashion. Learned at his mother's knee, he spoke it with a toothless Russian accent, just as his mother had spoken it, and the reaction this had on the many occasions we shared a table with relations and friends in Viareggio and Barga was hilarious. Sadly, both Gina and Charlie have passed away, but their daughter Gina, a successful Glasgow lawyer, remains a close friend and advises me in legal matters.

Alas, apart from myself and one other, Reidar Marthisen Cornillon, the 9.30 Society members have all passed away. Reidar lives alone on the island. His wife Grete died some years ago, and now at the age of eighty-two he plays a daily round on Son Vida, usually alone. On my visits to Majorca I ride with him on his buggy, for I have long since had to give up golf. Our talk is of the old days of the 9.30 Society, of the many visits he paid to Mary and myself in Scotland and of the memorable game we had on the Turnberry Links.

Steve Cusak, the American whose foresight and business acumen brought wealth and luxury to the arid Son Vida valley died too, just some months ago. Fortune had come his way, but the last years of his life were filled with tragedy. Ten years or so ago the elder of his two sons took his own life. The young man committed suicide by hanging himself in his parents' bedroom, Freud make of that what you will, and the distraught mother, out of her mind with the grief of it, spent the rest of her life cared for in a nursing home. Cusak himself spent his last lonely years in a multi-million euro mansion on the highest ridge of the Son Vida valley, undisputed King of all he surveyed.

❦ 12 ❦
Mary's Illness

At the beginning of the year 2000 I began to notice that Mary's car was uncharacteristically showing signs of minor scrapes and knocks, given that she was a good and careful driver who took care to keep her car in an immaculate condition. She explained these away as having occurred in the local supermarket car park, a perfectly acceptable explanation, considering the volume of traffic in the rather tight car park concerned. At that same time I had been experiencing some eye problems and had made an appointment to be seen at Ross Hall hospital by an ophthalmologist. I was advised to come by taxi or to bring a co-driver along, since I would be given belladonna eye drops for the purpose of the examination, and these would blur my vision. Mary came along with me, and I drove us there in her car. The examination over, I found that my vision had indeed become blurred, and I settled back in the passenger seat to be driven back home. Mary had some difficulty in exiting the hospital car park and getting into the traffic flow of the busy main road. She navigated the roundabout onto the motor road very slowly, straddling the white line in the process, and once on the road, began driving somewhat erratically at about forty miles an hour in the slow lane, her hands clenching the steering wheel, her eyes fixed staring at the road, with never a word being uttered.

She was obviously having difficulty in driving, so I made her pull over to the hard shoulder, and despite my blurred vision, took the steering wheel myself and drove home. Mary made no objection and sat impassively at my side. Driving with belladonna drops in the eyes and with blurred vision is not as difficult as you might think, at least on a motor road. I just kept at a steady fifty in the left hand lane and reached home without incident. Next morning an appointment was made with our GP, who examined Mary's reflexes, gave her one or two simple coordination tests, and pronounced that pending further tests Mary should no longer drive.

Test followed test, and Mary was diagnosed as having the beginnings of Parkinson's disease, and suitable medication was prescribed. The condition slowly worsened, the first diagnosis was put aside, and a series of other labels was put on her slowly deteriorating condition. Over a period of a few months she deteriorated quite rapidly, and began to show signs of disturbing mental and physical changes. A series of brain scans and ultrasound examinations followed, and a final diagnosis was made. Mary was suffering from a Leowy Body Dementia, which meant that parts of her brain were literally in the process of calcifying. Although I realised that her condition was progressive and that eventually she would have to be put permanently into care, I did everything to keep her at home as long as possible. I advertised in the local press for a part-time housekeeper, and was lucky to find a young ex-nurse from Islay, Colina Leslie, to keep house and look after Mary in the mornings, which gave me gave me some free time in the forenoon. Mary's condition had by now, eighteen months or so after the original diagnosis, deteriorated to the extent that round-the-clock help and supervision had to be provided. It was then that I began to realise what excellent social services the local authority could provide. Two carers came in the morning to shower and dress her. Two more came in the early afternoon to change her, for by now she could no longer attend to her own bodily needs, and two more came at night to change her once again and to put her to bed.

This routine carried on for about six months, until early one morning I awoke to find her still and motionless in bed beside me and showing no sign of breathing or of a pulse. I could not rouse her and phoned for assistance. Within minutes a doctor had arrived and he was of the opinion that she had suffered a stroke during the night. An ambulance rushed her to a ward in Stobhill hospital, where she came under the care of Dr Davie, a consultant in geriatric medicine. She regained consciousness, and although she seemed to be aware, could not communicate in any way. She was kept in Dr Davie's ward for six weeks, and from there she was taken to Four Hills, a nursing home in Bilsland Drive for long term patients. At Four Hills she was given her own room, and there I could visit her whenever I wished and stay by her bedside for as long as I cared to. The accommodation was of the highest standard, as was the care and attention that Mary was given. No amount of money could have provided any better medical and personal care than were on hand at Four Hills.

On 14 September 2003, eighteen months after her admission to Four Hills, Mary passed away. During this time her condition had deteriorated to the point that she could no longer make any coordinated movement and could do nothing for herself. For a year and a half she had been well looked after and her nurses and carers could not have been more dedicated. She was fed and washed and changed several times each day and lay on an airbed to prevent the formation of bedsores, and had been made as comfortable as was humanly possible. I visited her twice each day, morning and afternoon. She could not communicate in any way, her facial expression never changed and it was impossible to say to what extent she was aware of her condition and of her surroundings, if at all. She slept most of the time, but in her waking moments her eyes followed my movements around the room and I like to think that she was aware of my presence and that my being there beside her was of some comfort to her. During Mary's long illness

I had the unstinting support of my daughter Laura, who also visited her mother on an almost daily basis and was a comfort to me in those traumatic days. As the end drew near Luisa and Linda came from Italy and Majorca respectively and we were all at her bedside as she sank into a coma. Finally, Mary passed away, leaving an emptiness and an ache in my life which will never leave me. I would like to believe that Mary was aware of the presence of myself and of her three daughters at that moment. Her ashes now lie buried in the Old Aisle Cemetery in Lenzie.

It is a terrible and harrowing thing to watch a person you have loved and lived with for more than 50 years disintegrate and decline in such a fashion, but the pain of seeing her so had dulled somewhat over the long months of her illness and I had been able to come to terms with the sadness of her condition and the certainty of the final end. In this I was helped by the sympathy and understanding of old friends and of the many new friends I made at Four Hills amongst those who ministered to her needs. All of us grow old, take ill, and will be in need of care and attention. When the inevitable comes knocking at my door I could hope for no better place to be admitted to than Four Hills Nursing Home, and to be placed under the dedicated care of the management and of the nurses there.

Perhaps the one thing above all else that helped me come to terms with the fate that had befallen Mary is the friendship I made with a long term resident of Four Hills, May Chesser, who during her active years was the secretary of a school in Cumbernauld. May was widowed some thirty years ago and has one son, an electrical engineer who works and lives permanently in the Dominican Republic. She is a woman of seventy-four years of age whose smooth unwrinkled face belies her years. For twenty years she has suffered from multiple sclerosis, and for more than fifteen of those years she has been left completely paralysed from the neck downwards, unable literally to move a finger. Everything has to be done for her. She has to be fed, washed and dressed and hoisted into a specially constructed electrically-powered reclining wheelchair which she controls by the movement of her mouth on a projecting lever.

May's mind is completely unaffected by her illness. Mentally alert, she makes full use of her every waking moment. She listens to the news on the radio and keeps abreast of world events. She listens to music, watches chosen programmes and videos on TV and is particularly fond of romantic musicals. Her current favourite is an old film of forty or more years ago, *Three Coins in the Fountain*, which she asks to be shown time and time again. She does not like to watch sad films, for she cannot wipe her own tears from her eyes and has to wait for a passing carer to perform that simple task for her. She takes a keen interest in the happenings at Four Hills and is always concerned about the wellbeing of the staff and of other residents. She has never been heard to utter a single word of complaint. I can think of no greater tragedy than to be a thinking, living, reasoning personality, with a brain imprisoned for evermore in a wasted unresponsive body, and yet May is tranquil and happy in the acceptance of her fate. She is a joy to be with and to talk to, and radiates an inner serenity which reflects the depth of her religious belief. On my way to visit Mary I used to stop at her room every morning for a chat, and never ceased to marvel at the happiness and peace of mind with which she greets the arrival of a new day. My contact with her has enriched my own life, for she is a shining example of how a person can come to terms with adversity. May has been an inspiration to me, as she has been to all who come into contact with her.

Mary's stay in Four Hills was to bring yet another element into my life. At the entrance to the home there is a reception desk where visitors are asked to sign in, and each day on arrival I was greeted cheerfully by a stocky, powerfully built man of about sixty or so, in charge of the reception area. His name was Archie Morrison. We exchanged pleasantries, which, as time went by, expanded into longer conversations and into an exchange of confidences about our respective families and general background. Archie's life had been an interesting one. His upbringing in the Maryhill district of Glasgow of half a century ago had been a rough and tumble one, to put it mildly, and a series of dead-end jobs after leaving school at the age of fifteen were leading him nowhere. In answer to a notice in an evening paper he trained as a croupier in the Stakis hotel and casino organisation and then plied his trade as a dealer and croupier around the world in gambling casinos in places as far apart as Glasgow and Las Vegas, with periods in the Bahamas, and on cruise liners in between. I began to question him at length about his experiences, for his stories were interesting and colourful and an idea had begun to take shape in my mind. Archie's reminiscences fascinated me. They were packed with incident. Why not have a book written about your experiences, I asked him. Raised in poor circumstances, self-taught, ambitious, becomes a croupier in the Stakis casinos, works in Las Vegas, in the Bahamas, on cruise ships, and now, in a somewhat startling change of occupation, in charge of security at Four Hills Nursing Home. Great material there for a book, I said. Instead of reading about other people's lives, why not a book about your own? It took a bit of coaxing, for Archie is by nature a modest man, but as the idea took hold he became as enthusiastic as I was about the project.

And so we started. Every morning as regularly as clockwork I would appear at Archie's desk with a little tape recorder and we would chat about his early life in Maryhill, his various jobs there as a teenager, his progress as a croupier in the Stakis organisation and then on to casinos in the Bahamas, the cruise ship *Oceana*, and in Las Vegas. Finally, his new career as the person in charge of security at a nursing home in the neighbourhood where he was born. As our conversations went on and as a result of my incessant questions, Archie began to remember long-forgotten events and to live again the days and nights spent behind the baccarat tables and the roulette wheels of the many casinos he had worked in. Fifteen minutes or so of talk and of questions and then I would go to sit by my Mary's bedside for the rest of the day and transcribe our conversation. I produced a page or two each day for Archie to pass judgement on, and in the space of a few months *The Wheel of Fortune*, the story of Archie's life, took form and was published in 2004 by Mercat Press of Edinburgh. The paths each of us takes in life, the manner in which they cross the paths of others and the results of such chance meetings are indeed strange. If my Mary had not been brought by her illness to finish her life at Four Hills, Archie and I would never have met and his story would never have seen the light of day.

I still visit Four Hills very frequently. I pause for a word with Archie, then go to sit and talk for a while with May Chesser. The nurses and the carers are still the ones who ministered to Mary, and over the past year I have come to look upon my friends at Four Hills as my family, for, as I shall explain, incredible and senseless though it may seem, contact with the only family I have left in Scotland has been denied to me.

❦ 13 ❦
Happenings

The day after Mary's funeral I left for Majorca with my daughter Linda, my son-in-law José and granddaughter Xisca, who had all come to Glasgow for the ceremony. There I was happy to see my other granddaughter Maria-Luisa, and stayed with them in Palma for a fortnight, after which I returned to Glasgow, only to leave again after a few days for Italy to seek solace there with Luisa, her husband Ennio and my two grandchildren, Paolo and Alessandro, both of whom were born in Scotland. I have nine grandchildren, but because of distance factors, I see some more frequently than others. Three of them, Joseph, Jessica and Rebecca, Lorenzo's children, live in Harrogate, and I have not seen them for some time. Xisca and Maria-Luisa, my Spanish connection, I stay with on my many visits to Mallorca; Xisca has just finished a course at University College London, where she has added an LLM to her Spanish Law degree, and during her stay in London she spent many a weekend with me here. The grandchildren I saw most of, however, almost on a daily basis since they lived just a street away, were Laura's children, Carlo and Daniela. Often Mary and I would collect them from school and often too were the occasions when holidays were spent together, in Majorca and once in Florida's Disneyland. Carlo was keen on all sports and I enjoyed playing golf with him. He learned to play with some clubs of mine cut down to suit his height, and showed great promise in the game, as he did in all of the activities he participated in. When I gave up the game a few months before Mary took ill, I presented him with all of my golf trophies, including a large silver cup, the Jim Large Trophy, which I won outright at the Son Vida 9.30 Society's last official tournament. It was the last meeting of the society, down now to three members, myself, Reidar Mathisen and George Turner.

Mary's death left a huge void in my life. When one has lived with a person for more than fifty years, that person becomes part of you and the loss is immense. I tried to fill the ache and the emptiness by immersing myself in writing and by taking refuge in the company of Laura's family and by increasing the time I spent with her and my two grandchildren. I was very fond and proud of all my grandchildren, especially of Carlo and of his achievements in school and in the field of sport. I took pleasure in telling him stories of the great golfers of the past, of how, when I was a boy of about his age I had seen the great Bobby Jones win the British amateur championship at St Andrews on his way to achieving his feat of winning four major championships in the one year: the Grand Slam, as the feat became known. I spoke of Walter Hagen, Henry Cotton, Joe Carr, Max Faulkner and of all the great golfers of the past I had seen play, and of how Bobby Jones' legacy to the golfing world was the Masters Tournament, played each year on the course he had designed at Augusta. Carlo one day asked me what ambition I had left in golf. I thought for a moment and replied that since I had been present at every Open played in Scotland since 1935, I would have liked to have been present at least one Masters tournament.

Some time passed, and to my astonishment one day Carlo presented me with two tickets for the practice rounds of the Masters tournament, to be played shortly over the Augusta course! Carlo, at that time a boy of only twelve, had, on his own initiative, written to the Augusta national club, telling them that he had an old grandfather who had known Bobby Jones and Walter Hagen and that he wanted to make him a present of tickets to view the Masters tournament. Would they please send him two tickets by return? In due course he received a reply, to the effect that all tickets to the Masters had been long since allocated, but that in view of the special circumstances, they were happy to enclose two tickets for the practice rounds for his grandfather to enjoy. He proudly presented me with the tickets. Needless to say, I was astonished and overwhelmed, and Mary and I were able to spend a wonderful week in Augusta, walking the fairways behind some of the greatest names in golf and taking in the wonderful sights I had become so accustomed to seeing on television. Not many twelve-year-old boys would have been able to show such initiative as Carlo did. An old man takes a great pride in his grandchildren, and my pride is well-founded, for they are all fine boys and girls and show great promise. I was very fond of Carlo, as indeed I still am, although I have not seen or spoken to him or my granddaughter Daniela for nearly three years now. For an extraordinary and unbelievable event was to result in my being completely ostracised from and denied all contact with Laura's family.

About three years ago, about four weeks after the death of Mary, at a time when I was at the lowest emotional point in my life and trying to come to terms with my sorrow, I was asked by my son-in-law, Aldo Ceresa, to undertake a course of action, which, after due consideration and after taking advice, I felt it impossible for me to agree to. During the course of several visits, intense pressure was put on me to do as he wanted, and after my final exasperated refusal he stormed out, leaving behind him an extraordinary letter addressed to me, in which he excoriates me for not giving in to his demand and then, for no reason whatsoever, since they had nothing to do with the matter on hand, other members of my family were also mentioned and traduced. From that day on I have been cut off from all contact with my family here, presumably as a punishment for not acceding to Aldo's request, and have not seen my two grandchildren, Carlo and Daniela, since. To say the least of it, I remain exceedingly bitter and angry about the whole affair and wonder what the grandchildren have been told to have them stay away from me.

However, as I did during Mary's illness, I sought refuge in my word processor and tried to escape from reality by applying my mind to writing. For a long time a theme for a book had been simmering at the back of my mind, and after some six months or so of intense work which helped to quell the grief in me, I had put together a manuscript entitled *They Took the High Road*, an attempt to show the connection which has existed between Italy and Scotland since the time of the Romans. In the first chapter I dealt briefly with the Roman occupation of the Scottish borderlands and then went on to talk of the presence of Scottish mercenaries in Italy during the Middle Ages and beyond. I recounted the legendary story of the Zeno brothers, the two Venetians shipwrecked on the Orkney Islands in the fourteenth century and I told of the legacy left to those islands by Italian POWs 600 years later. I wrote also of the connection between the Stuart Kings of England and the city of Rome. Then I came to more modern times and described in some detail the stream of immigration to Scotland in the last century from Barga, the little town in Tuscany, and finally I attempted to show the effect that Italian emigration to Scotland has had on their adopted country and the success achieved in all spheres of life by the children of those early settlers. The manuscript read well and was full of a great deal of historical detail gleaned and distilled with patience and application from various websites, both British and Italian. Gone are the days when hour after hour had to be spent in the Mitchell Library to check and verify one's information, as I had to do in the writing of *The Big Men*, the book dealing with the Glasgow police. In the writing of that book I had to spend laborious weeks going through microfilms of past newspaper editions to check on the authenticity of some of the stories I had been told by the retired policemen who had supplied me with some lurid accounts of happenings they had been involved in. Now, with a click of the mouse and a question to Google, a mass of information is immediately to hand on any subject, without having to move from one's chair.

Mercat Press of Edinburgh liked the manuscript and offered to publish it, but with a change to the title, and last year my book appeared in print, carrying the title *The Scots-Italians: Recollections of an Immigrant*. The publication of the book was followed by some rather unexpected results. The Press in general gave it very favourable reviews, and in particular the *Scotsman* ran a double page feature on the book. Their article was entitled 'The Triumph of the "Tallies"', with a photograph of myself holding my old Aliens registration book and a double-sized photograph of the beautiful and talented Nicola Benedetti, the young eighteen-year-old Scots-Italian violinist prodigy who had given a concert at the opening of the new Parliament building in Edinburgh at the beginning of the year. The article was seized upon by the Italian press, which gave it extended coverage, and came to the attention of Umberto Sereni, the *Sindaco* (Lord Mayor) of Barga, who then wrote me the following letter:

> *Dear Mr Pieri,*
>
> *News has reached me from the Scottish press of the good news of the publication of your book 'The Scots-Italians'.*
>
> *I note with pleasure that the book has aroused great interest in the general public. This interest is well merited, because your recollections are writings of extraordinary value in reconstructing the history of our community in Scotland.*
>
> *I take great pleasure in thanking you also because of your mention of my father Bruno, who long ago worked for a time in your father's shop and for whom those years, although hard, were of inestimable value in the school of life.*
>
> *I shall be in Scotland from the 25ᵗʰ to the 27ᵗʰ November for the 'Barga Night' festival in Troon. I would like to meet with you there, to present you with a token of the gratitude of the town of Barga.*
>
> *Umberto Sereni*
>
> *PS— Your book will have pride of place in the exhibition 'Barga-Scotland Connection', which is about to open here in our museum.*

I shall digress here for a moment to write a few words about the Sereni family. Bruno Sereni, the father of Umberto, the present *Sindaco* of Barga, has now become a legend in the little town where he was born. Well educated and well read at a time when many of his fellow citizens were barely literate, he was in his late teens when Fascism took hold in Italy in the 1920s. Ten years later, Sereni had developed well formulated Socialist ideas of the type which Mussolini was trying to stamp out. This was being achieved either by assassination, as was the case in the murder of the left-wing journalist Matteotti, or by exile to some remote part of Italy, as was the case with Carlo Levi, the writer who was later to tell of his exile in his book *Christ stopped at Eboli*, or by permanent incapacitation by the administration of large doses of castor oil, which was a punishment meted out to anyone who dared disagree with the Fascist regime. Sereni chose voluntary exile rather than run the risk of any of the above. He came to Scotland, and in 1934 or thereabouts, he went to work for my father in our newly acquired Savoy. I was about fifteen or so at the time, and I remember him then as a cheerful and powerfully-built young man with an infinite capacity for hard work. He also bore a startling resemblance to a film star of the day, Spencer Tracy. He fitted in well with the family and I remember clearly the political discussions he used to have with my father, who had no formal education of any kind, but who, because of his bitter experience in the bleak Italy of his own youth, shared Bruno's socialist philosophy.

Bruno once taught me to sing *L'Internationale*, the communist hymn, and I can remember him thundering out the stirring words:

> *Arise ye workers from your slumbers,*
> *Arise ye prisoners of want,*
> *For reason in revolt now thunders,*
> *And at last ends the age of cant.*
> *Away with all your superstitions,*
> *Servile masses arise, arise.*

That same year, I was going to Italy with my mother for a short visit, by train, of course, and we stopped at Domodossola, the frontier station between Switzerland and Italy. Italian frontier guards in their black shirts and tasselled headgear entered the train to examine passports. Two of them came into our compartment, and possessed by I know not what idiotic urge, I began to whistle the communist hymn. One of them frowned, but the other burst out laughing. He ruffled my hair and said. 'Better not to whistle that song here, sonny, it could get you into trouble.' He kept on chuckling as his silent companion sternly examined our passports. I recounted the incident to Bruno on our return. 'Some of them are black only on the outside,' he said 'some of them still have a good heart.'

In 1936 the civil war broke out in Spain, and Bruno promptly enrolled in the International Brigade to fight for the principles he so strongly believed in. He saw two years of bitter action, and on the Guadalajara front found himself fighting against Italian regular troops who had been sent by Mussolini to help his friend Franco. On the defeat of the Republicans, Bruno had to take refuge in France, where he stayed until 1939, when Mussolini declared a amnesty for all exiled political opponents. Bruno thereupon returned to his beloved Barga, where he kept his ideas and his recent exploits to himself and took up work in the small printing shop which he eventually was to own. His troubles were far from ended, however. On Italy's capitulation in 1943 the Germans descended into Italy and took control of the central and northern part of the peninsula. Bruno was denounced to the Gestapo as a communist, and was put in prison with several other political prisoners. There were five in his cell, and from time to time one of them was taken out at random and executed, until Bruno alone was left. Just hours after the last execution, there was the sound of shelling and of gunfire in the streets outside, and the prison doors were thrown open by the liberating forces of the Eighth Indian division of the British Army.

I saw Bruno for the first time after his 1936 departure from Glasgow in Barga when Capitanio and I visited there in 1948 during our long stay in Italy. Bruno had just founded Barga's own newspaper, *Il Giornale Di Barga*. The paper still flourishes, is published monthly, deals mainly with stories of local interest, and is mailed each month to the many Barghigiani who live in the four corners of the world. A tradition was in the process of being formed whereby the returning pilgrim to Barga has his or her name inserted in the next edition of the paper, together with details of the country they had emigrated to. A banknote from their country of origin would be placed under the glass top of Sereni's desk, and I duly inserted a Scottish pound note to join the many banknotes from the many countries already there. He was still a powerful figure, but lines of suffering were clearly etched on the strong face and his once dark-brown hair had turned white. I continued my visits to him each time I found myself in Barga, and saw him for the last time about fifteen years ago just before his death at the age of eighty. *Il Giornale di Barga* continued to be run by his son Umberto, who eventually was elected *Sindaco* of Barga. Since he took office, Umberto has done much to publicise and to encourage tourism to that part of Tuscany.

Luisa had picked up the news of my impending presentation from the Italian press, so my phone call telling her the news came as no surprise. She had already arranged for leave of absence from her duties as a lecturer at Pisa University to come to Glasgow for the occasion and arrived with my grandson Alessandro. Xisca, my Spanish granddaughter, who at the time was doing a stint in the legal department of Sotheby's in London, also came for the weekend, and so I had the pleasure and satisfaction of sharing the occasion with some members of the family. At the ceremony I sat at the top table, flanked on the one side by Mario Conti, Archbishop of Glasgow, and on the other by the Lord Provost of Edinburgh. I could not but chuckle silently at the thought of myself, son of a mezzadro from Bacchionero, and dispenser of fish and chips in the Savoy, in such august company. Umberto Sereni made a flowery speech (par for the course for an Italian) and duly presented me with a scroll and a gold medal of St Chistopher, patron saint of Barga. Not to be outdone I replied as follows, in Italian, of course:

Signor Professor Sindaco,
I do not deserve the great honour you do to me in the presentation of this medal, for in a sense, I am not the writer of this book. The book has been written for me by the hundreds and thousands of emigrants who left the hills of Barga in the early years of the last century to escape from the grinding poverty of their land to seek work and a better life in other lands for themselves and for their families. From their native Barga those emigrants

travelled to the four corners of the western world, but most of all we came to Scotland, a distant land in the north of Britain, to escape from poverty, and in search of a better life than we could find in our native Italy.

The Glasgow many of us came to was not the modern and pleasant city we know today. It was a foggy city of dark tenements and darker factories, and we can imagine the culture shock it must have been for our parents, with little or no knowledge of the language or customs of the country, to find themselves in an environment so different from the sunny Tuscan hills where they were born, and how difficult it must have been for them to adapt to their new environment. But in Scotland we found an ordered land, where everyone was indeed equal under the law, where a man had the freedom to speak his mind without fear of reprisal and where hard work had its reward.

It was to defend these values, Signor Sindaco, that your father Bruno had to suffer exile for many years far from his beloved Barga.

But we Italians are nothing if not workers and adapt we did, and we worked hard in our little fish and chip shops and cafés. Through our work we prospered, and over the years we became an accepted part of the Scottish scene and Scotland became our home. Our sons and daughters were born here and educated here and grew up here as a new breed, as Scots-Italians, proud of their Italian heritage and equally proud of their Scottish background. Many of our sons and daughters have made their mark here, not only in business, but also in the professions and in the Arts. Scotland has been the land that gave us the opportunity to work and to prosper, and for that we are indebted to her and I like to think that through our presence and work here we have given back something to Scotland in return.

So it is on behalf of those of us who first took the high road from Barga to Scotland, the early immigrants, the real writers of this book, that I accept this medal, and I shall wear it proudly, both as a Barghigiano and as a Scots-Italian.

Professor Sereni, Mayor of Barga, I thank you.

Mary would have been very proud.

❦ 14 ❦
Bacchionero to Bishopbriggs

In the summer of 1959, during our annual holiday with the family at our father's place in Viareggio, we decided to pay a last visit to Carletti, the mill house where the mezzadri of the area and the Carani family of Bacchionero took their grain and chestnuts to be ground into flour. By that year Bacchionero had been long abandoned. My male cousins who lived and worked there had been called up for military service during the war, and two, Franceschino and Vittorio, had been wounded during the conflict, one in the North African desert and one in Russia, and none of the remaining family cared to continue with the back-breaking work of their ancestors. With the post-war development of industry in the valleys below, well paid and much easier work was now available in the Barga and Lucca districts, and one by one the sharecropping families of the high hills abandoned the area for the more rewarding and less demanding work to be found in the towns of the Tuscan valleys. The Santi family of the the Carletti millhouse still lived there, but they too would soon be abandoning the area, for as a result of the work opportunities opened up by the newly formed European common market, the entire family of my aunt Rosa, my mother's sister, had found work in Verdun in France.

My father was in his eighties by then, and mother was in her middle seventies, and this was the last opportunity for our two families to meet. Carletti was situated about 8 kilometres and 300 metres above Renaio, the last place accessible by car, and the trek from there to Carletti had to be made on foot over rocky and sometimes dangerous paths barely fit for goats to negotiate. Mother was still in excellent health and felt capable of facing up to the climb, but there was no way father could have gone on foot for more than a few metres; age and a cardiac condition had taken their toll. The solution was found in the form of a sturdy mountain pony provided by a cousin, which stood passively with ears twitching as my father climbed slowly into the saddle. We set off, with the pony and its load, guided over the stony paths by my cousin Rocco, followed by the rest of the family: mother, myself and Mary with the four children, to whom all this was a great adventure, skipping along merrily behind. All except Laura that is, who, the youngest at three years of age, tired after a hundred yards or so of stumbling along the rocky trails and had to be hoisted on to my shoulders for the rest of the journey. The trek took about three hours of painfully slow progress, the occasional stream had to be crossed, which, although in most cases just a trickle of water over some flat stones, constituted a hazard to the pony with its precarious cargo.

Carletti was finally reached and tears flowed at the reunion of my mother and her sister Rosa, both of whom had given up hope of ever seeing each other again. Rosa was seventy-six, two years older than my mother. Although born in Bacchionero, Rosa had lived in Carletti since her marriage and had never moved from that area. She knew little of the outside world. Although she had seen many aeroplanes during the war as they strafed and bombed enemy positions in the surrounding hills, she had never seen a train. She had seen motor cars on the few occasions she had descended down as far as Barga, but had never been in one, apart from rummaging around in the wreck of a German jeep which had been destroyed by partisans in a neighbouring valley in 1943. The dynamo taken from that vehicle and driven by the Carletti millwheel was still supplying light to the house at the time of our visit in 1959!

We stayed there for four days, and the children played happily with their cousins in the lush meadows by the side of the clear mountain stream which ran under the house to give power to the heavy millwheel. They thought it great fun to use the outside dry lavatories and to participate in the milking of the few sheep and goats which represented the wealth of the Santi family. During these days Mary and I trekked back and forth from Bacchionero, a distance of half a kilometre or so, breathing in the scent-laden air and listening to the whispering of the breeze in the branches of the huge chestnut trees as we walked the floor of the valleys carpeted with the many years residue of ungathered chestnuts. We sat in the tiny square in front of the now derelict chapel and watched as nesting birds flew in and out of the deserted building. The floor inside lay covered in broken plaster, the wooden altar was no longer there and the body of the church had long been stripped of anything of value, possibly by the few backpackers who used the trail through Bacchionero to climb over the Apuan Alps in order to reach the picturesque volcanic lake known as *Il Lago Santo* (Holy Lake). I had a ciné camera with me, and was able to film a three minute 8 millimetre cassette before the light meter failed, thus putting an end to the exposure of any more film. This film was subsequently transferred to a video cassette which has now become a family heirloom. The grainy and, at times, indistinct images give an indication of what life was like for those of my ancestors who were born and who lived and died in that remote corner at the foot of the Apuan Alps.

Forty-eight years afterwards, just some months ago, the above scene was repeated in the ruins of Bacchionero, but in a modern context. During my last visit to my daughter Luisa some time ago, I had reminisced about the year I had spent as a boy in Bacchionero and had bemoaned the fact that at eighty-six years of age I was no longer capable of climbing up there to see my birthplace for one last time.

The family took note and hatched a plan. On my arrival at Luisa's house in Massa Macinaia, where I had gone again for a short visit some weeks ago, I was presented with a *fait accompli*. To retrace the paths I had trodden forty-seven years ago and to repeat the journey I had made with my parents and my own children, Luisa and her husband Ennio had arranged a trip to Bacchionero for their family, with myself as the guest of honour. The trip had been organised by Luisa, who by means of numerous phone calls to friends in Barga had been put in touch with a family in Renaio by the name of Moscardini, who knew Bacchionero, and who would be pleased to help Luisa in her plan.

Modern times being what they are, no horse was available to carry me up the mountain, but a much surer and more potent means of transportation had been arranged. A land rover was to take the place of the horse which had carried my father on its back, and this vehicle was to take us all from Renaio over the rough and steep terrain to a point as near as possible to the ruins of Bacchionero. It was already hot at 8 o' clock when Ennio's car left the Lucca plain for the winding climb up the valley of the Serchio river to Barga, and when about an hour later we had reached an agreed meeting place there with one of the Moscardini family, the thermometer registered more than thirty degrees, with the sun even more scorching than it had been in the denser air of the valley below. There we were met by a young woman, Nadia Moscardini, who was to guide us further up the valley to the point where ordinary cars could no longer go and where the land rover was to take over. I could not but marvel at the fact that these friendly and helpful good-hearted people had given half a day of their time over to escorting a group of perfect strangers headed by an old man through difficult and dangerous terrain, simply for them to view a cluster of ruined buildings. It was a pleasure, said Nadia, when I was profuse in my thanks for their kindness. She had heard through a friend that a family in Massa Macinaia were looking to hire a horse or a pony to take an old man up the mountain to visit the place where he had been born eighty-six years ago. Marvelling at such a request, and knowing that horses and mules were no longer available, she had offered the services of her uncle Modesto, a retired steel worker who lived in Rennaio, who owned a land rover, and who knew the area well. There was absolutely no question of any payment for his services. Modesto as a boy had known many of my relations and he considered it a pleasure to take a Signor Pieri, whose mother had been a Carani of Bacchionero, who himself had been born there and who was now such an old man, to see for one last time the place of his birth. We followed Nadia's car to a point where ordinary cars could go no further, and there we all piled into Modesto's land rover. The next couple of kilometres were indescribably difficult. Crawling at barely walking pace, the land rover inched its way along the steep rock-strewn path, its wheels barely a yard away from precipitous slopes whose danger lay hidden by the stunted shrubs and bushes at the path's edge.

Finally even the land rover could go no further and about two hundred yards remained to be traversed on foot. The incline was of forty-five degrees or so, and two streams of water had to be crossed, but finally we emerged on to what had been the piazzetta in front of the tiny church of Bacchionero. Choked with ferns and weeds, the area seemed smaller than when I had last climbed there some ten years ago. The heavy wooden church doors had disappeared, probably taken down and cut into firewood by backpackers on their way over the Apuan mountains to the *Lago Santo* (Holy Lake) the picturesque and remote beauty spot on the other side of the mountain. The interior was a complete ruin; broken rafters hung down and the sun shone through gaping holes in the roof. The balcony where I used to work the bellows handle to pump air into the church organ was still there, but the wooden steps leading up to it had vanished, as had the organ itself. Chiselled into the stone doorframe of the church there is the name 'Pieri', cut into the solid rock by my brother Ralph on a visit there forty or more years ago. On the inside of that doorframe a traveller has written a few words with some kind of indelible material:

> *O tiny chapel in the middle of nowhere*
> *What memory your stones must have*
> *Of persons who lived and worshipped here*
> *Of prayers said and hopes expressed*
> *In times and ages now long past.*

The simple lines bear the name 'Manzu' and a date 1990.

The farmhouse and barns still stood; there are no doors there either, but the stone walls of the church and the outhouses are so thick that they will stand until some cataclysm topples them a thousand years from now, or until a bulldozer demolishes them to make way for some sort of modern development to satisfy the needs of the waves of tourists who now flock to the Tuscan hills. An eerie silence prevails, and half a century of unhindered natural growth has obscured what was once a magnificent view into the valley beneath.

I sat and reminisced aloud for a while and spoke of the chestnut gathering time of long ago and of the wheat harvest which we threshed with primitive wooden poles in the tiny square in front of the church and of the hours spent bringing in the sheep and goats from the now overgrown pastures above, and of the times I tramped those hills with my cousins in search of mushrooms, and of the division of everything we produced into two parts, so that one half could be taken away by the landowner's agents. I called to mind the Sundays when the priest from Renaio would arrive by mule to say Mass, and I remembered the shrill, high-pitched voices of the women as they intoned their hymns and responsorial chants, and I spoke of the parishioners who had trekked for kilometres with their families to hear Mass and who afterwards loaded the priest's mule with gifts, to the extent that he had to make his return journey to Renaio on foot. I then sat awhile in silence and in nostalgia, and while my companions chatted and while my two grandchildren excitedly explored the ruined houses, I daydreamed about those days of fifty-six years ago when Mary and I had visited here as part of our honeymoon trip, and of the enchanted hours we had spent walking in the silent chestnut forests. We then left as we had come, and returned to the valley below.

I have lived in a wonderful and history-making century. I can think of no other in the history of mankind which has seen as many material changes or as much social progress. The twentieth century has been a century of life-changing inventions; the telephone, the radio, the aeroplane, the television. It has seen the development of the motor-car and the miracle of the personal computer and instantaneous communication between every corner of the planet. The internet has seen to it that the accumulated knowledge of mankind is available to all at the mere touch of a keyboard. This century has seen the beginnings of travel in outer space, with men landing on the moon. It has seen two apocalyptic world wars in which tens of millions died, and it has witnessed the formation of a European union which has ensured that there will never be a repeat of those two disastrous wars, at least between European nations. It has seen advances of inestimable benefit to mankind in the medical sciences, and it has seen social change which has made these benefits available to all, regardless of social status. It has seen the elimination of the slums that characterized almost all industrial cities, and seen the social and economic development in the developed world giving the ordinary citizen the opportunity to live and to prosper in a manner which was once the preserve of the so-called upper classes. I can relate all these changes to my own life. I can look back and remember the poverty and deprivation of Bacchionero and of the other crofts above Barga. I can look back over the long journey I have travelled by way of the squalor of Surrey Street, Crown Street and the Gorbals and the relative comfort of the Cowcaddens to the affluence of Bearsden and Milngavie, and can compare my beginnings to the comfort and amenities with which I am now surrounded. I can vividly remember when the streets and tenement houses in Glasgow were lit by gas, when in winter for days on end a well nigh impenetrable fog blanketed the dingy city, when the diseases of deprivation, rickets and tuberculosis, were rife, and when a man of sixty-five was considered old. I remember the days when radio, the 'wireless', was just beginning to make an appearance, when motor cars were few and far between, and an aeroplane flying overhead gave cause for marvel. To have made that journey possible for me in the manner in which I have travelled it, all credit must go my parents. Had they not had the drive and the ambition and the courage which drove them to leave their homeland for the strange and the unknown, I might well have had to earn my living as a *carbonaro* in the hills of Bacchionero and might have finished my life in the north African desert or on the Russian Steppes as fodder in a fascist army, which was the fate of some of my relatives. As it was, because of their emigration, I was given the opportunity of growing up in two cultures, Italian and Scottish, and of understanding and appreciating the rich and diverse qualities of them both. Also, during the war years, had they not, with great sacrifice, kept the doors of the Savoy open so that their two sons could have a workplace to come back to after the war, things could have been very different. The Savoy, with all its great potential, was there waiting for us in 1945 when Ralph and I took up the interrupted thread of our lives, and served as a springboard for all that followed. What faith and and courage and certainty those two old people must have had. During the war years there was no doubt in their mind but that their sons would return home, and no sacrifice was too great for them to make as they waited for that day to come.

I have had a long, and in the main, a good and happy life. The passing years have been kind to me. I have had fifty-three years of happy married life, and Mary and I had the joy and the pride of seeing our children grow and achieve scholastic success in their chosen subjects, and if they have not achieved all that I had hoped for them in their lives, it is they who have to be satisfied with the paths they have taken. Mary and I had a wonderful twenty-four years of retirement together. New horizons, the Majorca days, were opened up to us during that period, with all the experiences Mary and I encountered there. But nothing can last forever, and Mary's harrowing illness and death signalled the end of it all. Even before Mary passed away I had decided that a final change of home would be necessary for me. Our apartment in Lenzie held too many memories and loneliness filled all of its rooms. Luisa and Linda both have invited me to live with them. I know I would be welcome, and I have thought hard and long about it. Life with either would have been pleasant. In Massa Macinaia with Luisa and her family I would have been amongst 'my ain folk' and not far from the hills where Barga and Bacchionero lie. In Majorca with Linda I could have shared her home in Son Vida and would have been perfectly at home with her Spanish family and friends. With either of them I would have been with family, a way of life engrained in me after fifty-three years of marriage and thirty-three years of family life before that.

But as long as I am capable of maintaining it, independence is of paramount importance to me, as it is to every other old person I have spoken to. To use a well hackneyed phrase, I have no wish to be a burden to anybody, and whenever the day comes that I can no longer take care of myself, there will be social services to take over. In saying this, I show a lifetime of conditioning and the Scots side of me. In Italy, as is the case in Spain, it is taken for granted that the elderly and infirm will be taken care of within the family, and in every home you will find an old person sitting patiently waiting for death in a corner by the hearth, as much part of the family as the young and healthy. But even there, the pace and the affluent values of modern life are catching up and purpose-built retirement homes for the elderly are beginning to make their appearance in the neighbourhood of Palma and of Lucca. And so I have come to live in retirement flats in Bishopbriggs, which have every convenience required by those who, like myself, are not as agile nor as capable as they once were. It is said that the changing of one's home is the second greatest trauma in a person's life, the first being the loss of a loved one, and I have certainly found it to be so. After the trauma of Mary's death and subsequent family events I could never have managed a change of home on my own, and I have to thank my daughter Luisa for having taken a month away from her own affairs in Italy to spend it with me in Lenzie in order to attend to the hundred and one problems involved in the selling of a house and the move into smaller accommodation. For the three week period when I was literally homeless, since my Lenzie flat had been sold and my new one was not yet ready, I went to Majorca to live with Linda, whose help and support has also been invaluable. During that time I left all my affairs in the capable hands of Margaret Duckworth, my friend and immediate neighbour in Lenzie, who took charge of the storing of furniture and all the details involved in the taking over of new accommodation. It was she who synchronised every detail during my absence and summoned me back from Majorca when all was complete. I may not have hit the jackpot as far as my family here is concerned, to put it very mildly, but no-one could have hoped for any better friends than I have around me. Moreover, during the various difficulties that have beset me during the past months I have received invaluable support from Mary's side of the family. Her cousin, Mary McLernon, and her husband James, the family's lifelong friends who live close by in Kirkintilloch, have been of great moral and practical help. Mary supplied the moral help through her sympathy and understanding concerning my family situation, and James was the practical one, putting up shelves and hanging heavy mirrors and pictures on the walls of my new apartment, tasks which, alas, I can no longer cope with on my own. Looking back over the distress caused by Mary's death and the family happenings that took place afterwards, events which still make me seethe with irresolvable anger, I realise that I probably would not have survived without the moral support and sympathy received from friends and from Mary's side of the family. However, all that is water under the bridge and there is no point in wallowing in the angry memory of it. I am comfortable and well-ensconced now in this little community whose residents come from all walks of life, and who are bound together by these common factors: the encroachment of old age and, in many cases, bereavement.

Numberless times during my life I have been asked whether I feel myself to be either Scottish or Italian, and my answer has always been that I am neither one nor the other, but a mixture of both. Perhaps the answer lies in the fact that I have chosen Bishopbriggs rather than Bacchionero in which to spend the rest of my life.